Distancing

Distancing

*Avoidant Personality Disorder,
Revised and Expanded*

MARTIN KANTOR

Westport, Connecticut
London

BP53

Library of Congress Cataloging-in-Publication Data

Kantor, Martin.
   Distancing : avoidant personality disorder / Martin Kantor. — Rev. and expanded
      p. cm.
   ISBN 0–275–97829–X (alk. paper)
   1. Avoidant personality disorder.   2. Avoidance (Psychology).   3. Remoteness
(Personality trait).   I. Title.

RC569.5.A93K35   2003
616.85′8—dc21   2003052894

British Library Cataloguing in Publication Data is available.

Library of Congress Catalog Card Number: 2003052894
ISBN: 0–275–97829–X

First published in 2003

Praeger Publishers, 88 Post Road West, Westport, CT 06881
An imprint of Greenwood Publishing Group, Inc.
www.praeger.com

Printed in the United States of America

11/14/07

To M.E.C.

Let us not forget that the motives behind human actions are usually infinitely more complicated and various than we assume them to be in our subsequent explanations . . .

—Dostoyevsky, *The Idiot*

Contents

Preface

In today's world, avoidance, distancing, removal and isolation have become so widespread that people assign greater importance to their possessions than they assign to their relationships. This is not surprising. What will startle us, however, is the extent to which laypersons, clinicians, and researchers alike have overlooked, misunderstood, or downplayed avoidance, even though, like sex or hunger, it serves as a primary determinant of behavior, creates as much interpersonal difficulty as schizoid remoteness, depressive withdrawal, and borderline ambivalence, and causes as much social distress as ignorance and poverty. Avoidants themselves (I use the term *avoidants* to refer to patients with an Avoidant Personality Disorder) think they are happy as things stand, or, if they feel unhappy, blame their unhappiness on their stars or on their fate. Victims of avoidants remain convinced that something is wrong with them, and try to do better, when it is the avoidant who has the problem and should be the one making the improvements. Psychotherapists treating avoidants often have too narrow a view of what causes and constitutes avoidance. In the realm of what causes avoidance, they often focus exclusively on the avoidant's fear of criticism, humiliation, and rejection, without considering other equally important reasons to be avoidant, such as the paranoid tendency to assume criticism, humiliation and rejection in their absence, or the histrionic tendency to rage mightily over the most insignificant and unimportant of interpersonal events. In the realm of what constitutes avoidance, they focus almost exclusively on two groups of avoidants: individuals who are timid and shy in their relationships, and individuals with a Social Phobia such as public speakers with stage fright. Virtually overlooked are avoidants whose social anxiety is displayed in other ways. Particularly overlooked are those avoidants who are neither shy nor phobic but who form unstable relationships characterized by a fear of closeness, intimacy, and commitment.

In its turn the scientific literature overlooks much of the valuable work already done on avoidance, often simply because it is otherwise labeled. For example, what scanty literature there is on avoidance fails to mention that as early as 1945 Otto Fenichel described a group of individuals who suffer from "social inhibitions consisting of a general shyness ... [that may lead to withdrawal] from any social contact [because] they anticipate possible criticisms to a degree that makes them hardly distinguishable from persons with paranoid trends" (p. 180), or that in 1953 Harry Stack Sullivan devoted substantial portions of his text *The Interpersonal Theory of Psychiatry* to the subject of avoidance. Karen Horney's contribution to the concept of Avoidant Personality Disorder (as outlined in Chapter 2) is generally downplayed, and Eric Berne's (1964) *Games People Play*, although it describes a number of what are essentially avoidant transactions substituting for real intimacy, is not as renowned as it should be as a treatise on interpersonal distancing. As usual, although Sigmund Freud has done much of the seminal work on avoidance, he gets little, or none, of the credit. For example, in *Totem and Taboo*, Freud (1950) was one of the first to use the term "avoidance," trace the "ancient history" or "phylogenetic" origin of "avoidance" (his word), and analyze "avoidance," in this case as it took the form of that notorious negativity we so often see between a man and his mother-in-law.

My book *Distancing* makes a break from tradition in order to provide a fresh, in-depth descriptive, dynamic and therapeutic look at avoidance and Avoidant Personality Disorder (AvPD). *Descriptively*, I delineate four types of avoidants. Collectively, all primarily suffer from social or relationship anxiety leading to distancing. Individually, each is distinguished by the specific way they distance.

Type I avoidants are removed avoidants who distance by withdrawing. There are two subtypes depending on the specific nature of the withdrawal: shy social isolates and social phobics. Shy social isolates stay at home living by themselves or with their family, either rarely socializing or socializing but within limits—making a few distant contacts and keeping a few old friends while having great difficulty meeting new people and even more difficulty sustaining close, intimate relationships. As Theodore Millon and Roger D. Davis (1996) say, these are the *"conflicted avoidants* [who] would like to be close and show affection but anticipate experiencing intense pain and disillusionment" (p. 268). Therefore they "precipitate disillusionment through obstructive and negative behaviors" (p. 268). In contrast, social phobics package their social anxiety into discrete quanta. Their anxiety appears in specific situations where they are called upon to perform, for example, when they are called upon to speak in public. They then withdraw, but they do so only in these special circumstances, in the main sparing other, more intimate, aspects of their relationships. As Millon and Davis (1996) say, these phobic avoidants "disposed to find highly specific phobic precipitants" (p. 269) "turn their attentions to finding a symbolic substitute, some object or event onto which they can displace and funnel their anxieties" (p. 270) by "a psychic displacement and condensation of [their] internal and generalized anxiety onto a symbolic external object" (p. 270).

Type II avoidants are ambivalent avoidants who distance by having numerous superficial but few or no close intimate relationships. Typical Type II avoidants include my mingles avoidants, serial daters who meet new people easily but have difficulty sustaining and developing old relationships due to a fear of closeness, intimacy, and commitment.

Type III avoidants are also ambivalent vacillating avoidants who, however, distance by first forming what at least appear to be satisfactory relationships that seem to do well (if only superficially) and last. Then, after a shorter or longer period of time, they do an about-face and demean, devalue, and disavow those relationships—even when, or just because, they seem to be working. These are the seven year itch avoidants who form a long-term relationship with a lover, then one day announce "I need a hiatus from this relationship." Or they get married, then one day either file for a divorce out of the blue or just disappear forever out of the life of a significant other, often one who truly loves them.

Type IV avoidants are dependent individuals who distance by becoming deeply involved with, or immersed in, a regressive relationship with one other person or with a closed group of individuals. These individuals are exemplified by the codependents described by Melody Beattie (1987). Their goal is to get close to one in order to reduce or eliminate worldly contact with all. (All of these types and subtypes will be discussed more fully in Chapter 4.)

Dynamically, I view the distancing of Type I–IV avoidance as the product of multiple social/relationship anxieties—not just one. In addition to anxiety about criticism, humiliation, and rejection (the official avoidant dynamic), avoidants suffer from anxiety about being flooded by out-of-control instincts rushing out should they open up their inner Pandora's box full of dark sexuality and anger; anxiety about being depleted of life-energy as a result of letting go of their feelings; and, the *opposite* of anxiety about rejection, anxiety about the possibility of *acceptance*. This latter anxiety—a most important, and often downplayed, anxiety—is in turn due to one or more component anxieties: anxiety about becoming dependent; anxiety about being controlled, and as a result being overwhelmed by, trapped in, and engulfed by the closeness and intimacy of a committed relationship; and anxiety both about winning (a fear of success) and about losing (a fear of failure). My definition of AvPD is therefore much broader than the narrow definition of AvPD found in the *DSM-IV*: "AvPD is a pervasive pattern of social inhibition, feelings of inadequacy, and hypersensitivity to negative evaluation . . . present in a variety of contexts" (p. 662).

In *Distancing* I supplement clinical material gleaned from the avoidant in the therapist's office, on the structured psychological test, and in the research lab to include a perspective on the avoidant that the serious student of personality disorder too often discounts because of its informal, anecdotal, and so supposedly unscientific nature—a study of the avoidant in the real world, in his or her native habitat, in a place where he or she acts spontaneously, thereby producing material useful for bringing the scientific approach to the patient into line with the normal proband. I observe avoidant behavior in everyday life. I watch avoidants doing real, avoidant things without necessarily being aware that they are being studied. This way they reveal themselves without posing and without playing up to an audience, presenting a fleshy and true picture, not one that is suitable only for framing. I observe avoidants at home, on the dock on a summer's day in a singles' resort, at the rail on a winter's morn in a singles or gay bar, and in the supermarket, missing the people around them as they obsessively shuffle their two-for-one coupons. I also observe them in the gym, doing precisely three sets of twelve reps each, deliciously contemplating how their body will look six months from now when they should be even more deliciously contemplating the person at hand, the one right before them, the one waiting impatiently for the machine. I watch them fight for the machine, not for the person about to take it away from them, as they tell the interloper, "Go away and come back when I'm done," instead of turning the situation around to their nonavoidant advantage by saying, "Come here; let's not fight over gym machines; let's talk about us, and our getting together for a date, perhaps tonight."

My goal is to evolve a dedicated, eclectic, holistic, action-oriented therapeutic approach to treating the avoidant/AvPD patient, a therapeutic approach I call *avoidance reduction*. My therapeutic approach is *dedicated* because it is focused on the distancing process in all its aspects. It is *eclectic and holistic* because it deals with a broad range of core avoidant issues, including but not limited to the developmental, psychodynamic, cognitive-behavioral, interpersonal and existential-philosophical basis of avoidance, that is, it covers the main components of avoidance that go into making up the whole avoidant picture—the avoidant gestalt. It is *action-oriented* because it emphasizes doing as much as thinking. It goes beyond the more passive techniques such as those that emphasize developing understanding into the psychodynamics of avoidance, its developmental origins, and its basis in cognitive illogic, to include and emphasize the more active techniques such as exhorting patients to convert from avoidance to nonavoidance by facing their fears now, as best they can, by exposing themselves directly to situations that make them anxious so that they can make that all-important leap from understanding to action.

My approach contains little that is new. I have scanned the various schools of thought for proven techniques that might be helpful for isolated remote patients having difficulty becoming meaningfully interrelated. I have come up with a compendium of relevant methods and techniques borrowed from the major schools of psychotherapy in use today, and cut and pasted them together to form a collage dedicated to helping patients become less shy, more outgoing, and increasingly comfortable with closeness, commitment and intimacy.

My text is intended for at least three audiences:

Therapists and other mental health workers who want their descriptions and dynamics rooted not merely in psychological test protocol/associative anamnesis but in everyday behavior in the real world, less tethered to theory than to earth, and who are looking for a practical, step-by-step guide they can use to help patients with Avoidant Personality Disorder conquer their distancing.

Avoidants themselves, stuck in heterosexual or homosexual distancing patterns, who can learn from its pages how to get beyond self-defeating, painful avoidance to extend a pseudopod to at least one other person in life: a friend or, to quote the personals column, "perhaps. . . . more?"

The victims of avoidants, who can infer from its pages what is troubling and eating at their potential or actual avoidant partners. Now they can make an intelligent decision about whether to try to turn a difficult relationship around to become one that is pleasurable, rewarding, satisfying, and even permanent, or to stay out of or get away from a problematical relationship that is unlikely to be salvageable. Victims who choose the former course can adapt my methods to help the avoidants in their lives become less distant. Victims who choose the latter course can make a more informed decision to either stay or go and, if they decide to stay, can infer methods for better coping with the avoidants in their lives who cannot or will not change.

I especially dedicate this book to a group of avoidants mostly ignored by a psychological literature preoccupied with shyness and specific social phobic symptoms such as an inability to speak or sign one's name to a check in public. My book has a special place for avoidants whose problems consist of fear of attachment, intimacy, closeness and commitment: straight men and women, gay men and lesbians, whose social anxiety is characterized in the main not by shyness or anxiety aroused by specific, identifiable trivial prompts such as having to speak in public, use a public rest room, or enter a crowded room where there is a party going on, but by a deep, ongoing, pervasive, multilayered *relationship anxiety* that makes it difficult for them to meet, connect with, and get close to someone, to form meaningful permanent relationships, and to then maintain and sustain them over time. To date, scientists just do not seem to take their problems seriously. They do not seem to find them sufficiently worthy of their attention and study. They dismiss people with such problems by calling them, pejoratively, the "walking well," then, relegating a discussion of their problems to the self-help literature, banishing the discussion to that inferior place on the bookshelf where they believe treatises on people with mere problems of living belong. In contrast, I view such avoidants, though survivors, as survivors with significant deficit. I take their problems seriously, and attempt to develop a useful, accessible, doable approach to solving them. My goal is to help those who suffer from avoidance, in whatever form, free themselves from their painful shyness and self-destructive distancing, to emerge from the dark shadows of isolation and loneliness into the bright light of warm, close, satisfying, loving relationships, relationships that can even last for a lifetime.

PART I

Description

CHAPTER 1

Why Has Avoidant Personality Disorder Received So Little Attention?

Avoidant Personality Disorder, along with Passive-Aggressive Personality Disorder, might be called a stepchild, or orphan, personality disorder. The aptness of this label is revealed by the attitudes of all-concerned—their friends and family, psychotherapists treating them, their victims; the avoidants themselves, and the scientific literature on avoidance and AvPD—towards the avoidants. Friends and family tend to discount and minimize avoidant behaviors in those close to them. One avoidant teenager had no friends and never said hello to his fellow students. At home, he regularly failed to even make eye contact with the neighbors. His fellow students, the neighbors, and even his parents did not think him at all remote. Instead they discounted his behavior as "typical of teenagers" and confidently predicted that he "would just grow out of it."

Psychotherapists treating patients with AvPD often fail to identify the problem and so overlook the diagnosis. The tendency to do so is revealed in an experienced colleague's remark, "I have never made the diagnosis of AvPD in my life," and by Frances and Widiger's (1987) observation that "several distinguished colleagues find themselves making the AvPD diagnosis rarely or never at all" (p. 279). Avoidants who apply for treatment run the risk of having the therapist view their presenting problem as insignificant, dismissing their avoidance as normal shyness, reticence, unfriendliness, cliquishness, just part of growing up, or even as socially accepted bigotry to be condoned as normal, justified, and even romantic. The psychotherapist then sends the avoidant off with reassurance that all is well, and that no therapy is necessary.

The victims of avoidants, uncomprehending and unprepared, remain in the dark about the nature of and reasons for their loved-ones' remoteness. When a Type III avoidant told a partner "out of the blue" that "our relationship is over," the partner, who until that very moment thought that things were going well, was so surprised and stunned that she took to bed for a month and was not able to resume working for almost half a year. As she put it, "I still cannot believe it. He just fell apart—and took me down with him."

Avoidants themselves, unaware that they have a problem, continue to annoy, frustrate, and hurt themselves and the others in their lives. Some avoidants are isolated individuals who, unmindful of the pathological nature of their avoidance, cite, and live by, its presumed advantages, and eventually even come to believe that their isolation from family, friends, and potential intimates is a good thing.

A big-city man did not speak to his neighbors because "not talking to them is the one and only way to handle living in such close proximity." He believed that to be a social success he must first cut all ties with his family of origin deemed socially inferior so that he would not be embarrassed by them in the circles in which he hoped and planned to travel. Though he knew that his mother, to make him dependent on her so that he would devote his life to caring for her, isolated him from the rest of the family by repeating everything negative he said in passing about his relatives to his relatives, instead of putting a stop to her misbehavior by telling the relatives his side of the story, he allowed, and even encouraged, her disruptive ways. He reasoned that what she was doing was in the long run actually a good thing "because it's unhealthy for a young man to be too involved with his family."

Other avoidants, less isolated, get involved in relationships that are unstable and dysfunctional, like the man who married a remote and unattainable partner because he found her more challenging and consequently more alluring and desirable than he found partners who were interested in, involved with, warm towards, and available to him.

A good part of the "responsibility" for this stepchild or orphan status of AvPD belongs to the scientific literature and its tendency to diminish the status of AvPD or threaten its very existence as a syndrome by obsessively questioning whether or not AvPD is a discrete, identifiable personality disorder with inclusive and exclusive syndromal boundaries. The mighty struggle is not, as it should be, against AvPD as the common enemy. Rather it is between *believers* who identify a discrete syndrome, and *nonbelievers* who do not. The nonbelievers form into two camps. The *first* camp claims that there is no discrete Avoidant Personality Disorder because in their view avoidance is little more than a pathological personality trait or defense mechanism. (As they see it, avoidance may either be primary, that is, may occur de novo as a fundamental behavior in its own right, or be secondary, that is, may be a manifestation of another personality disorder, so that avoidance is really paranoid anger or obsessive-compulsive uncertainty—e.g., a kind of final common pathway response found in anyone who fears or distrusts other people for any reason whatsoever.) The *second* camp claims that there is no discrete Avoidant Personality Disorder because in their view avoidance is a nonpathological trait or even a useful defense mechanism, both of which are to be found in almost everyone in certain stressful situations. In this view avoidance is a healthy, justifiable, self-protective response whose admirable goal is warding off anticipated humiliation or rejection by critics, and protecting oneself from the intrusive threats of overeager suitors. Unfortunately, such an ongoing struggle does not provide refinements that strengthen, deepen, or broaden the concept. Rather, with all concerned sidetracked onto clarifying secondary issues, the primary issue—the avoidant's interpersonal angst—is almost completely overlooked.

Of course, some of the "responsibility" for the stepchild or orphan status of AvPD resides in the nature of the disorder itself. First, since AvPD causes only relatively mild impairment, it is unlikely to be responsible for the hospitalization that so often brings patients into close proximity to researchers. Second, because AvPD is inherently undramatic in its presentation—more a chronic diathesis than an acute encapsulated symptom, it is more elusive and less startling in nature, and so less attention-getting, than its sister disorder, Social Phobia—the disorder that these days seems to garner all the attention.

Third, avoidants do not present for evaluation and treatment because they avoid therapeutic contact just as they avoid all relationships, and essentially for the same reasons. When they do present for evaluation and treatment, they keep their avoidance to themselves during the clinical interview. They hesitate to reveal intimacies due to embarrassment and shame, because past criticisms have caused them to fear new disdain, ridicule, and humiliation at the hands of everyone, therapists included, and because previous therapists treated them as bad, not sick, and gave them punishment instead of offering them help. One avoidant was "thoroughly tired," as he put it, of having people call him names like "compulsive loser, wallflower, and wimp," and of having his therapist tell him that he was too passive for his own good. If they do reveal the intimacies of their avoidance, they make excuses for them and for themselves. They often do this by blaming their biology, not their psychology, closing off an in-depth discussion of psychological factors with a statement like, "It's inherited, I was born this way," or "It's my chemical imbalance." Therapists often share the view of avoidance as purely biological. Pharmaceutical companies, for obvious reasons, successfully convince therapists that a chemical imbalance is the main cause of Social Phobia. Therapists arrive at the same conclusion on their own, though via a different route: a form of von Domarus or "similar-things-are-the-same" illogical thinking where they equate two things with each other because of their resemblance to a third thing. Some therapists think specifically, "Biological processes are bereft of psychic representations; avoidants are often silent about the psychology of their avoidance; therefore avoidance is a biological process."

Fourth, symptoms of AvPD clinically resemble, overlap with, and so are often misidentified as symptoms of another disorder such as depressive withdrawal; hysterical frantic gregariousness characterized by "hypomanic pseudorelatedness"; hysterical sexual anesthesia when the anesthesia is created primarily to drive a partner away; the dependency of dependent personality disorder, a diagnosis that emphasizes less the withdrawal from mature than the attachment to immature relationships; and the narcissism of Narcissistic Personality Disorder where self-love more than interpersonal anxiety is the main mover in the distancing process, as illustrated by the following story, told by one of my patients:

A narcissistic woman decorated the public hall in her apartment building with drawings by her 2 year old, doing so in spite of the neighbors' complaints that, as one put it, "I dislike primitive art." Pressured to take the drawings down, she complied, only, however, to start the process over again by replacing the drawings with a basketball hoop for her son's practice shots. As she later confessed, "People say I'm just thinking of myself. I am."

Fifth, and partly as a result of the clinical overlap just mentioned, avoidance is often diluted in mixed syndromes like Millon's (1981) "avoidant-borderline mixed personality" (pp. 314–315). In the AvPD/BPD (Borderline Personality Disorder) admixture, avoidance and the distancing that results is subsumed diagnostically into the characteristic distancing of the object satiation/emerging phase of borderlines, the kind that is in turn cyclically undone by the overly close intense relationships characteristic of the object hunger/merging phase of borderlines.

A borderline individual in the emerging phase confined himself to behaviors that had little inherent interpersonal interest—dull, lonely things, like watching television from the couch, or self-destructive lonely things like excessive drinking and/ or taking drugs. In contrast, in the merging phase he instead indulged in frantically promiscuous party-time excesses such as constant bar-hopping. This cycling between emerging and merging was both diversionary for him and off-putting for others, the latter because it kept people at bay by keeping them off-guard, not knowing what to expect from him next.

In the recent literature AvPD has been subsumed into, and really swallowed up by, the diagnosis of Social Phobia. As I will elaborate further in Chapters 2, 4, 10, and 12, I believe that while all social phobics are avoidant, not all avoidants are social phobics. For example, a patient with a Social Phobia that takes the form of a fear of public speaking is technically an avoidant because he or she avoids relating to others, if only in a limited way. But many patients who are shy and withdrawn do not complain of being afraid of speaking in public, or of anything like that. Indeed, as many actors point out, as shy people they actively come alive when on stage, only to revert to type when the play is over. Henry P. Laughlin (1956) called this anti-phobia, the converse of a phobia, a "soteria" (pp. 198–201). In contrast, I emphasize not the descriptive and dynamic overlap but the descriptive and dynamic differences between the two disorders, and hence the distinctiveness of AvPD. As first mentioned in the preface, AvPD patients primarily are not bothered, as are social phobics, by reactive situational anxiety attached to discrete "trivial prompts"—that is, by situations not particularly meaningful in themselves that become meaningful only because they are invested with catastrophic implications. Rather, the life of the typical patient with AvPD primarily is consumed by diffuse, ongoing dysfunctional relationships characterized by remoteness, shyness, and/or a tendency to recoil from closeness and intimacy. Therefore, while social phobics and patients with AvPD both avoid out of fear, the social phobic's fears mainly arise in the clinical context of feeling, or actually being called upon to perform in ways ranging from giving a speech to urinating in a public washroom. In contrast the avoidant's fears generally arise in the context of interpersonal relationships, the main marker I look for in making the diagnosis of AvPD.

Sixth, avoidance tends to be illusory because it can be transient, selective, intermittent, reactive, or age-related. As for *transient*, avoidance can improve so rapidly on its own that the problem disappears before it is identified; or it can be mastered by an act of will, a possibility familiar to anyone who has been able to talk his or her way through the initial phase of stage fright or of meeting someone (though this is both difficult to do and often temporary in its effect).

As for *selective*, the avoidant is often bold when relationships don't count, but shy when they do:

One timid had no problem with positive feelings as long as he could express them to a third party, or have them about a stranger where there was no possibility of consummation, as when he had them about women he merely passed on the street. A single man, he readily admitted, "I like her" to his friends, but never to the people he liked. With people he really liked, to use his own words, when he "got past first base" and was "in a position to score" he "completely froze up." Also, timid and shy with friends and family, he was bold and forceful with waiters and hat-check girls—comfortable with those whom he perceived to be "less threatening" because "from a lower social order, from an underclass."

As for *intermittent*, avoidance can appear and disappear cyclically for no seemingly apparent reason (endogenously)—so that for what appear to be indeterminable reasons avoidants have some days when they are less avoidant than they are on other days. As for *reactive,* avoidance often comes and goes in response to external provocation (exogenously)—so that avoidants are more avoidant in some than in other situations. Typically, avoidance thrives when others are rejecting and diminishes when others are accepting and give positive feedback. Vicious cycles to which others contribute often affect the presence and severity of avoidance. Perhaps the most devastating vicious cycle for the avoidant is the one surrounding fear of rejection. The avoidant's withdrawal is the result of this fear of rejection, and the counterhostile response of others, who take the withdrawal personally (often properly so). Therefore, the avoidant actually becomes rejecting, and more fearful of relating due to more and more fear of rejection.

As for *age-related,* there can be marked differences between early (acute) and late (chronic) AvPD. Late AvPD is early AvPD altered and transformed by maturity, adaptation, syndromal admixtures, resignation, and therapeutization.

AvPD can diminish with *maturity,* with or without treatment. In one pattern, an increasing self- and other-forgiveness that comes (at least with nondepressives) with mellowing over the years allows an asocial, off-putting, fearful, angry youth/adult to go on to become a self-confident, related, sociable elder. (Not all personality disorders improve with maturity. As Henry Pinsker suggests, antisocial/psychopaths such as CEOs out to raid their own corporations for personal gain may get worse as they grow older as they become simultaneously needier and cleverer [personal communication, July 2002].)

Adaptation can occur through changes in the defensive structure. In the life of all avoidants defenses against the fear of rejection soon appear. We might see defensive misanthropy that in essence says, "Who cares if you reject me—I have already rejected you," or a frantic desperation to connect manifested by panicky, often futile, attempts to "meet someone before it's too late." Sometimes the avoidant, instead of frantically searching for new relationships, strives for familiarity and sameness, avoiding rejection by retreating into routines with the same few, old friends, as Frances and Widiger (1987) note, "going to the same restaurant, the same table, and eating the same entrée" (p. 280), developing what Jerome Kagan as quoted by Ruth Galvin (1992) calls a fear of the unfamiliar (p. 43). (This fear of the unfamiliar, or of newness, is discussed further in Chapter 2.)

Often defensive acting-out develops. In one form of defensive acting-out the avoidant provokes others to get annoyed with him or her so that he or she can abandon them, and thus look not like an avoidant but like the victim of avoidance. A husband wants to go drinking, but his wife disapproves. He has no trouble antagonizing her by picking on her for small things like vacuuming when he is trying to watch television. She gets defensive, saying, "Who else is going to clean around here?" and now he has the reason he was looking for to go out. She looks to the world like a harpy. He looks to the world not like an avoidant but like a hen-pecked husband.

In another form of defensive acting-out, avoidants get others to display their avoidance for them. It was pets for the patient who kept a half-dog, half-wolf that he taught to snarl at passers-by, and for the man who let his dog off the leash so that it might wander about and soil and uproot his neighbors' lawns and gardens. It was the spouse for the man who appeared to the world to be the "perfectly delightful one" while he egged his wife on to be the troublemaker of the family. It was the children for the avoidant who publicly played the role of "pillar of the community" while privately encouraging his children to cut the neighbor's flowers (by wishing aloud for a certain bouquet) and to shout anti-gay epithets (by criticizing homosexuals within the children's hearing range). It was the underlings for the boss who used them to live out his own petty inter-personal antagonisms, taking A into his confidence, making nasty com-ments to A about B, then behind A's back making nasty comments to B about A, getting them fighting. It was colleagues for an employee who provoked fights among his coworkers by misquoting them by "quoting" passing comments out of context and without qualifiers, and by otherwise subtly changing in the telling the meaning of a comment from positive to negative. It was a patient for a therapist who, unable to get the divorce he longed for, fulfilled his wishes in fantasy by encouraging the patient to act out against her own spouse instead of encouraging her to smooth things over and attempt reconciliation.

This therapist took sides with his patient based on material she deliberately skewed to have an antagonistic effect. He encouraged her to see to it that her husband, an alcoholic, was sentenced to jail for a behavioral peccadillo, not let off on psychiatric grounds, because "it isn't wise for him to constantly evade the consequences of his behavior." The therapeutic principle was good in theory— alcoholics must face the consequences of their alcoholism—but the real intent showed in the results—the husband started drinking again and, unable to forgive his wife for her heartlessness, filed for divorce.

It was the mother for a psychiatrist with marked self-destructive tendencies:

The mother of a psychiatrist who was about to join the staff of a psychiatric hos-pital was best friends with the mother of an inpatient currently admitted to the psychiatric ward that the son would soon administrate. Just before the psychiatrist was to arrive at the hospital to begin his tenure, he discovered that his mother planned to go through the entire ward and introduce herself to all the patients, telling them, "I am the mother of your new doctor," an action that was likely to create transference problems for the patients and countertransference problems for the son. Not only did he do nothing to discourage/stop her, he thought aloud in her presence, "Maybe it's a good idea—perhaps they will respect me even more when they see what a fine family I come from."

The appearance of second-line defenses is also discussed in Chapter 8.

In the realm of *syndromal admixtures,* as previously suggested, in time most avoidants bring other personality disorders into play to coexist with their AvPD, transforming the classical syndrome. Here I cite two of the commonest syndromal admixtures: the above-mentioned Borderline Personality Disorder, which adds a dimension of "now you see it, now you don't" unpredictability to the avoidance (as the individual swings between separation-individuation or emerging, and nonseparation-nonindividuation or merging); and Passive-Aggressive Personality Disorder—Millon's (1981) "avoidant-passive-aggressive personality" (pp. 313–314)—which adds a new dimension of thinly disguised hostility to the thinly disguised hostility already expressed in distancing patterns. Comorbid disorders and the mixed personality pattern that results are discussed in detail in Chapters 9–11.

In the realm of *resignation,* timid-shy avoidants commonly give up after months or years of fear of, and actual, negative feedback, replacing fear, timidity, and shyness with a general sense of doom associated with existential hopelessness and pervasive anhedonia. Paraphrasing Berne (1964), who refers to the lonely consequences of playing off-putting games, because they are "not stroked [their] spinal cord . . . shrivel[s] up" (p. 14).

Finally, in the realm of *therapeutization,* avoidance often yields to the treatment of other, related disorders, such as chronic fatigue or sexual impotence, if only because therapists, friends and family rally round, take pity, and cheer on. Unfortunately, avoidance can also worsen if the therapist neglects the avoidant component of another clinical or personality disorder, or offers treatment that helps overcome a primary disorder at the expense of intensifying the avoidance—a common, unfortunate, and generally unavoidable complication of treating schizophrenics with high-dose pharmacotherapy.

In conclusion, my experience accords with that of Frances and Widiger (1987), who suggest that AvPD "does appear with some frequency in systematic studies . . . and seems to be a frequent diagnosis in our own outpatient departments and in our private practice" (p. 279). As I hope will become clear, I believe that there is a discrete, identifiable, Avoidant Personality Disorder, and that it is a diagnosis that is both appropriate and useful for those individuals whose lives are marred by social/relationship anxiety in the form of distancing, a problem that I believe to be as important as any other significant mental health problem patients, their real or potential loved-ones, and their therapists face today.

CHAPTER 2

The Literature

While at first glance the scientific literature on avoidance/AvPD appears scanty, in fact many authors have contributed, though in writings that are manifestly on other topics. Once we think to look for a discussion of avoidance/AvPD in the works of personologists like Ernst Kretschmer and Timothy Leary, in Freud's (1950) *Totem and Taboo,* in Sullivan's (1953) *The Interpersonal Theory of Psychiatry,* and in Berne's (1964) *Games People Play,* we find a great deal of value, little of which has found its way into the mainstream.

DESCRIPTIVE ASPECTS

The Historical View

Historically, many personality classification systems have included a personality type that closely approximates AvPD. According to Millon (1981), Kretschmer's asthenic individuals are "inclined toward an introversion, timidity, and a lack of personal warmth—that is, lesser intensities of the more withdrawn and unresponsive schizophrenics to whom they were akin" (p. 34). Of Kretschmer's four fundamental reaction types, one, the sensitive type, is "distinguished by a brooding, anxious, restricted, and unconfident behavioral style" (p. 35). William H. Sheldon describes cerebrotonia, which he defines as a "tendency toward restraint, self-consciousness, introversion, social awkwardness, and a desire for solitude when troubled" (p. 35). Henrik Sjobring describes subvalid personalities defined as "cautious, reserved, precise, industrious and scrupulous"

(p. 36). Eugen Kahn describes dysphoric types, whom he characterizes as anxiously timid and peevish (p. 37). Moritz Tramer describes a hypo-thymic personality whom he characterizes as "withdrawn and schizoid" (p. 37). Raymond Cattell uses the term *schizothymia* for those who are "reserved, detached, aloof" (p. 40). Hans Eysenck's dimensions of personality include "introversion-extroversion" (p. 41), which is founded in concepts of "autonomic nervous system reactivity and ease of condition-ability" (p. 41). Eysenck also states that "those who readily form conditioned responses are inclined to introverted behavior" (p. 41), and that "people at the high end of both conditionability and autonomic reactivity are disposed to develop fears and compulsions" (p. 41). Maurice Lorr and Leslie Phillips categorize personality types according to the dimensions of "socialized-unsocialized," (p. 41) and one of their interpersonal styles is characterized by "avoidance of others . . . withdrawal behaviors, fantasy preoccupations, or other indices of social detachment" (p. 42). Henry J. Walton and his associates specify a withdrawn type "noted [for] being socially isolated and emotionally inhibited" (p. 44). Leary presents an "interpersonal typology [that is] based on two dimensions, dominance-submission and hate-love" (p. 55). He defines a rebellious-distrustful personality who handles "anxiety and frustration by active distancing from others and by displays of bitterness, cynicism, and passively resistant behaviors. . . .Experience has taught [the rebellious-distrustful personality] that it is best not to trust others, to be skeptical of the so-called good-will of others, and to be alert to and rebel against signs of phoniness and deceit" (p. 55). The New York Medical School, collaborating with the Menninger Foundation, notes that some children "reached out for everything presented, others avoided anything new . . .[They] exhibited withdrawal reactions to new stimuli, showed minimal flexibility in response to change, and expressed intense and often negative moods" (p. 38).

Modern Formulations

Fear of Newness

John M. Oldham and Lois B. Morris (1995) describe comfort with routine, Lorna Smith Benjamin (1996) notes that avoidants "don't often try new situations" (p. 297), and, as previously mentioned in Chapter 1, Kagan, as quoted by Galvin (1992), emphasizes how some patients strive for familiarity and sameness, for example, "the same restaurant, the same table, the same entrée" (p. 280). In my experience, this fear of newness can readily change over to become an equally avoidant fear of sameness as patients go from being Type I avoidants, who fear the new, to become Type II avoidants, who feel a discomfort with the old.

A patient kept the same routine for months or years, not only eating in the same restaurant every night but also ordering the same food and drinks. Then afterwards he would do an about face and, fearing stagnation, suddenly and without warning change restaurants on a slim, slightly paranoid pretext, once, for example, because, "The waiter hustled me for drinks, and the baked potatoes today were smaller than the baked potatoes yesterday."

Codependency

In Beattie's (1987) *Codependent No More* the syndrome called codependency is an "odd mixture" of nonavoidant and avoidant traits reflecting the tragic conflicts of real life Type IV avoidants with their strange, ambivalent admixture of dependency and withdrawal—avoidants who sink into one relationship in order to hide out from all others. They hide out for the same reasons other avoidants hide out: shame, low self-esteem, a paranoid tendency to take things too personally, fear of rejection, depression due to the lack of compliments and praise (stroke deprivation), and the pessimistic view that there is no sense trying to relate widely since the chances of being loved are at best narrow.

Social Phobia

The modern literature devotes considerable (some would say excessive) attention to differentiating Social Phobia and AvPD. David H. Barlow (1992) notes that the distinction between Avoidant Personality Disorder and Social Phobia is not clear. He suggests that the two disorders may actually represent points on a continuum of severity (most observers consider AvPD to be more severe than Social Phobia). In contrast, Millon and Davis (1996) distinguish Social Phobia from AvPD, as follows: First, in AvPD "there is a pervasiveness and diffuseness to the personality's socially aversive behaviors, in contrast to the [social phobic's] specificity of the phobic object and the intensity of the phobic response. Second [in Social Phobia] the phobic symptom is not associated with the broad range of traits that characterize the [avoidant] personality, such as 'low self-esteem' [or] the 'desire for acceptance'," (p. 274), or, as Benjamin (1996) notes, the AVD's (AvPD's) sense of being "socially inept [and] personally unappealing, or inferior to others" (p. 297). As a result, as Benjamin suggests, the patient with AVD "is less likely to be married, [and more likely to be] content (even relieved) to stay home by himself or herself" (p. 298).

I suggest that the problem of differentiating Social Phobia from Avoidant Personality Disorder is partly a specific instance of the wider problem of determining the relationship between any Axis I (Clinical Disorder) and its related Axis II (Personality Disorder), not only Social Phobia and AvPD but also Obsessive-Compulsive Disorder and Obsessive-Compulsive Personality Disorder or Conversion Hysteria and Histrionic Personality Disorder. The core dynamics of an Axis I and its related Axis II disorder are very similar. The distinction between the Axis I and the Axis II disorder resides in the way that these similar dynamics present clinically. In both Social Phobia (an Axis I disorder) and AvPD (an Axis II disorder) social anxiety is the "core lesion" with withdrawal a key defense mechanism used to cope. But while social phobics choose to express their social anxiety indirectly and symbolically in the form of withdrawal from specific trivial prompts, avoidants choose to express their social anxiety more directly, in the form of ongoing interpersonal withdrawal behaviors including shyness, as well as problems with meeting, mingling with, moving close to, and remaining intimate and involved with, actual people.

DYNAMIC ASPECTS

The Historical View

Karen Horney

According to Isidore Portnoy (1959), Horney identified a group of individuals with "'basic anxiety'" (p. 315), individuals who "feel helpless, isolated, and afraid in a potentially hostile world" (p. 315). Horney believed that "parental neurosis [is] the major factor determining [how] the child seeks safety" and if the child seeks safety through "detachment" (p. 316). Horney "noted the frequency with which such [safety-seeking] children grow up in the shadow of an adored parent, self-sacrificing mother, or preferred sibling [and how] affection of a kind was attainable at a price: that of a self-subordinating devotion" (p. 316). Many such individuals as adults "soon adopt as their basic safety pattern a compulsively compliant attitude toward their human environment. Their dominant needs focus on being loved and lovable, being protected and taken care of, being inoffensive, pleasing others, avoiding all friction and conflict with others. Here the groundwork is laid for the dependent pattern and the need to repress assertive and aggressive as well as autonomous strivings. The major possibilities of anxiety come to be rejection or disapproval by others and hostile impulses from within the self" (p. 316).

Clara Thompson

Thompson (1959) states, "Problems of intimacy are among the most disturbing interpersonal difficulties. [A] form of interpersonal difficulty is that of isolation. The inability to make contact may be due to a hostile or even a destructive attitude. The individual feels so threatened by others that he must either drive them away or destroy them altogether" (p 239–240). Thompson is in effect describing my Type II avoidants when she notes "there are also detached people who are not particularly hostile, who live as onlookers to life. They have an impersonal warmth so long as no closeness is involved, but they fear any entanglement of their emotions. They are lonely people, but unable to remedy their state through their own efforts. Again, the solution must come from a radical exploration and alternation of the character pattern" (p. 239–240). Thompson adds, "Many of these people get along very well in more superficial relationships. In fact, they may be the 'life of the party' or 'the hail fellow well met' so long as no permanent warmth or friendliness is demanded. However, some have difficulty in even these tenuous contacts and succeed either in making enemies through their arrogance or hostility, or in withdrawing so completely that no one feels the urge to seek them out" (pp. 239–240).

Eric Berne

Berne (1964) describes a number of interpersonally off-putting games such as the essentially sadomasochistic "Why Don't You—Yes, But" (pp. 116–122). In this game, interpersonal intimacy is avoided via a process of asking for specific suggestions, then rejecting one after another as unacceptable, in order to wear the other person down and out. A significant advantage of Berne's "game," or "transactional," analysis, is that each member of a dyad is asked to own up to his or her role in creating interpersonal difficulty. As such, Berne's transactional analysis is particularly therapeutic for those avoidants who blame others for their loneliness and isolation without acknowledging the active role their off-putting behavior plays in causing their own rejections.

Sigmund Freud

Freud's contribution to understanding avoidance/AvPD generally goes unappreciated by both the scientific and by the lay literature. One difference between the scientific and the lay literature is that the former, as exemplified by the *Diagnostic and Statistical Manual of Mental Disorders*, 4th edition (*DSM-IV*), and Martin M. Anthony and Richard P. Swinson (2000), eschews Freudian dynamics almost entirely, believing them either unverified or unverifiable, or both. In contrast, the lay literature freely borrows from Freudian concepts such as mother fixation and incest taboo, usually, however, without giving Freud much credit.

A review of Ernest Jones (1953–57, vols. 1–3) and Freud's original writings indicates that Freud made a number of contributions to the science of avoidance and AvPD.

Transference Trauma. In many of his writings Freud emphasizes the central role early experience plays in the development of emotional disorder later in life. For example, a fear of rejection now might originate in an actual or imagined rejection in the past, revived by a current prompt that resembles, and so reminds of, an old rejection.

Anxiety. In Freud's (1936) paper *The Problem of Anxiety,* written in 1926, he noted that all symptoms serve a defensive purpose (i.e., exist solely to avoid anxiety), pursued the question of the nature of the danger with which anxiety is concerned, and suggested some reasons for interpersonal withdrawal. As Jones (1953–57, vol. 3) summarizes it, Freud noted that *"real* anxiety differs from . . . morbid anxiety in that the nature of the danger is evident in the former, whereas in the latter it is unknown. In morbid anxiety the danger may emanate from dread of impulses in the id, from threats from the super-ego or from a fear of punishment from without, but with males [the fear of punishment] is always ultimately a fear of castration [whereas] with females more characteristically [it is] the fear of not being loved" (p. 255). This formulation anticipates my more modern one: that avoidants shrink from relationships not only because they fear criticism, humiliation, and rejection, but also because they fear that their romantic and hostile instincts will break through to roil a punitive conscience, disappoint an ideal self, flood or deplete them, and/or expose them to actual punishment.

Primitive Genital Phobia. Freud (1957g) in his 1908 paper "On the Sexual Theories of Children" anticipated Sullivan's (1953) concept of "primitive genital phobia" (p. 376) (also discussed below). Freud implicated the sadistic conception of coitus in the inhibition of the capacity for sexual excitement later in life. The sadistic conception of coitus originates from primal scene observation, unceasing quarrels overheard during the daytime and extrapolated to become the "night time fight," and the observation of spots of blood in the bed or on the linen.

Excessive Masturbation. Jones (1953–57, vol. 2) notes that in a 1910 discussion in the Vienna Psycho-Analytical Society on onanism and other forms of autoerotic activity, inadequate satisfaction, the habitual (characterological) attitude of seeking of self-gratification without making any efforts in the outer world to find a partner, and the favoring of infantile aims and the retention of psychical infantilism are considered harmful effects of excessive masturbation (p. 301). While it is simplistic to view excessive masturbation as the cause of avoidance, most observers would agree that avoidance is at times associated with a preference for masturbation over sexual relationships, and the ability to reach orgasm via masturbation more readily than via sexual intercourse.

The following discussion of jealousy, masochism, narcissism, libidinal types, those wrecked by success, and neurotic exogamy constitutes the main body of Freud's contribution to the study of the characterological aspects of avoidance.

Jealousy. In his 1922 paper "Certain Neurotic Mechanisms in Jealousy, Paranoia and Homosexuality," Freud (1957a) divided jealousy into competitive or normal, projected, and delusional types. The first was connected with a sense of loss and narcissistic wound, as well as enmity against the successful rival; the second was a projection of one's own temptations (that may have been repressed), with flirtations a safeguard against actual infidelity; and the third was associated more specifically with projection of repressed homosexuality. These three forms of jealousy help explain an avoidant's special difficulty with criticism and rejection. Competitive or normal jealousy leads an avoidant to fear being criticized and rejected out of the fear that he or she will be thrown over for someone else. Projected jealousy leads an avoidant to fear being criticized and re-jected due to having projected self-criticism for his or her own sexuality to become criticism from others for his or her sexual feelings. Delusional jealousy leads an avoidant to fear being criticized and rejected due to having projected his or her unconscious forbidden homosexual wishes onto others, changing "I hate myself for being homosexual" to "You hate me for being queer."

Masochism.   In his 1924 paper "The Economic Problem in Masochism," Freud (1957c) described moral masochism, which he defined as a need for punishment and suffering due to an unconscious sense of guilt, which plays an extensive part in social life. In such cases, interpersonal anxiety would result not only from a fear of rejection, but also from the possibility of gratification without the possibility of punishment. I believe this ex-plains the avoidant's rarely mentioned *wish* for rejection (that is, fear of acceptance) that accompanies/underlies his or her more familiar *fear* of rejection, and partly accounts for the provocation of punishment in the form of abandonment. That is, when it comes to relationships, the avoid-ant "must do something inexpedient, act against his own interests, ruin the prospects which the real world offers him, and risk the possibility of destroying his own existence in the world of reality" (pp. 266–267).

Narcissism.   In his 1914 paper "On Narcissism: An Introduction," Freud (1957f) discussed egoism and its inverse relationship to object love. He noted that bodily ailments, sleep, hypochondria, neurasthenia, and anxiety neurosis banish the readiness to love. He considered overesti-mation of the sexual object to be narcissism born again. For some avo-idants overestimation of the sexual object is a factor determining their particular vulnerability to rejection.

Libidinal Types.   In his 1931 paper "Libidinal Types," Freud (1957d) distinguished among *erotic* types whose main interest is focused on love, with loving and the desire to be loved the most important thing in life and with loss of love a cause of dread; *obsessional* types who fear their conscience more than the risk of losing love, exhibiting an inner rather than an outer dependence; and *narcissistic* types, who show no tension between ego and superego and no preponderance of erotic needs, with the need to love subordinate to self-preservation. These narcissistic types are independent people not easily overawed, leaders capable of consid-erable aggressivity who, according to Jones (1953–57, vol. 3) can "benefit their social surroundings through stimulation or injure it through their ruthlessness" (p. 261). I believe that Freud's first category, the erotic libidinal, overlaps with my category of overcompensated, hypomanic avoidants; Freud's second category, the obsessional libidinal, overlaps with my category of vacillating Type II and unpredictable Type III avoidants who avoid out of a sense of guilt; and Freud's third category, the narcissistic libidinal, overlaps both with my category of narcissistic Type II and III avoidants who use people for their own emotional benefit, then drop them, and with my category of psychopathic/antisocial Type II and III avoidants who use people strictly for what they can extract from them—for example, using their shoulders to climb higher on the corporate ladder, then ignoring them after getting the boost they need to the top.

Those Wrecked by Success/Criminality from a Sense of Guilt. In his 1915 paper "Some Character-Types Met With in Psycho-analytic Work," Freud (1957h) described three character types: "exceptions," "those wrecked by success," and "criminality from a sense of guilt." The character type which he called "those wrecked by success" are happy until they have achieved some important goal; then they fall ill because they are unable to endure bliss. As an example, Freud cites a woman who went to pieces when her longtime lover decided to make her his wife. Fantasy goal is permissible, but the reality of achieving the goal is not; therefore, the patient collapses on achieving his or her aim. Dynamically, the forces of conscience forbid the person to gain long hoped-for enjoyment. The conscience says, "I let you play with that wish, but it must not be actually gratified." I like to call this problem successophobia, and emphasize the role it can play in Type I shyness, Type II ambivalence associated with commitment phobia, and Type III seven year itch instability of long-term relationships.

Freud's third kind of "character-types," those who suffer from "criminality from a sense of guilt," commit a criminal act to provoke a punishment to ease their conscience. I suggest criminal avoidants who abandon their spouses and children without means of support, harass others sexually, rape their dates, or molest children sometimes transgress for this reason.

Neurotic Exogamy. (Freud collected the following three papers under the title of "Contributions to the Psychology of Love," which can be found in *Collected Papers* Vol. 4, published in 1957.) In 1910, in the first paper, "A Special Type of Choice of Object Made by Men," Freud (1957i) anticipated the modern literature on relationship problems when he noted that for the type of man in question four "conditions of love" have to be fulfilled before he is moved to fall in love, and at first sight these conditions appear to be very disparate. Passionate attractions of this kind are repeated with one woman after another—with a whole series of women that fulfill the necessary conditions.

1. The woman has to belong to some other man—engaged or married, or a friend of a friend, what Freud calls "the need for an injured third party" (p. 194).

2. Her reputation must be not entirely chaste. Her fidelity and loyalty must admit of some doubt—the "love for a harlot" (p. 194). When jealousy and distrust develop, these are often exhibited not for her legitimate partner but for new acquaintances or strangers—so that a woman who is in an adulterous relationship with a married man can accept his present wife but not a new lover.

3. A sense of preciousness and uniqueness is attached to her being a "light woman" (p. 195) in contrast to her being a woman with sexual integrity.

4. The man's constant phantasy is to save her from the fate of loss of respectability—a "rescue phantasy" (p. 195). The free, chaste, ordinary woman will not be found attractive. It is necessary to "induce the loved one to 'keep in the path of virtue'" (p. 196).

According to Freud, men with such passions are mother-fixated individuals for whom each woman is merely a substitute for the truly irreplaceable unconscious image of mother. Of course, mother belongs to another man, is not chaste, and is precious and unique. The fourth criterion, the need for the disreputableness of the object, comes from the discovery that mother is not a virgin and is untrue to her son. I classify men with a mother fixation as histrionic Type II or mingles avoidants who cannot get close to women because every woman they meet is not as good as their mother. Also every woman they meet, should they get involved with her, would take them away from their mother, and that means being unfaithful to mother. I believe another dynamic also applies: histrionic men avoid every woman they meet because all women remind them of their mothers, and that is incestuous. (Freud [1957e] discusses the incest taboo in the next paper cited, "The Most Prevalent Form of Degradation in Erotic Life." Type II histrionic women have parallel problems with men and father.)

Impotence, Frigidity, Abstinence, Cheating.   In 1912 in his second paper, "The Most Prevalent Form of Degradation in Erotic Life," Freud (1957e) discussed male psychical impotence, which he viewed as being caused by the difficulty in fusing tender affectionate feelings, such as are appropriate toward a loved mother, with sensual feelings, which seem incompatible with them and meet the barrier of incest. In such people the sexual instinct is "capricious, easily upset, often clumsily carried out, and not very pleasurable" (p. 207). There is "a sensation of holding back" (p. 203) and the man perceives a "check within him" (p. 203). "Above all, however, [the sexual instinct] avoids all association with feelings of tenderness. . . . The sensual feeling that has remained active seeks only objects evoking no reminder of the incestuous person forbidden to it; the impression made by someone who seems deserving of high esteem leads, not to a sexual excitation, but to feelings of tenderness which remain erotically ineffectual. . . . Where such men love they have no desire and where they desire they cannot love" (p. 207). As Jones (1953–57, vol. 2) suggests, the unfortunate result is that "no civilized man is completely potent, [and] no man can enjoy intense love together with the maximum of sensual pleasure. The respect for the partner that the former [tenderness] brings always inhibits to some extent the latter [sensual urges], and many men are only capable of intense physical pleasure with a woman socially, morally, or aesthetically of a lower order" (p. 299). I believe that Type II avoidant male serial daters serial date as a way to avoid forbidden closeness—with closeness forbidden because it is viewed as incestuous—and suffer from a commitment phobia for the same reason. I also believe that some homosexuals who pursue serial affairs with rough trade do so partly because they are unable to fuse their tender with their sexual feelings and so are unable to experience intense physical pleasure with someone socially comparable to themselves. Similarly, open marriages, gay or straight, are often the individual participant's way to keep tender and sexual feelings apart. As Freud (1957e) notes, the lack of stability in object-choice as evidenced by a neophobic "craving for stimulus" (p. 215) can be the product of a need to have an "endless series of substitute objects, none of which can ever give full satisfaction" (p. 215), because the ultimate object is incestuous.

In this paper Freud explains frigidity in women—an attitude toward love that can be equated with psychical impotence in the male—as being due to long abstinence from sexuality prior to marriage and to the sense of forbiddenness that was an actuality in the years before marriage. This sense becomes so closely associated with sensual longing that the woman can become anesthetic. Therefore, such women can enjoy intercourse with a lover but not with a husband for "the condition of prohibition is restored by a secret intrigue" (p. 212). Type III avoidant adulterers often state that a good deal of the excitement associated with having an affair comes from the forbidden nature of the relationship and the secret plotting that goes into maintaining it.

In the same paper Freud suggested that something inherent in the nature of the sexual instinct "is unfavorable to the achievement of absolute gratification" (p. 214). He blames this problem on two factors: (1) the two separate phases of human sexual development—infancy and puberty, "together with the intervention of the incest-barrier between the two" (p. 214) leading the individual to require "an endless series of substitute-objects, none of which ever give full satisfaction" (p. 215) and (2) the anatomical proximity of the genital to the excremental organs.

In 1918 in the third paper, "The Taboo of Virginity," Freud (1957j) discusses the relationship between defloration and sadism via the ideas of inflicting pain and causing the "destruction of an organ" (p. 228). I believe that when a sadistic concept of defloration persists in the adult it can take the form of an avoidance of sexuality due to the belief that having sex means hurting or being hurt. This attitude surfaces in the abnormal "hostile embitterment displayed by [seriously emotionally troubled avoidant] women against men" (p. 231) (and also by men with a similar problem against women).

Inhibition. In 1908 in his paper "'Civilized' Sexual Morality and Modern Nervousness," Freud (1957b) studies "undue suppression of the sexual life in civilized peoples" (p. 80). He remarks on the "spiritual disappointment and physical deprivation [that is the] fate of most marriages" (p. 90) and notes that the "behavior of a human being in sexual matters is often a prototype for the whole of his other modes of reaction to life" (p. 93). His suggestion that abstinence predisposes "to the numerous forms of neurosis and psychosis" suggests a possible connection between AvPD and the comorbid disorders so commonly found in avoidants.

Taboo. In his 1913 paper "Totem and Taboo" (published in 1950) in the section entitled, "Taboo and the Ambivalence of Feelings," Freud (1950) discusses how taboos are ceremonial performances designed to undo a harm feared, a deprivation that renounces a forbidden temptation resulting in an inhibition. Along similar lines, Fenichel (1945) equates avoidance with inhibition (p. 169), while other observers suggest that the term *inhibited personality* could substitute for the term *Avoidant Personality Disorder*; that is, as I suggest throughout, avoidance is a kind of ritualistic inhibition that renounces forbidden temptations of both a sexual and hostile nature.

Hostility. Freud has touched on, if only peripherally, the relationship between hostility and avoidance. In 1915 in his paper "Thoughts for the Times on War and Death," Freud (1957l) noted "there adheres to the tenderest and closest of our affections a vestige of hostility which can excite an unconscious death wish" (p. 315). He also suggested that "Our unconscious is just as . . . divided or ambivalent towards the loved, as was man in earliest antiquity" (p. 316). A possible conclusion is that avoidance is an unsatisfactory way to master and control those underlying hostile instincts that are always present in close relationships.

Harry Stack Sullivan

Sullivan (1953) described an asocial personality who avoids others out of a fear that relationships will evoke feelings and desires that ultimately will lead only to conflict and frustration. Sullivan distinguishes *conjunctive* from *disjunctive* behaviors, terms that parallel the terms *nonavoidant* and *avoidant.* Sullivan's conjunctive forces include the need for interpersonal intimacy, tenderness, adult participation, and exchange with a fellow being, a chum, a friend, or a loved one—all to avoid loneliness, which he believes is more terrible than anxiety. He contrasts these conjunctive forces with the disjunctive disintegration of intimacy, a process that he refers to as a "somnolent detachment" (p. 57). He believes somnolent detachment is called out by:

1. Prolonged severe anxiety induced by interpersonal situations.
2. Revulsion, a sort of chilled turning away from things.
3. Dissociation between lust and the need for intimacy.
4. Hostility, the disjunctive nature of "malevolence. . . . Once upon a time every-thing was lovely, but that was before I had to deal with people" (p. 216). A reason for hostility is to maintain self-esteem by pulling down the standing of others via disparagement and ridicule. Sullivan emphasizes the role "forbid-ding gestures" (p. 86) play in the expression of hostility. I refer to forbidding gestures as nonverbals.
5. Defensiveness. Although avoidance can be a potentially conjunctive force, as when it is used to conceal extreme vulnerability to anxiety at the hands of practically anyone, it is mainly a dysfunctional force, as when low self-esteem is dealt with by the concealment of defensive social isolation—a ritual avoid-ance machinery put into place to maintain one's security by avoiding a partic-ular field or a particular subject. This looks like a specialization but it is really a limitation. An example of such a limitation is the inability to enter a certain (occupational) field because any interest in moving toward the field immedi-ately arouses anxiety, which prohibits any further movement in pursuit of information.
6. Taboo, or phobic mechanisms, the prevailing mechanism in Social Phobia, where large numbers of aspects of living are avoided.
7. Isolating social rituals like gang formation and ostracism. Sullivan notes that out-group youngsters improve their sense of self-worth (at the expense of pro-ductive interpersonal relationships) by having interpersonal relationships ex-clusively with one another. Another isolating social ritual is the "pseudosocial ritual" (p. 306), or Fenichel's (1945) "substitute gratification" (p. 180), a con-suming interest that appears to be conjunctive but is in fact disjunctive—a re-striction in disguise. Here the individual is "busily engaged with people [and things], but nothing particularly personal transpires" (p. 306).

Otto Fenichel

Fenichel (1945) views avoidance as the product of a tendency to neu-tralize wishes defensively—that is, with countercathexes, or equal but op-posite forces. He equates avoided situations with inhibited functions and notes, "Analysis always shows that the specifically avoided situations or the inhibited functions have unconsciously an instinctual (sexual or ag-gressive) significance. It is this instinctual significance against which the defense [of avoidance] really is directed. What is avoided is an allusion either to a temptation for the warded-off drive or to a feared punishment or both" (p. 169).

Also, Fenichel (1945) speaking of what is, in essence, hidden avoidance notes: "instead of a full avoidance, there may be a decrease in functions or a specific lack of interest. . . . an intense dislike of formal parties, a shyness at such affairs, a lack of interest in or understanding of music, a feeling of fatigue and lack of power on occasions where others would feel rage, and a psychogenic sexual impotence . . ." (p. 169).

Modern Formulations

The Quality Assurance Project (1991)—a paper which, as we shall see, suggests that "Individual psychoanalytically-oriented psychotherapy is the treatment of choice for [Avoidant Personality] Disorder" (p. 405)—describes the core dynamics of avoidance as extreme interpersonal sensitivity to perceived rejection and a tendency to interpret developing involvement with others as hazardous. This paper is one of the first, and possibly the only one in the scientific literature to refer to "fear of commitment" (p. 410) and to assign it a role in the dynamics of avoidance.

As mentioned in my preface, I go beyond the narrow view of AvPD as the product of a fear of criticism, rejection, and humiliation from others to offer further reasons for social anxiety. These include a fear of self-criticism (condemnation by one's superego) associated with a fear of loss of self-pride (disappointment in oneself); a fear of flooding due to over-stimulation; a fear of depletion due to letting go to the point of dissipating one's life energy; and a fear of acceptance due to a fear of becoming dependent, being controlled, and becoming destructively rivalrous in situations of closeness, intimacy, and commitment.

Current observers tend to downplay the role anger plays in avoidance, mentioning it, if at all, only in passing. The *DSM-IV* merely hints that problem anger can be a component of avoidance. In contrast Fenichel (1945) suggests that avoidance is an anger equivalent—that is, it appears "on occasions where others would feel rage" (p. 169). In speaking of the anger in patients with a Posttraumatic Stress Disorder, Edward C. Norman (1990) notes that the "popular word 'stress' [puts] the emphasis 'out there' rather than facing the fact that we are not stressed but angry" (p. 1255). As Norman suggests, we should "talk openly about anger and accept its value" (p. 1253). Millon (1981) describes an avoidant-passive-aggressive mixed personality and notes that a threat equal to personal humiliation or social rejection is the avoidant's own aggressive impulses. In some models avoidants and passive-aggressives are placed side-by-side as both likely to be high on hostility. Aaron T. Beck (1990) notes that "dysphoric thoughts and . . . negative feelings [in the avoidant consist of] sadness, fear, or anger" (p. 273). Benjamin (1996) says, "I believe that the DSM should add angry outbursts to the description of AVD [AvPD]. Occasionally AVDs will identify with their humiliating and rejecting family members, and become quite commanding and judgmental themselves. Usually they restrain this aspect, but clinicians should be aware of AVD's tendency to become indignant about alleged humiliations" (p. 293).

DEVELOPMENT

Elisabeth Rosenthal (1992), in the *New York Times* describes new studies that show how the early "interplay between young siblings exerts a powerful lifelong force" (p. C1) as people "keep the relationships they had when they were young—such as rivalry or bossiness—. . . color[ing] all their interactions in the adult world" (p. C1). Millon (1981) speaks of the importance of parental rejection and deprecation (p. 318), along with peer group ridicule (p. 320) in the later development of relationship difficulties. Benjamin (1996), linking early developmental history to later avoidance, notes that patients with "AVD began the developmental sequence with appropriate nurturance and social bonding [giving the avoidant-to-be] a base of attachment that preserved normative wishes for social contact" (p. 292). However, the AVD-to-be was "subject to relentless parental control on behalf of constructing an impressive and memorable social image. This led the AVD to be "concerned about public exposure" (p. 292) and to make "impression management" (p. 292) a priority. As a result the AVD developed "strong self-control and restraint to avoid making mistakes that might be humiliating or embarrassing" (p. 292). There was also "degrading mockery for any existent failures and shortcomings" (p. 292) backed up by "shunning, banishment, exclusion, and enforced autonomy" (p. 293). When internalized, such a situation made the individual sensitive to humiliation, leading to social withdrawal in anticipation of rejection and humiliation (p. 293) and an "unwilling[ness] to reach out unless there is massive evidence that it is safe to take the risk" (p. 293).

CONSTITUTION AND TEMPERAMENT

Constitutional/temperamental factors may be suspected when avoidance does not seem to be subject to conscious control; is not apparently the result of, or influenced by, experience; or seems to originate in a primitive, ur, Jungian "collective," or intergenerational, unconscious.

Millon (1981) postulates a "genetic or hereditary . . . interpersonal aversiveness" (p. 316) displayed in an early hyperirritability, crankiness, and tension, and in withdrawal behaviors. We see "easily frightened and hypertense babies who are easily awakened, cry, and are colicky [and who] rarely afford their parents much comfort and joy [but who rather] induce parental weariness, feelings of inadequacy, exasperation, and anger [accompanied by] parental rejection and deprecation" (p. 317). Millon (1981) also speculates that anatomical (an "'aversive center' of the limbic system" [p. 317]) and hormonal-biochemical factors ("excess adrenalin . . . rapid synaptic transmission" [p. 317]) might account for avoidant behaviors.

James Ballenger (1991) views avoidance as a way to deal with anxiety/ panic attacks that appear when a "brain alarm system . . . fires . . . too easily" (p. 4) so that the patient responds to the events of everyday life with excessive anxiety. According to Ballenger, panic attacks commonly lead to an avoidance of certain situations "because [the patient] fear[s] that if a panic attack occurred in these settings, it would be embarrassing, frightening, or both" (pp. 4–5).

Kagan, according to Galvin (1992), says that at one time he assumed that "timidity was acquired through experience, the repeated avoidance of challenge strengthening a childhood tendency to withdraw. Now he . . . wonder[s] whether he had overlooked something: temperament" (p. 43). He describes a "small group of people . . . who are born with a tendency to be shy with strangers and cautious in new situations, a temperamental quality Kagan calls "inhibition" (p. 41), which is related to shyness. He remarks how some children, like some puppies, are born inhibited and remain so throughout their lives. Kagan believes that this temperament is inherited. As he puts it, "Every dog owner knows that it's hard to make a terrier behave like a police dog" (p. 41). He says that what is inherited is a "lower threshold for arousal of the sympathetic nervous system. . . . There are even indirect signs that [the] brain chemistry may be different" (pp. 41–42). Kagan, like Millon, suggests a limbic origin of the fear behind inhibition. Doing a kind of about-face, Kagan also notes "although society sees [shy people] as underreactors, inhibited persons may actually have a *stronger*-than-normal response to novelty— too strong, in fact, for their brains to tolerate, with inhibition and shyness appearing as the self-protective result" (p. 41).

Larry J. Siever (1992) presents a serotonergic hypothesis of "externally oriented aggression, [e.g.] fights, temper tantrums" in patients with affective and personality disorders. Studying the noradrenergic system in these patients, he notes that "reductions in noradrenergic efficiency may lead to disengagement from an environment . . . while increased responsiveness of the noradrenergic system may contribute to increased irritability in response to provocation" (n.p.). (These ideas are briefly revisited in Chapter 18 on pharmacotherapy).

PSYCHOTHERAPY

Psychoanalytic and Psychodynamic Psychotherapy

Millon (1999) notes that therapists who use psychoanalytic approaches attempt to uncover childhood memories at the roots of avoidance. They explore the avoidant's anxiety-provoking fantasies as they occur in the patient's present life as well as in his or her transference to the therapist (p. 324).

Anthony and Swinson (2000), while giving the nod to the (as they put it, "waning") popularity of psychodynamic approaches, take a negative view of psychodynamic psychotherapy. They insist, somewhat too strongly in my opinion, that psychological therapies other than cognitive-behavior therapy are "not proven when it comes to treating Social Phobia and other anxiety-related conditions" (p. 78). They feel that little evidence supports the theoretical assumptions of psychodynamic psychotherapies. They believe that these assumptions cannot be tested because they are based on unconscious motivations that cannot be measured. They note that the goals of psychodynamic treatments are often not well defined and they suggest that psychodynamic psychotherapists are relatively unconcerned with treating specific features of a condition. They believe that there is little evidence supporting the effectiveness of psychodynamic psychotherapies for specific psychological problems. They emphasize that psychodynamic psychotherapy tends to be expensive and impractical. They note that psychodynamic psychotherapists take an unacceptably dark view of human nature, assuming that all human behavior is driven by primitive drives, including aggressive impulses and the drive for sex, so that little room exists for the role of individual choice in determining behavior. (They do not explain why they equate "sexuality" with "dark," and fail to note that Freudian psychology also mentions non-drive ego-psychological determinants of emotional disorders such as "punishment from without" and "not being loved"—formulations that are very close to modern ones.) Finally, they note that in psychodynamic psychotherapy the therapist is seen as the expert so that there is a risk of interpretations being biased by the therapist's subjective viewpoint (pp. 100–101).

Interpersonal Therapy

Sullivan (1953) places the focus of therapy on anxiety. He suggests "confronting anxiety" (p. 302). By that he does not mean exercising the will or pulling oneself together. Rather he means not "running away from minor anxiety" (p. 302), an unprofitable approach in the "sense that it is not changing things for the better" (p. 302). Frieda Fromm-Reichmann (1960) describes the goal of treatment as a "potential freedom from fear, anxiety, and the entanglements of greed, envy, and jealousy. This goal will also be actualized by the development of [the] capacity for self-realization, [the] ability to form durable relationships of intimacy with others, and [the ability] to give and accept mature love" (p. 34). She defines mature love, in accordance with Eric Fromm and Sullivan, as "the state of interpersonal relatedness in which one is as concerned with the growth, maturation, welfare, and happiness of the beloved person as with one's own" (p. 34). Fromm-Reichmann's definition of desirable relationships and mature love resembles Ludwig Binswanger's "philosophy of the 'loving together-ness'" (p. 34). Also, commenting on Wilhelm Reich's concept of genital maturity (genitality), Fromm-Reichmann adds that "a person who is rea-sonably free from anxiety, greed, envy, and jealousy and who is able to experience interpersonal intimacy will be capable of expressing this in terms of satisfactory sexual activities" (p. 35).

Millon and Davis (1996) suggest that interpersonal therapy involves having "a 'corrective emotional experience' with the therapist" (p. 283). Hopefully this will "generalize to contexts outside of the therapy hour" (p. 283) as the therapist serves as a mirror for other relationships.

Much valuable material on interpersonal therapy is to be found in the self-help and how-to literature under topics ranging from "how to meet and mate" to "women who marry their fathers." However, in some of these texts the descriptions and dynamics are naive and oversimplified, while in others perceptivity is a function of overinclusiveness; that is, so many dynamic speculations are advanced that some of them almost have to be right. Some of the lay literature ("how to deal with difficult people") tends to overblame intrapsychic problems on extrapsychic occurrences, encouraging the avoidant to view him- or herself, unproductively, as a nonparticipant in, or an "innocent victim" of, others' rejecting tendencies. As a result intervention is weighed too heavily away from self-exploration and too heavily toward changing one's environment ("take a cruise to relax," "get rid of your stress-inducing husband").

Cognitive-Behavioral Therapy

Beck (1999) notes that "in anxiety the dominant theme is danger" (p. 251) and that the "person with an avoidant personality simply minimizes her social interaction in order to protect self-esteem" (p. 53). In therapy he elicits the automatic thoughts that appear in difficult interpersonal sit-uations, then challenges those thoughts, particularly the ones related to the patients' conviction that they are viewed as socially inept and unde-sirable by people they are persuaded are superior to them, think critically of them, and are bound to reject them as they get to know them better. That is, the dominant theme in his treatment is the patients' image of low self-esteem as it accounts, at least in part, for their "unfriendly behaviors and actions" (p. 54). He reality-tests such negative thinking as it appears not only outside of therapy but also in therapy, in the transference. He reality-tests by asking patients to "apply . . . rules of evidence" (p. 252), "consider . . . alternative explanations" (pp. 252–253), and solve interpersonal problems by "putting aside the subjective meanings they attach to a communication and focusing on the objective content" (p. 254). He also uses behavioral techniques to help patients correct the consequences of their illogical thinking. For example, he might ask an angry patient to "divert discussion from a hot topic to a neutral one and postpone further discussion of the highly charged topic" (p. 262).

Ronald M. Rapee (1998) suggests a cognitive approach to shyness and Social Phobia utilizing the following techniques, among others:

• Motivate yourself by recording why you want to change.

• Develop self-control.

• Learn relationship skills.

• Learn how to interpret and think about situations and other people more realistically, for example, by learning that feelings and emotions are directly caused by thoughts, attitudes, and beliefs, not by the things going on outside.

• Identify and change basic beliefs and unwritten laws such as everyone must like me and if I am not liked I am worthless.

• Identify and challenge basic fears—the things that make you anxious.

• Don't overestimate the likelihood that bad things will happen in social situations. Ask, "What is the evidence for the expectations?" and, reassuringly, tell yourself, if the worst should occur, "So what?"

• Use meditation and relaxation to reduce anxiety.

• Practice attention-strengthening exercises to help pay strict attention to the task at hand.

• Engage in previously avoided behaviors gradually, one step at a time, stay in a situation until you start to calm down, and don't be discouraged by bad days.

• Enhance your results by getting feedback from people you trust and by videotaping yourself so that you can see yourself as others see you.

Anthony and Swinson (2000) cover much the same ground as Rapee. Additionally they ask their patients to expose themselves not only to uncomfortable external but also to uncomfortable inner sensations (interoceptive exposure) so that they can get used to and learn to tolerate their inner anxiety experiences. A prototype of interoceptive exposure involves hyperventilating to accustom oneself to the sensations of dizziness that can occur when a patient attempts to make social contact (p. 181). These authors also lay out specifics for teaching the patient how to interact and communicate effectively with other people. They offer patients social skills training, for example, they help them to learn to listen, modify off-putting nonverbal communication and develop conversational skills. They teach them how to go on job interviews; how to communicate assertively instead of too passively (hesitantly, shyly) or passive-aggressively; how to meet new people, make new friends, and date; and how to develop public speaking skills (pp. 193–219).

Benjamin (1996) suggests that therapists should help avoidants block maladaptive patterns with "desensitization" (p. 304). She recommends group therapy for some avoidants, noting, "new skills can be developed in the group [and] normal social development can follow" (p. 305). Speaking somewhat negatively about cognitive-behavioral therapy, she in effect notes that the patient's behavior is often too ingrained and unconscious for cognitive-behavioral therapy alone to be effective (p. 305). The Quality Assurance Project (1991), essentially agreeing with Benjamin, notes that sometimes "social skills training [can lead to] areas of increased social activities with decreased associated anxiety, a lessening of social isolation with diminished depression, and the loss of many irrational social beliefs" (pp. 404–405). However, that is not always the case. "From the literature it could be concluded that social skills training is the treatment of choice for Avoidant Personality Disorder and that graded exposure is likely to promote generalization of newly acquired social skills. Even so there appear to be major problems with the behavioural therapies in getting improvement to generalize outside of the clinic and in helping these people become comfortable with the intimacy they desire" (p. 405).

I believe that too often cognitive therapists treat avoidant symptoms out of context. A patient who is shy and withdrawn but not depressed is treated the same way as a patient who is shy and withdrawn and depressed. Also, most cognitive therapists recognize and treat Type I avoidants only—those suffering from social anxiety in the form of shyness and Social Phobia. Generally speaking they are not particularly directed toward treating Types II–IV avoidants, those avoidants whose social anxiety takes the form of a fear of commitment or defensive removal into codependency. Unconscious motivation, for which there is plenty of evidence—Anthony and Swinson (2000) notwithstanding—is downplayed in favor of a focus on conscious ideation, so that therapists challenge the intellect but not its irrational, emotional underpinnings. All patients are assumed to be cooperative and nonresistant, and the relationship between the therapist and the patient is neither explored nor used for such therapeutic purposes as giving the patient a corrective emotional experience. Behavior therapy in particular, as I see it, has very little to offer Type II–IV avoidants. Gradual exposure techniques suitable for shy avoidants and social phobics such as those afraid of public speaking do not work well for vacillating avoidants who cannot settle down, commitment phobics who fear closeness and intimacy, seven year itch avoidants who become restless in at least what appear to be steady, nonproblematical relationships and feel, to their own detriment and to that of their partners, that they simply have to move on, and dependent-regressed avoidants who hide out in one bodice to avoid ever having to face the world out there beyond their all-engulfing bosom.

Supportive Therapy

Benjamin (1996) notes that in therapy "the AVD's pattern is an especially intense version of the 'generic' patient position. He or she wants to be accepted and loved, and 'holds back' because of poor self-concept and fears of humiliation. The 'generic' therapist position addresses this 'generic' patient position [with] generous doses of . . . empathy and warm support . . . delivered without a hint of judgmentalism or rejection. Gradually, as the AVD shares intimacies and feelings of inadequacy or guilt and shame, the therapist can provide evidence of safe haven. The therapist's benign and nonjudgmental acceptance of the AVD helps the AVD begin to accept himself or herself. As the therapy relationship strengthens, the patient can begin to explore his or her patterns" (p. 302).

Eclectic Therapy

Oldham and Morris (1995) suggest an eclectic approach: "desensitizing [avoidants'] anxiety, [helping avoidants learn] social skills, [helping avoidants] consciously change . . . some of their self-destructive thinking patterns, [and using insight] psychotherapy," which they believe "can be highly beneficial for the Avoidant person who has the courage to face—instead of running away from—his or her problems" (p. 201).

Millon and Davis's (1996) eclectic schema for treating avoidance involves multitasking using individual behavioral, interpersonal, cognitive, self-image (self-worth-enhancing), intrapsychic, and pharmacological therapy (pp. 321–324). Millon and Davis (1996) also advocate group and family approaches for some patients (p. 284). Specifically, Millon and Davis (1996) suggest having avoidant patients: 1. understand their avoidance developmentally and dynamically; 2. focus on increasing pleasure; 3. increase contact to acquire critical social skills; 4. learn to understand others; 5. learn to differentiate between real, incidental, and imagined threats; 6. develop internal (and internalized) realistic reference points by which to judge their own behavior; 7. use cognitive corrections and rework aversive schemas cognitively and behaviorally; 8. use distraction methods, such as positive social interaction; 9. improve self-image; 10. learn to control fretful-expressive behavior while simultaneously establishing and improving friendships; 11. try new experiences, which can help both directly and indirectly by maintaining motivation, and providing the opportunity to monitor behavior and correct maladaptive, automatic thoughts and irrational beliefs; and 12. use pharmacotherapeutic agents when indicated, such as beta blockers, monoamine oxidase inhibitors (MAOI), or serotonin uptake inhibitors to reduce anxiety (pp. 282–284). Millon and Davis (1996) recommend that these therapeutic modalities take place in a supportive setting where the therapist counters apprehension with "freehanded empathy and support" (p. 283), the "therapist's only recourse" (p. 283).

Widiger (1988) also recommends an eclectic approach for the treatment of avoidance. His approach offers a combination of uncovering/insight, cognitive-behavioral therapy including exposure to the avoided stimuli, and supportive therapy including empathic group therapy techniques. Additionally he suggests the use of anxiolytics to help patients cope with their fear and antidepressants to help relieve any superimposed panic disorder (pp. 638–639).

I recommend an eclectic, action-oriented approach to the treatment of avoidance/AvPD. In the realm of the *analytic contribution*, the therapist obtains and imparts insight from a study of the patient's past avoidances, current fantasies, and transference behavior. In the realm of the *cognitive contribution*, the therapist identifies and corrects negative interpersonal illogical distortions, particularly those with a paranoid caste, and emphasizes the positive aspects of those relationships the patient views as all negative. In the realm of the *behavioral contribution*, the therapist gives the patient a series of graded nonavoidant interpersonal tasks of progressive difficulty. In the realm of the *interpersonal contribution*, the therapist shows the patient how he or she makes others uncomfortable with his or her offputting shyness and recommends consultative action, asking the patient to share his or her fears with others, owning up to his or her interpersonal anxieties instead of retreating in silence to save face. This brings avoidance out into the open, both exposing it to the cleansing light of day and getting others to understand and sympathize rather than reacting negatively to the patient's shyness. In the realm of the *educative contribution*, a therapist increases motivation by enumerating the virtues of relating over being isolated. In the realm of the *supportive contribution*, the therapist provides the patient with a warm reassuring, healing environment, which helps reduce relationship anxiety directly with such reassurances as, "You will get over your anxiety if you patiently persevere." Pharmacotherapy, my next topic, is highly recommended for selected patients.

Pharmacotherapy

John R. Marshall (1992) suggests that beta-blockers, MAOI, benzodi-azepines, and possibly other agents are useful in the treatment of Social Phobia (p. A8). Glen O. Gabbard (1992), noting that Social Phobia is the result of "guilt feelings . . . entailing an aggressive demand for complete attention . . . associated with a wish to scare away or kill off all rivals . . . interwoven with a sense of shame. . . . " (p. A8), suggests diminishing anger chemically. Rapee (1998) discourages the use of pharmacotherapy. He suggests, I believe unwisely, that with cognitive therapy medication becomes unnecessary and so "if you are taking medication that was pre-scribed by a doctor, you need to go back to that doctor and ask him or her to help you stop taking the medication" (p. 116).

CHAPTER 3

The Mental Status Profile

Characteristic changes in the mental status profile help make the diagnosis of AvPD and help differentiate patients with AvPD both from patients whose avoidance is within normal limits and from patients suffering from another primary disorder with avoidant features. Patients whose avoidance is within normal limits experience a degree of interpersonal anxiety, but not of sufficient intensity to warrant the diagnosis of Avoidant Personality Disorder or require therapeutic intervention.

Patients suffering from another primary disorder with avoidant features may not yet be ready for avoidance reduction, or if ready, may require more than avoidance reduction alone. The latter was the case for an obsessive-compulsive patient who used a severe hand-washing compulsion not only to express her inner conflicts but also to annoy her husband and provoke him to lose patience with her, and the following schizophrenic patient, clearly a man who needed more than help to embrace the world in a burst of all-loving warmth and affection.

This patient raised his fist up more than once during the evaluation process, replied to the question, "Are you suicidal?" with, "I'd rather kill you than myself," not only spoke of his fantasies of raping old women but actually described several attempted rapes of old women he committed in the past, and pointedly noted that in his last relationship, desiring his lover's life insurance money, he poured gasoline on him and tried to light it, his victim escaping with his life only because the matches were wet.

Patients suffering from another primary disorder with avoidant features might even get worse when treated with avoidance reduction alone. This was the case for a depressed avoidant who responded negatively to avoidance reduction because he viewed his therapist's cognitive corrections as criticism, attempts to relieve his isolation by using total push/exposure as intrusive and controlling, and his own inability to follow his therapist's instructions the first time around as a sign of personal defect.

APPEARANCE

Changes in appearance are often absent in AvPD. If changes are present, they take one of several forms, each representing a different way to deal with social anxiety. Avoidants who withdraw and act shy to deal with their fear of criticism and rejection may appear unable to make eye contact or to offer a firm hand for a handshake. Or they may appear off-putting as they make themselves unappealing by using such props as unstylish clothing deliberately geared to drive others away. Ives Hendrick (1958) refers to off-putting changes in appearance when he notes that "A woman who is in danger of distressing anxiety or guilt from phantasies aroused by strange men looking at her can protect herself by avoiding public places, or by dressing herself so that no one will want to look" (p. 173).

A patient deliberately used little tricks to compromise his appearance. With legs, as he himself said, "bandy and misshapen," he nevertheless wore black socks and formal shoes with walking shorts to make himself look unappealing. He had a rhinoplasty that turned a handsome but big nose into a cute little nose but one that was inappropriate for his face and even for his personality, and he attempted to cover his bald spots in ways that were not only unsuccessful but instead called attention to them. Off-putting too were nonverbal communications like the hostile squint of the eye or the frown screwing up the face into a grimace; carrying tote bags whose logo proclaimed membership in a special group—avoidant because it in effect proclaimed a rejection of people outside of that inner circle; and boredom as manifest in hardly suppressed yawns that indicated his complete lack of interest in what others were saying to him.

Avoidants who also suffer from Posttraumatic Stress Disorder—the PTSD avoidants described in detail in Chapter 10—often put people off by dressing for the era when an original trauma took place. For some Vietnam veterans, wearing 1960s hairstyles/facial hair and "never forget" T-shirts is more than just a matter of nostalgia or being stuck in a traumatic time. It is also part of their plan to continue to live in a traumatic past in order to detach from relationships in the present.

Finally, avoidants who withdraw by becoming hypomanic to deal with their fear of criticism and rejection may overcompensate by primping excessively as their way to be liked, not rejected. They might overdress or use too much makeup hoping to be loved, if not for themselves, then at least for their looks.

BEHAVIOR

Not all avoidants act overtly shy and fearful. Some avoidants, particularly Type I avoidants, convert their shyness into nonverbal-expressive somatic displays of avoidant anxiety. They hide their anxiety as a sexual problem, such as a man's impotence or a woman's dyspareunia when used as a way to detach from a partner. Such sexual problems can appear in the personality as well, in the limp handshake of impotent avoidant men, or in the "interpersonal dyspareunia" of avoidant women who act as if they find personal intercourse as painful and unrewarding as they find sexual intercourse. In contrast, Type II "mingles" avoidants distance not by being fearful or shy but by withdrawing partially, not completely. They detach themselves either by making sensible choices of friends and lovers only to withdraw when closeness threatens, or by selecting friends and lovers whom they sense will be wrong for or unavailable to them right from the start. For example, they select partners who are too handsome or beautiful to be readily attainable. Type III avoidants distance by growing weary of perfectly good ongoing relationships and abandoning suitable partners seemingly without warning. Finally, Type IV avoidants distance by merging into a relationship with one person to detach themselves from the rest of the world.

All avoidants, Type I–IV, are capable of distancing by being either openly or covertly (passive-aggressively) hostile:

One patient expressed his hostility in the form of a body tic, a compulsive sticking his tongue out, easily misinterpreted (or interpreted correctly) as critical by the subjects of his action. He also turned every discussion into a debate by emphasizing B instead of A when it was a little of both; used conversation stoppers, really killers, like "If you would only wear black you would look thirty pounds lighter"; dismissed others by belaboring the obvious in a patronizing way, in one case telling a mental health worker colleague not to allow a patient to have his gun back after the patient was committed to a mental hospital for having shot his wife; and criticized everything and everybody, then thought to undo his hostility by criticizing himself with jokes made at his own expense. For example, he told a clever but revealing story that caused him to be treated as the class clown when it would have been better for him to be treated as the class Romeo: "My friend couldn't find her cat all day. Finally, after hours of hysterical crying and searching, she found the cat by accident, still alive, locked in the refrigerator. I myself would never have this problem, because if my cat were missing I would go right to the refrigerator to grab a beer to celebrate." This got the desired laugh, but people secretly thought him sadistic and wondered how he would treat them if they were in trouble.

On the job he struggled with clients because he resented their making him work. He would hold them to the specifics of an in-terminology that they had little way of knowing and no need to master. He knew, but refused to acknowledge, what the client meant and wanted, and held off giving it to him or her until and unless the client used exactly the right phraseology. To illustrate from a parallel case, a customer called up a bond fund for which a patient worked to ask what interest a specific fund paid. The recipient of the call knew what the customer meant but refused to answer the question until the customer recognized the distinction between interest, dividends, and total yield, and asked for the right one, and in so many words.

SPEECH

Rate

There are two groups of avoidants. The first tends to be silent, and the second tends to be overtalkative. In the realm of the silent avoidant, according to Galvin (1992), Kagan notes that, "For a rabbit, freezing on a lawn is a sign of fear. I believe that speechlessness is a similar diagnostic sign for us. . . . There's a circuit in the brain that controls our vocal cords, and becoming quiet can be one sign of fear . . . extreme introverts have a difficult time beginning conversation at a dinner party where they don't know anyone. The first hour can be painful" (p. 44). Millon (1981), along similar lines, notes how "exterior . . . sluggishness and inactivity [can be a] cover-up . . . [for] chronic tension" (p. 316).

In the realm of the overtalkative avoidant, here underlying interpersonal anxiety or panic is expressed not as impoverishment of speech or outright silence but as an effusive garrulousness often with overinclusiveness, tangentiality, and circumstantiality of speech that may be accompanied by a degree of disorganization of thought. This effusive garrulousness may originate as a direct manifestation of adrenergic discharge; in an affective process (hypomania); in cognitive error, for example, in the magical belief that, "If I keep talking I won't faint or die"; or as a denial defense against interpersonal anxiety, for example, as an attempt to be the life of the party to cover up the fear that one will not be entertaining enough to be invited back.

Content

Unendearing "foot-in-the-mouth" blunders and other off-putting conversation-stoppers are characteristic of the more hostile avoidants. These include throwing-cold-water-in-the-face retorts, insinuations/indelicacies, and outright social blunders. A psychiatrist told a colleague of the pleasure he derived from a recent visit to Cambridge, Massachusetts, because of the wonderful "ghosts of all the old analysts that inhabited the area," whereupon the colleague's first remark (really association) was, "What is the name of that man who just came out with another anti-Freudian book?" One woman called a slightly older but still young man "Pops." One man regularly asked the dreaded question, "What do you do?" when first meeting people socially, though by experience he knew that he would often elicit a negative response for being nosy and intrusive. Talking about oneself too much is a common method Type II avoidants use to put distance between themselves and others. Boring topics thrust on an unwilling listener also belong in this category, such as one man's need to debate, every chance he got, the long-ago-become-tiresome issue of whether George Gershwin's *Porgy and Bess* is or is not an opera. Off-putting verbal tics that drive others to despair are also found, such as calling everything "little" to devalue it; overusing the trite expressions "well" and "you know" or both together as "well, you know"; including all of one's second thoughts in every pronouncement for purpose of accuracy (really of obfuscation); and using the same questioning word or phrase over and over again, like the obsessional uncertainty/apology of ending every sentence with, "Is that right?" or "Is that okay?" to indicate personal hesitation and to express intrusively an excessive need for confirmation and love.

THOUGHT

Avoidant thought consists of a number of *cognitive errors* that lead the avoidant to conclude that he or she should fear relationships. These cognitive errors were referred to in Chapter 2 and will be discussed in detail in Chapters 12 and 15. To anticipate, avoidants who think catastrophically, in the "for want of a penny the ship was lost" mode, believe that any sign of uninterest in them becomes a turndown, a turndown becomes a rejection, and a rejection becomes an event of tragic proportions.

The inability in waking life to make and keep personal contacts has as its counterpart *dreams* whose theme is being unable to relate, being abandoned, being alone, and being lonely. In some dreams the sense of isolation/failure is expressed directly, while in others the expression is symbolic—as in dreams of running stuck in place and not being able to move forward; or waiting for the bus that never comes, then when it finally does come, it turns out to be the wrong bus; or if it is the right bus, it takes us to the wrong place, or to a dangerous place, where we get mugged. This symbolic expression often takes on a surrealistic cast:

A man dreamt of a street at the end of which was a welcoming bar, with welcoming neon lights, friendly music, and warm grog. One side of the street was brightly lit, and the other was completely dark. Unable to traverse the lit side he had to instead traverse the side that was dark. This side, however, held too many terrors and dangers for him to seriously consider making the attempt.

AFFECT

Some avoidants deal with their fears of being rejected by developing a protective bluntness of affect that comes across as a removal. Others deny the possibility of being rejected by becoming hypomanic. Still others become depressed in order to become inured to a rejection that they are certain will come. As mentioned throughout, many avoidants are hostile people. Thus Millon (1981) notes the presence of "tension, sadness and anger" (p. 303) in avoidants, states that avoidant profiles are often shared with passive-aggressives (he identifies an avoidant-passive-aggressive mixed personality), and notes that avoidants have "strong elements of counterhostility" (page 310). Frances and Widiger (1987) state, in referring to Widiger and Kelso's circumplex model, that avoidants are, like passive-aggressives, "likely to be higher on hostility" (p. 278) than dependents. Walter B. Cannon's familiar fight-flight dichotomy suggests that hostility and timidity are opposite sides of the same coin. A physician-patient himself forged an association between anxiety and hostility by comparing himself to a dog who "barks both because he is afraid and because he is angry," and by noting that after a mouse crossed his path, first he jumped in fear, and second he wanted to kill it.

Anger in avoidants can be part of their *temperament*; a defense against relating, for example, identifying with the aggressor and becoming critical of others (as Benjamin [1996] suggests, becoming "commanding and judgmental" [p. 293]) to cope with feeling criticized by others; or *rational* as distinct from irrational. In the realm of temperament, it seems as if some avoidants were born angry.

An avoidant drove a waitress to tears by telling her that she was a complete idiot for asking if she wanted her pork chops medium or well-done, even though the reason she asked was because management told her to inquire. Though she said that more than anything else she feared losing her on-the-job friends, she nevertheless told a coworker, "I don't see how you can come to work with such frizzy hair." The victim was so hurt by the remark that she spent all day looking in the mirror. To quote her, "Every fifteen minutes I went into the bathroom to check to see if my hair was straight."

In the realm of *defensive* anger, avoidants can retreat via becoming provocative, as a case of Hendrick (1958) illustrates: "To avoid the anxiety which threatens when impulses to love genital objects and friends are conscious, the individual may renounce love and camaraderie. . . . The man who was insolent to superiors as soon as he began to love them illustrates such a case" (p. 173). Shyness itself can be defensive, a cynically hostile critical aggressive pushing others away in order to make certain that, as one patient put it, there will be "none of that closeness that I fear."

In the realm of *rational*, that is *reactive*, anger, anger is sometimes a sensible response to others' hostility or counterhostility. However, so-called reactive anger must be differentiated from irrational anger—anger that is excessive and inappropriate. This is exemplified by anger due to a paranoid tendency to imagine reasons to get angry in the absence of such reasons, like the anger that originates in a correct but narrow and selective view of what others have in mind, or in an inability or a refusal to see another's benign as compared to negative motives, or good as compared to bad points.

A patient and his wife though estranged and living separately still attended social functions together. The wife of the estranged couple invited an intact couple over for dinner with her alone. When the husband found out about it he saw ulterior motives in her innocent behavior, and became suspicious and angry, thinking that at best he was being rejected, and at worst that his wife had something going on with the couple. So he called the couple up to rail against them for excluding him, and told them that he would no longer be their friend.

Irrational anger tends to flare most when the avoidant feels his or her *dependency* needs threatened; feels *controlled*; or when as an excessively competitive individual, he or she feels as if he or she is *losing out*.

In the realm of threatened dependency needs:

An appliance salesman was fired because his customers complained to management that when they asked him if he could cut the price on an item he stared them down. He later admitted that this was his way to tell them that he felt like strangling them for trying to deprive him of some of the commission he needed to feed his family.

In the realm of feeling controlled:

At work a physician looked for any excuse he could find to loaf, proclaiming that his favorite cartoon was one that said in essence, "Medicine would be fun if we didn't actually have to see patients." In his social life when at parties he cycled between fear and anger, now feeling shy and shrinking from desired contacts, and now thinking, "Who needs those people, they don't compare to me in brains or looks. They are just a bunch of slobs." On those rare occasions when he began relationships, he soon became angry that the other person was attempting to "make time with him." Then he expressed his hostility in the form of what might be described as a "fear of commitment aggressively communicated to a hapless partner." When he said, "I hesitate to be tied down," he in fact intended an attack, a slap in the face, a hurtful criticism that in essence meant, "I don't want to be tied down *to you*."

In the realm of feeling as if one is losing out competitively:

The colleague of a free-lance writer was hostile to anyone he perceived to be more successful than he. The writer said, "I'm writing an article on . . . ," to which his colleague replied, "It has been done before." Again the writer said he was writing an article, and this time the colleague replied, "That was just done recently in . . ." This only inspired the writer to become frantic in his need to get approval, so he continued much in the same vein, only to have his colleague reply this time, "That was an interesting topic, seven years ago."

Two sisters envied and angrily competed with each other. One sister, who lived in New Jersey, complained about the other sister, who lived in New York, saying, "She always sends her packages to my home in New Jersey. She says this is to save on New York sales tax, but I think this is merely a ploy to make me subservient. I feel like a doorman ordered to pick up her parcels. I envy her for having so much more money than I, enough to buy the beautiful things I can't afford." The New Jersey sister next refused to accept any more parcels, and that became the occasion for the two to stop speaking to each other. The New York sister complained, "I won't talk to anyone who refuses to do me a little favor," while the New Jersey sister complained, "I won't talk to anyone who treats me like a commoner."

Two other sisters fought constantly whenever they got together in person so, though they lived but ten blocks away from each other, they saw each other only twice a year, on July 4th for the family picnic, and on Christmas Eve. At other times there was contact, but it was by answering machine or e-mail only. A sample fight: "She doesn't want me to have what she has. So she recommends great new books knowing that since I can't afford them in hard cover, I will be tantalized waiting until they come out in paperback. I'll retaliate by forgetting to tell her about scheduled family events. This way she can be the only insider who is absent. When she finds out after the fact, she'll think that the whole family didn't want her to be there, not just me."

Two neighbors outdid each other in creating "the elegant country home." One waxed enthusiastic about staining his wooden floors white, the other about growing an indoor ficus tree so tall that it would reach to the two-story high ceiling of his living room. What started as constructive competition turned into a feud so intense that it resulted in their not speaking, each thinking, "If he wants to do battle, then it's war." Trivial slights, interpersonal faux pas, and/or characterological peculiarities were then cited for justification of what was already felt and planned. One said, "He talks about sex too much," the other, "He's making fun of me for serving English muffins instead of croissants," and, "How dare he take upsetting phone calls in my house, then cry when someone he loves cancels a date. After all, this is my refuge, not a place where I want to be bothered by someone else's problems."

A coworker became enraged because he believed another's skills, however peripheral to his own needs, highlighted his own failings. So he reacted to the discovery that a colleague could type better than he could by taking a speed-typing course, not because he needed to learn how to type fast, but because he needed to crush what he believed to be competition.

When a rabid stereo aficionado told a friend, "My sound system is great," he really meant, "Better than yours," and ultimately, "I am better than you are," a message not lost on the hearer. What was lost was the friendship, which crumbled in two stages—first with the initial bragging and second when the entire sublimation came unglued and raw competitive hostility erupted in an escalating battle of the stereos, one thinking, "I want more than anything to beat him," and the other thinking, "He is trying to castrate me—I can't allow him to have an amplifier bigger than mine."

Finally, as anger is a way to cope defensively with closeness, distance is a way to cope defensively with anger. As previously mentioned in Chapter 2, Fenichel (1945) implies as much when he refers to how a feeling of "fatigue and lack of power [appears] on occasions where others would feel rage" (p. 169).

INSIGHT

Good Insight

Avoidants with *good* insight are aware that they have relationship anxiety and that it is a problem for them. They read books about their avoidance, analyze themselves, and consult therapists for help in getting over their inhibitions so that they can be free to express the loving that they have inside.

Partial/Compromised Insight

Many avoidants lack a degree of insight into their avoidance. Their insight is partial or compromised in one of a number of ways. In one form of partial or compromised insight, avoidants do seek change for their difficulty relating, but they do not seek that change through treatment. Rather they seek it through discovering the new and better club, singles or gay bar, plastic surgeon, apartment, house in the country, clothier, hairstylist, or dating service. In another form of partial or compromised insight, avoidants have good superficial but impaired deep insight. Such avoidants may be aware that they are avoidant but not why. In another form of partial or compromised insight, avoidants are aware of their avoidance but not of its consequences and are aware of their inhibitions but unaware of how these compromise function, that is, of the effect their avoidance has on their lives and on others. They might say, "I admit I'm a perfectionist," but fail to recognize specifically how their perfectionism leads them to put off or discard suitable candidates for relationships. Or they might say, "I admit I'm fussy," while failing to recognize how their fussiness makes them impossible to live with. In still another form of partial or compromised insight, avoidants admit to their problems but make "not-me" excuses for having them. They view their inability to connect as a natural, expected response to inner or outer circumstances beyond their control. They blame their biology ("my chemical imbalance"), physical problems ("I am ugly"), or advanced age, or remain convinced that bad luck, fate, and the stars explain why they cannot meet Mr. or Ms. Right and develop a long-term committed relationship or get married.

Nancy Hass (2002), in an article in the *New York Times* entitled "A Haven for Women Is No Longer Quite Home," speaks of buildings in New York City that were a magnet for women who were seeking an independent life. In her article she quotes a retired teacher who is in her early sixties explaining away a lifetime of staying single: "I never found anyone who was interesting or creative enough. They just wanted me to move to Scarsdale or Riverdale or somewhere and be a house mouse. I never found a good enough reason to leave this nice place" (p. 6).

They frequently blame geography for a failure to connect. A common scapegoat is the environment in which they live, such as the city in which they feel stuck ("You can't meet anyone in New York"), or the place they go to try being nonavoidant ("None of the bars in this town are any good").

Such avoidants are typically unaware of how they engineer the very rejections they claim to fear. They typically say "I tried but it's not to be." They fail to see that they pick unavailable people for partners or actively provoke available people to reject them. Many claim that others are aggravating their paranoia when in fact they are aggravating the paranoia of others. Unconsciously, rather instantaneously, by a glance, a backward look, a flash of disdain, they enable others, particularly sensitive others, to read their avoidant minds and to know in an instant what they are thinking and plan to do, until others, quite naturally, counterrespond also instantaneously, accordingly, and negatively. Hypomanic avoidants are routinely unaware of how their frantic but meaningless counterphobic/hypomanic/compulsive/driven homosexual or heterosexual activity (with or without cyclic removal) is ultimately a way not to connect but to distance themselves from close meaningful relationships by driving off serious suitors.

To anticipate my therapeutic approach to avoidants who unconsciously engineer their own loneliness, such avoidants must accept a degree of responsibility for themselves and for their avoidant behavior. Avoidants who continue to believe they are alone because they haven't hit the right club yet, live in the boondocks where it is impossible to meet people because there is no one there to meet or live in the big city where it is impossible to meet people because everyone is unfriendly, have discouraging parents who defeat them at every turn, or have a job that makes them too tired to socialize after work, should just admit to themselves, "it's me," and do something about it. They should ask themselves, "What do I do that makes me unable to meet people and/or causes me to lose them after I have met them?" and answer this and other related questions intelligently and perceptively, then use their answers as the basis for creating a new nonavoidant plan. This new plan should be based on the realization that they are acting the part of the captain of a sinking ship who runs the ship onto the rocks of his or her own making following a map of his or her own design, then blames the choppy and shallow water instead of his or her own inability or refusal to steer the ship away from the rocky shoals. In my experience, most avoidants could overcome their relationship anxiety and meet people if only they could muster the strength and courage to overcome the main thing holding them back— not the small town they live in full of undesirables, or anything like that, but themselves.

In still another form of partial/compromised insight, avoidants permit themselves full insight as long as it does no good. They freely acknowledge their avoidance, understand its origins, and recognize its consequences, yet they steadfastly maintain that they are helpless to cope with it. As one patient put it, "I know I turn people off, and I do it in this and that way, but I can't do anything to change, and years of therapy hasn't helped."

Finally, partial/compromised insight is often the product of a comorbid emotional disorder. For example, in depressed avoidants insight is typically present but self-punitive. Depressed avoidants do not, like paranoid avoidants, externalize their forbidden impulses so that they may attribute them to others and criticize them accordingly. Rather they heap abuse on themselves for their difficulties. As a result they close off constructive dialogue by viewing themselves not as troubled and conflicted but as too dim-witted to be helped.

Poor Insight

Still other avoidants have *little* insight, superficial or deep:

An avoidant man who refused to let a penniless friend borrow a book because he feared that the friend might soil some of the pages was only aware of the fate of his book, not of the fate of his relationship. He followed this pattern throughout life, never making the connection between his avoidance and the loneliness and isolation of which he complained.

Characteristically, uninsightful avoidants have simply built their avoidance into their lives, unquestioningly, with little or no idea of why they are so uncomfortable and dissatisfied with their existence. As Fenichel (1945) suggests, these avoidants "avoid certain situations or objects or activities or fields of interest or qualities of feeling . . . without being aware of the avoidance" (p. 169). They have relationships, but they are unaware that what relationships they have are not truly intimate. Rather their relationships are what Sullivan (1953) has called "ritual preoccupations" (p. 308), and what Fenichel (1945) has called "substitute gratifications" (p. 180). As mentioned throughout, many disguise their avoidances as *preferences* or *tastes*. As an example, one avoidant who nightly dreamed that he wanted to, but was afraid to, meet people, daily rationalized his avoidance as follows: "I prefer to live alone because I can fill the refrigerator with what I want to eat, drop my clothes wherever I want to drop them, play my sound equipment when and how it suits me, and when I go to work and leave a soda behind know it will be there when I return." Others disguise their avoidance as *appropriate*. An avoidant went to the greatest lengths to justify his competitiveness as "normal professional rivalry." A composer, he railed against live composers and believed that the only good composer was a dead one, not because he thought modern music had no value, but because he saw modernists as live competitors, not safely tucked away underground. Such avoidants may justify a sadistic inhumanity to man according to high, lofty principles that are only part, and often a small part, of the picture. Here I include doctors refusing to "addict" terminal patients to opiates even though there are no practical negative consequences of such an addiction, and the gay journalist whose real reasons for outing closeted homosexuals in the public eye (beyond the sociocultural excuses he made) were revealed when he said, "Moral judgments must be made about gay men and women who hide their sexuality." Avoidants who justify their avoidance as appropriate might cite their avoidant behaviors as being "in" and therefore nonavoidant because it's currently popular, that is, because "everybody is doing it" (for example, the do-your-own-thing or me-ism avoidances of the recent past, and the schadenfreude avoidance rife in today's world). Other avoidants justify their avoidances as *rational* responses. They believe that some of their prejudices, such as homophobia, are an appropriate negative response to real, unlikable behaviors on the part of gay men and lesbians when in fact they are just another excuse to hate and discard people. Some complain of sexual harassment, viewing their complaints as perfectly justified even when they are little more than paranoid misattributions to others of their own forbidden sexual desires, or an overreaction to sexual approaches that are appropriate and would not be unwelcome to other people under some circumstances.

The following are examples of patients who might have or who actually benefited from developing more insight into how they put distance between themselves and others.

One narcissist was very unpopular at the gym because of his habit of selecting a machine, doing a set of exercises, then going off to find a pad or weight for the machine, or going to the lounge to rest between sets, all the while retaining the machine in his fantasy as "reserved for me" so that when he returned he expected to find the machine unoccupied and waiting. If he found it occupied, he became enraged that it was "taken from him." Now he interrupted the "interloper" with an all-too-transparent passive-aggressive question, "How many more sets do you have to do?" really, "And when are you going to get off my machine?"

A patient who came to therapy claiming "I dislike being alone, help me get connected" lived near his psychiatrist. A few months after therapy began, he became preoccupied with the possibility that he and his therapist might meet by accident, and that his therapist might catch him in compromising behavior and throw him out of treatment. So he became very hostile to his therapist, giving as his reason, "You charge too much and I am saving my money for my old age." His hostility was part of a plan to provoke his therapist to interrupt treatment so that, as an ex-patient, he would have less reason to feel sheepish about meeting his therapist outside of formal sessions.

An ambivalent avoidant put ads in the personals column deliberately worded to show uncertainty of purpose—ads that were both welcoming ("wants to meet") and off-putting ("Manhattan only.") She joined groups manifestly designed to help people meet people but with a latent agenda: to maintain the integrity of the group. The individuals in the group encouraged each other to throw cold water on any relationships that came the way of the other group members. When she was not in a committed relationship she complained about being lonely, but when she was in one she complained of feeling overwhelmed. She accepted blind dates from sources that had proved unreliable in the past, but refused blind dates when she sensed that they might work out. When they seemed not to be working out she made another date to see if she could make repairs, but when they seemed to be working out, she looked for something about the individual that would allow her to express a preconceived negative notion about how most blind dates are "bad news"—for example, blemished on "account of not already having a date," that is, on account of needing the blind date in the first place. To the dates themselves, she made it clear that she felt that "accepting a blind date is a desperate maneuver for people who can't do any better." For good measure she used her date's minor flaws to illustrate what she meant, adding, in a further rejection, "Here are some suggestions for how you can improve yourself, if not for me, then the next time, for the next person."

In her therapy she made appointments, then forgot them, called to make another one and broke that, came late (calling to say she was just leaving from home about the time she was expected in the office), or came at the right time but on the wrong day—all the while apologizing, yet continuing to repeat her actions. She spent the few sessions that actually took place criticizing her therapist. For example, he was damned if he did and damned if he didn't—if he pushed her too far and too fast, he was making her anxious, and if he was too accepting of her and of her resistances to getting out and meeting people, he wasn't doing enough for her. Eventually, looking for something concrete to justify a hostile attitude already in place toward him, she began to criticize him personally, along the following lines: on the days she thought that he was a married man, she suspected him of having an extramarital affair or of trying to seduce her, while on the days she thought he might be single, she suspected him of being abstinent or homosexual.

Here is a letter I received from an ex-patient, presented without comment.

There is not much action in the town and since most of the gays are in the closet meeting people is very difficult. I have taken your advice—I do not frequent too many bars and of course, I never drank. I am still single. I have had a few flings, but they were just that, flings. I am still very serious about meeting someone and establishing a monogamous relationship. But I can't seem to meet the right person. Maybe I am simply not receptive enough. I seem to have a propensity for being attracted to divorced or soon-to-be divorced men with children, who may or may not be homosexual. I suspect that they are, but nothing seems to happen. I really think that I am wasting my time.

JUDGMENT

Bad judgment is a frequent companion of bad insight. Indeed, avoidance is by definition an act of bad judgment. Additionally, avoidants deliberately if unconsciously cultivate bad judgment for purposes of further avoidance.

The above-mentioned estranged avoidant couple lived together in a house divided into two parts. The man, who no longer had sexual intercourse with his wife because "the romance has gone out of our marriage," took on a lover and invited her to stay with him in his part of the house, in full view both of his estranged wife and of their children.

One woman described her failure plan as follows: "I will go to New York, have a sophisticated career and lifestyle, give it up to get married, then move to the suburbs, get a dog, and have children when, unhappy about and bored with being a housewife, I will hire help to care for my children and resume working at something more gratifying than housework. My outside work will then give me the money I need to become independent and my independence the emotional foundation I need to get a divorce. After my divorce I can again return to the place of my birth, home to my family, whom I should never have left in the first place."

Bad judgment is often fueled by comorbid affective disorder. *Depressed* avoidants display bad judgment by living out self-defeating and self-destructive beliefs such as the conviction that "I can spot the good pickup from superficial inspection, for if he's clean and handsome then he is safe." Or they display bad judgment by living out low self-esteem by desperately pleading for attention in a way that makes them look weak and vulnerable, and elicits not love but ridicule from others. Or they live out bad judgment by displaying self-hatred by relating to people who are too different from them to be compatible.

A northern attorney told of how he joined a gun club in the South to escape the oppressive sophistication of New Yorkers. Then he laughingly admitted, "They could tell I'm not one of them anyway, no matter how hard I tried to disguise it." But what was he doing there, why did he want to be one of them, and why was he trying to disguise who he was? Analysis revealed that it was his inability to self-accept that made him desire to hide his true identity by joining a group whose members seemed as unlike himself as possible. Predictable were his sense of panic and self-disgust when he found he "couldn't make it there because these people are not like me," and his defensive disdain of others, thinking, "These people are no good anyway" in order to avoid recognizing the anger and disappointment he felt about not fitting in.

Hypomanic avoidants, who look conjunctive while actually remaining disjunctive, display bad judgment by devoting themselves full-time to being nonavoidant, too frantically intensifying the search for love in order to hide their fear of actually finding it.

One individual's life consisted of a concentrated, compulsive, driven, single-minded distractive searching for partners that forced connecting instead of letting it go at its own rate. Wherever he was and whatever he was doing, he stared directly at an attractive individual or, thinking he could contemplate the mark leisurely without his being noticed (untrue because the mark invariably sensed he was being looked at), fixed him in his peripheral vision. He attended singles bars every night and stayed up late drinking and searching, a practice he continued even though, really because, he knew that even if meaningful liaisons did begin in such places at such times he would do his career serious damage if night after night he deprived himself of the sleep he had to have to effectively concentrate on his work the next day.

Such individuals go to all the right places, then do all the wrong things when they get there, such as focusing on matters tangential to their stated purpose, getting drunk, or improving their self-esteem by satirizing/humiliating/vilifying potential suitors, often for nothing more than minor physical flaws or trivial character imperfections. Equally self-defeating is their propensity to fall in love at first sight after attributing special qual-

ities to others that they don't really have, and the opposite tendency—
simultaneously operative— to hate others before they even get to know
them. An avoidant who alternated between these two positions went to
singles bars where she either "met the love of my life" or saw only "the
worst dorks I have ever encountered." Many choose the classic hypomanic
geographical "solution" to relationship problems—rushing about from
town to town, impotently trying to change their luck by changing their
locale.

One man's fantasy was that in the Big City he would find a better, more suitable
woman than he could find in his home town. For this man the small-town woman
was too poor, too unsophisticated, too uneducated, and not beautiful enough to
warrant his attention. That this was a critical man who, having eliminated all
women at home, was also likely to eliminate all women in the Big City, is evident
from his subsequent assessment of the Big City woman: "too sophisticated, edu-
cated, and beautiful to be as warm and welcoming as the women back in my
hometown."

Such hypomanics are well-represented among the avoidants who become one with groups, or gangs, who say they want to "meet others" but
who put group cohesion before self-realization. At the gym I attend there
is a hard-core of in-group singles I overhear telling each other, loudly,
volubly, and continuously, how much they long to meet someone right
for them, while complaining to each other that they cannot find Mr. or
Ms. Right even though they hit the bars every night and cruise constantly
for love. Apparently the solution is more obvious to me than it is to them:
stop hitting the bars every night, stop socializing exclusively with each
other at the gym, and start talking to some of the hundreds of other people
on the floor that until now they have been completely ignoring.

Bad judgment often takes the form of using the personal ads not to
meet someone but to act out one's avoidance. Avoidants act out by placing
ads virtually guaranteed to defeat their stated purpose. Instead of presenting their case, they present their case history. Instead of acting resolutely nonavoidant they place ads where their ambivalence shows—the
familiar "caring sharing, no one over 25" admixture. Instead of placing
ads indicating a willingness to expand their horizons they place ads that
narrow or eliminate good possibilities right from the start. Two ways they
do this are through displays of compulsive preferences and by making
nonnegotiable demands for others with identical interests. Compulsive
preferences are preferences chosen for, not by, the one expressing the preference. A common compulsive preference involves the compunction to be
associated with status and power—the "wow" or "varsity letter" standard
for relationships. Here avoidants demand grandness in others in order to
simultaneously divert themselves from and compensate for their own feel-

ings of being personally defective, the typical "I won't relate to him/her unless his/her family meets certain lofty standards." Identical interests, though much in demand by ad-placers, are also a trap for the unwary, being as much a reason for exclusion as they are for inclusion.

Self-defeating too is not presenting oneself in a positive light but instead offering bad presentations of good qualities, as when high self-esteem comes across as narcissism. Also self-defeating is a failure to steer a moderate course between excessive modesty and immodesty. Both excessive modesty and excessive immodesty are off-putting, the first because it suggests feelings of inferiority directly and the second because it suggests that the individual is attempting to overcompensate. Also self-defeating are ads that masochistically beg, putting the ad-placer in a particularly bad light as he or she desperately and in a self-humiliating way pleads for help or proclaims a willingness to take anything he or she can get. Such self-demeaning ads provoke a sadistic counterresponse. The reader may be inspired to rub it in in the reply—by writing back of his or her lack of interest in "someone with your undesirable characteristics," or by making a first date, then breaking it before it takes place. Some sadists even keep the first date just so that they can hurt their victim by refusing to make a second date.

Also self-defeating are ads that are off-putting because they overuse diverting humor, though romance is rarely a laughing matter and laughing matters are rarely romantic. Humorous ads that make the clever hook and the bon mot more important than the potential relationship lose sight of the original purpose for placing the ad. All of us have witnessed the off-putting effect of the good joke made on the self as a misguided attempt to get points for being able to take a little self-kidding. In this behavior others see not humorous deficiencies/uproarious foibles, but disqualifying lesions. One fellow said in his ad, "I love lobster so much that I even eat the shells." Analysis revealed that saying he loved lobster was a misguided attempt to be sophisticated, while saying he ate the shells was an equally misguided attempt to take it back in order not to appear excessively proud of himself and insufficiently "down to earth." In the same category are ads that are marked by a superficial self-conscious feyness— the classically cited, "I love midnight walks on the beach, and yellow candles." This feyness diverts from more important personal qualities such as the capacity for warmth, empathy, and love, or undoes desirable traits by caricaturing them, giving them an overdone, hard-breathing, melodramatic, "I want someone who is all heart" quality.

Unwelcoming ads that are hurtful to others are particularly unproductive. The people who read these ads view aggressively put age and body habitus preferences not as suggestions about what the ad-placer would like but as comments on what they as potential applicants don't have. This makes potential applicants, many of whom already feel hopeless and depressed, believe that they do not match up. Now they feel even more hopeless and depressed. They do not respond to the ad in question and may even give up all attempts at socializing, thus reducing the pool of available candidates. (To my way of thinking, avoidants have a social responsibility to help other avoidants out. Listing others' possible flaws is the opposite of helpful.)

Finally, some ads are ultimately self-defeating because they are selfishly manipulative rather than straightforward and honest. The ad-placers are just looking for someone to make a current partner jealous, to hedge bets by having someone in reserve in case what they have now does not work out, or to notch their gun, along the lines of "see how many people are interested in me, that must mean that I am interesting." Some ad-placers even put in ads never intending to reply to any takers. They merely want to be entertained. They get sadistic pleasure out of others' desperation, and out of gloating how they are better off than the losers out there. Or they are just attempting to win points with their friends by collecting replies and passing them on.

CHAPTER 4

Types of Avoidants

I distinguish four types of avoidants according to the specific way their underlying social or relationship anxiety becomes manifest clinically:

TYPE I: SHY/SOCIAL PHOBIC AVOIDANTS

Type I avoidants are distinguished by their use of withdrawal mechanisms to manage their social anxiety. There are two subtypes: shy avoidants and social phobics. *Shy* Type I avoidants have difficulty forming relationships. Some Type I shy avoidants are seriously isolated individuals:

A patient, after having gone to a great deal of trouble and expense to move from the crowded large city in which he lived to a small town with fewer people, could do no better than to complain about the daytime noise in his new hometown—the leaf blowers, the gas company repairing the mains, and the like, really because they were the accoutrements of life and living. To get away from all the activity he moved again, this time to a farmhouse surrounded by acres of land and enclosed by a high fence to keep intruders out—only to move still again to an even more remote place in the desert because "On the farm I'm frightened by the shadows in the woods at night."

After years of being unemployed he took a job working in the mail room of the post office. He took that particular job even though it was beneath his capabilities because it allowed him to have as little contact as possible with his coworkers. He wanted to avoid contact with them because he took their minor slights and rejections so personally that after arriving home after a day's work he began to brood about who said, meant, and did what to him. Unable to sleep that night, he was too tired to function effectively the next day and so unable to concentrate on his work. As a result, he became so distraught that he called in sick the day after that, only to become so guilty for calling in sick that he was once again unable to sleep at night, and had to call in sick the day afterwards as well. Eventually he became a secretive, isolated, sullen and uncooperative worker who was diagnosed as having burnout and put on disability leave. In response, he quit his job, and returned once again to his lonely, completely isolated life.

Other Type I shy avoidants are less isolated than he:

A woman stayed at home with her parents, being the good, dutiful, but resentfully compliant daughter who drew a magic circle around herself, letting no one important in. She had a few friends whom she saw occasionally but no close intimates. Her life was mainly filled with impersonal interests such as collecting things and attending craft shows. While sometimes she complained about being lonely and isolated, at other times she convinced herself that she was enjoying her life, living it exactly the way she wanted to.

Still other Type I shy avoidants do manage to get out, and even go to singles bars, mixers and parties. However they function poorly once they get there, standing off completely by themselves, or speaking only to the person they came in with. They regularly complain that they are dissatisfied with the narrowness of their lives, but just as regularly add that however hard they try to change their luck they can never seem to do any better.

Social phobic Type I avoidants also use withdrawal mechanisms to handle their social anxiety. However, they display their withdrawal mainly symbolically, and they do so specifically in situations where they feel called upon to perform—such as being asked to write a check or speak in public. I discuss the differences between patients with AvPD and patients with a Social Phobia in detail in Chapters 1, 2, 10, and 12.

TYPE II: "MINGLES" AVOIDANTS

While Type I shy avoidants tend to be, and come across to others as, self-conscious, introverted, and lacking in self-confidence, Type II, or "mingles," avoidants give just the opposite impression. They look, at least superficially, as if they are well-related, and sometimes even better related than average. Unlike Type I shy avoidants, who are *neophobes*—that is, individuals who cannot initiate relationships because they fear what an unknown fate holds in store for them, Type II "mingles" avoidants are very comfortable socializing and are even *neophiles* who want to, can, and like to attend social functions and initiate relationships once they get there. However, while they find it easy to form new relationships, they find it hard to keep them going. There are several subtypes:

The Anxious Type

Anxious Type II avoidants are too fearful to maintain new relationships both because they are too highly attuned to the possibility of being criticized, humiliated, and rejected and because they take actual criticisms, humiliations, and rejections too seriously. Some are rejection-sensitive because they expect too much from the world. They forget that rejection is part of life's give and take. Expecting life to always be fair, rewarding, and complete, they have become highly vulnerable to the first signs of life's inherent unfairness. Expecting miracles on a regular basis, they go to mingles events/singles resorts/share singles homes in country resorts thinking, "Tonight I will connect for sure," then, even though they know intellectually and from experience that they cannot count on connecting every night, let one night's failure or one turndown become a commentary on how they are completely wasting their time, and how no one will *ever* love them. In many cases a catastrophic reaction follows. They panic, pull back, give up, and cry, "Never again." Others are rejection-sensitive because their self-esteem is very low. They anticipate rejections and take those that actually occur much too seriously, believing that that means that their greatest fears have come true.

The Ambivalent Type

Ambivalent Type II avoidants are too uncertain to pursue relationships without seriously vacillating. Among these individuals are the grass-is-always-greener singles who place personal ads even when they have currently successful relationships going, then view those who reply positively to the ads as less exciting than those who are still out there. Also among them we find the bachelor who can never be captured, at least for very long, or the seductive woman who breaks off a relationship as soon as it appears to be getting serious. On the one hand, they condemn others for being too remote and unfriendly; they act very dependent and beg others to love them, saying, "Please, I cannot live without you." Then, doing an about-face, on the other hand they condemn others for coming too close— for moving and closing in on them, and occupying their space; they become remote and threaten to break off the relationship complaining that they are being forced into something they want no part of. They resemble the fictional hard-to-get Holly Golightly in Truman Capote's (1993) *Breakfast at Tiffany's*, and Rodolphe in Gustave Flaubert's (1964) *Madame Bovary*, whose ambivalent delaying tactics (meant to postpone and ultimately avoid running off with Emma Bovary) were described thus by Flaubert:

He [Rodolphe] needed two more weeks to wind up some business. Then, after one week had passed, he asked for two more. Then he said he felt ill. Then he took a trip. The month of August passed. After all these delays, they decided that it would be, without fail, Monday, September 4 (p. 193).

The Masochistic Type

Masochistic Type II avoidants prove the truth of the Freudian formulation that behind every fear is a hidden wish. While they manifestly complain about fearing rejection, they secretly desire it, because they fear acceptance even more, and with it the success that acceptance brings. As such they arrange to have their relationships fail. They might arrange to fail by pursuing quantity over quality. Or they might arrange to fail by joining groups of other avoidants with the same or similar problems. Now they all head for, but never seem to find, a conquest. All concerned roam around in "packs," saying that they hope to "snare a man" or "finally pick the right woman." Instead they relate as a collective—to only other members of their group, each group member seeing to it that the other members meet no one outside of the group. Such groups typically maintain their integrity by ostracizing people outside of the group, making certain that no one not already in the group is ever admitted into their magic inner circle. Often heavy drinking is part of the picture, and can even become the main purpose of the group, the group's real, or even only, "social" activity.

Or they might arrange to fail by selecting distant unavailable people to relate to, or people with a fatal flaw, such as those who dislike them or those who are already taken, for example, because they are married. They often have rescue fantasies in which they long to turn impossible situations around, then make efforts to do so, even knowing that their efforts are virtually certain to come to naught. A familiar example is the woman who selects a married man to change from polygamous/promiscuous to monogamous/faithful, forgetting, really remembering, that this man is already a proven cheat on account of his record with her, and so is unlikely to be ready, willing, or able to, be rescued from himself.

The Dissociative Type

Dissociative Type II avoidants, when faced with the danger, as they see it, of being accepted and getting what they want, go into a trance or enter another one of their multiple personalities.

One patient's dissociation/trance behaviors reminded him of the rabbit freezing instead of running, a trance that was meant to be protective but was actually self-destructive just as it is when it occurs in a rabbit who happens to be in the middle of the road, in the path of a car. He denied closeness as other people deny ill health or an accident about to happen. Like these people he thought, "This isn't happening to me" or "It's happening to me but it is of no consequence." For him success in relationships was the danger in question, and success was dangerous because of the forbidden positive feelings aroused. When these feelings appeared he shrugged them off with a "yeah, sure," acted silly and giggly, or became preoccupied and remote—his mind wandering to other things, often (perversely) to a future affair with a mysterious stranger. In extreme cases, as when introduced to someone he really liked, he became defensively hazy, actually fainted dead away, or called on one of his multiple personalities to save him—one of the reserve second personalities or alter-egos to which he reverted on a temporary basis at times of danger—created by suppressing parts of his old personality; by borrowing new personality parts through identification with someone else; or by becoming once again like himself as he once was but was no longer. Only later, after he had eliminated any possibility of forming a relationship, did he come to his senses, wonder what he was thinking about at the time, and "kick himself" for allowing the one that got away to get away. Then he pressured himself to "go out and meet someone," starting the entire process again from square one.

The Hypomanic Type

Hypomanic Type II avoidants never seem to be able to settle down. Many of them are overly active in the singles' scene. They frantically socialize looking for a mate only to jump from one situation that does not work to another that works just as badly, continuing that pattern in spite of its obvious futility. They juggle many ongoing but resolutely superficial relationships. A chic and sophisticated lifestyle often fills their days with insignificant others who function for them as mere hood ornaments: pretty girls or handsome men on the arm, worn like a badge that says, "View me favorably, because if I can get something this stunning I must be someone special myself."

One such Type II avoidant's main goal in life seemed to be to impress people. He decorated and redecorated his apartment so that it would look "stunning" when people came to visit. This preoccupation went nicely with his belief that where he went was more important than what he did when he got there, associated with an all-consuming and all-surpassing desire to be where it's at, in with the in crowd, at in resorts, rubbing elbows with celebrities, not low-lifes, in the trendy bar or restaurant that not everybody knew about. He was also preoccupied with finding the perfectly-honed bon mot, often nothing more than a hostile put-down in flimsy disguise. Sometimes it was reverse chic that he favored, bragging, "I wouldn't be caught dead in the yuppie bars of Hoboken—I prefer the places the locals go"; "I never buy things wholesale—I like to pay too much for everything"; "I want a house in a working-class town so I can enjoy the primitive delights of living with the peasants"; "It's back to nature for me—to an undeveloped part of the world where I can lie on a slab under mosquito netting, without the usual conveniences, like refrigerators and toilets, just to get away from those fey summer resorts, just so that I can get some backbone"; and his favorite in-joke (really a paraphrase of a famous pianist's remark), "I hate Mozart—he didn't die too young; on the contrary, he lived to be too old."

When actually rejected, hypomanic Type II avoidants make an especially frantic attempt to feel loved once again. They rush about even more looking for lovers, grabbing the first accepting person who comes along, not for any winning quality that person might have, but to get unrejected, and to undo a sense of despair and a feeling of emptiness. They become the life of the party in order to deny the feeling that no one has invited them to the ball. Sometimes they even become rejecting themselves, so that now if they cannot get accepted, they can at least get revenge.

TYPE III: "SEVEN YEAR ITCH" AVOIDANTS

Type III, or seven year itch, avoidants are able to form more-or-less full and satisfactory relationships, but they can only do so for a finite period of time. Unlike Type II avoidants, who have some difficulty committing fully right from the start, they commit fully, or at least they appear to do so, and they do so for a long time. Eventually, however, they feel restless, question their commitment, and opt out, often rather precipitously, saying things like, "I want some down time to think," "I want to be free," or "I met someone new and fell in love, so I want a divorce."

Type III avoidants fear not rejection but continuance. Unlike Type II avoidants who are neophiles because they long for newness, Type III avoidants are neophiles because they fear oldness, that is, familiarity. This principle is illustrated by the joke about the woman who tries to reintroduce romance into her marriage by dressing seductively only to have her husband say, "You are attractive, and I would sleep with you, if only you weren't my wife." In long-term relationships they feel controlled, fear losing their identity, and complain that there is no challenge to be had from steadiness and that without challenge nothing means anything. As successophobes they are unable to tolerate the pleasures and rewards of a comfortable serious relationship. A need to suffer makes it difficult for them to accept being happy and feel fulfilled. When these avoidants say, "This relationship is wrong for me" they really mean that it is too right—too threatening because it is too intense. Growing impatient with the old, they grab at the new. Becoming restless and impulsive, they act contemptuous of the familiar, telling present company that they are defective compared to past or future company, discarding present partners summarily, and saying that they plan to look for someone new who can better serve their needs. Convinced that it is easier to find a new love than it is to tolerate an old relationship, they begin to date again, to go out into the world to "find themselves and be me," forgetting, as did many of my patients in the late 1970s and early 1980s, that disco fever is benign in the young, malignant after a certain age.

One patient after postponing getting engaged for years did get engaged then, after a three year engagement, seemingly without warning, announced that he was taking a hiatus from the relationship and would call again after a few months time, which he said he needed to work things out in his mind. A year later he still hadn't called as promised.

A gay patient, who, as it was subsequently revealed, kept his fingers slightly crossed during the wedding ceremony, told his long-term lover he was leaving him because one day instead of being there to greet him when he arrived home from work, the lover had gone out to do some errands and didn't leave a note saying where he was going, "forcing me to come home to an empty house, causing me to panic about having to stay there by myself for who knows how long."

After a series of unhappy love affairs one avoidant finally settled down with a man a few years his senior, only to announce after ten years of successful marriage, "I refuse to spend the rest of my life with that silly old bald man just because he is disease free, loves me, and never causes me any problems . . . except for the big one—he is dull, dull, dull!"

Edith Wharton (1987) in her book *The Age of Innocence* describes a main character whose Type III avoidance we might infer from his almost compulsive dislike of his attractive, well-bred, society wife whom he considers dull compared to a more exciting, exotic countess. Type III avoidance may also be the reason for Emma Bovary's compulsive need to take a lover associated with an equally compulsive dislike for her "pedestrian" country doctor husband, however devoted to her he might be (perhaps *because* of that very devotion).

Often ambivalence about the new relationship follows shortly upon its formation, making the next relationship just as straitjacketing as the last:

A successophobic man married on the rebound when his little girl left him. Throughout his five years of subsequent marriage the only way he could be sexually potent with his wife was by fantasizing his lost little girl while he was having sexual relationships with his wife. Later, he and his wife divorced. By coincidence, the very day of the divorce the little girl called, and they arranged to meet again. Alas, to quote him, she "had a mole on her forehead that had grown an inch, and had become excessively obese." Bravely, he "smoked a joint, drank, took her to dinner at a romantic hideaway, took her home, put make-out music on the stereo, turned down the lights, and forced himself to have intercourse with her." But, to his consternation, he found that the only way he could have satisfactory sexual relationships with his little girl was—by fantasizing having sex with his former wife.

TYPE IV: DEPENDENT/CODEPENDENT AVOIDANTS

Obviously avoidant are those Type IV dependent avoidants who, too close to their parents, live at home with no lover or spouse. Not so obviously avoidant are those Type IV avoidants who move away from home and in with a steady partner or spouse but never actually "cut the apron strings." This was the case for the man who after years of refusing to marry a woman because he didn't want to hurt his mother finally married that woman but never told his mother, or the rest of the family, that he was married. Instead he hid his wife from all concerned so as to not hurt his mother's feelings and thereby make her sick. Even less obviously avoidant are immersion codependent avoidants who seem nonavoidant because they are in a close, all-encompassing loving, permanent relationship, but are, however, not so much relating to one as they are hiding from all. Sometimes these bosom relationships work, and last, but if the number of books written on how to overcome codependency is any indication, all is not well in codependent relationships. So often these are not as loving as they seem to be. So often they are not the healthy if overly dependent relationships they appear to be at first glance, but are rather unhealthy hostile-dependent relationships. Here the hostility, at first submerged in the dependency, will out. When it does, it becomes directed at the significant other who has "taken me away from everybody." We next see fights provoked to regain one's freedom, accompanied by threats to leave for good. These predictably weaken the relationship until it fragments and suddenly and explosively dies, the familiar "one day he just up and left me, and without even telling me where he was going."

CHAPTER 5

Healthy Avoidance

We must distinguish not only between the incapacity for forming relationships that characterizes the schizoid patient and the fear of relating
that characterizes the avoidant patient, but also between both of these and
the reasonable desire to be alone that characterizes some perfectly healthy
individuals. These are the individuals who are healthfully avoidant, that
is, they are avoidant without actually having a problem with avoidance.
Their avoidance can be healthy because it is *preferential*, that is, something
they believe to be both good and good for them. Solitary by choice, they
have built their aloneness comfortably into their lives. They truly view
isolation as splendid. They are not rationalizing when they say that they
like being self-sufficient, independent of others, and their own master, and
speak eloquently of how they enjoy the peace that comes with removal
and detachment. One such individual even proudly referred to herself as
a Greta Garbo, or "I want to be alone," kind of person, and quoted for
explanation, self-justification and self-defense the lyrics of the song that
refers to jangling spurs that say you should roll merrily along being glad
that you are single. They argue persuasively and convincingly that marriage isn't right for everybody, especially for them, and note that as single
people they can come and go as they please, being me by being free. Hence
we see them in public comfortably eating dinner in a restaurant, all by
themselves, reading the Sunday newspaper on Saturday night. Or we spot
them fishing by day, day in and day out, alone by the seashore. They like
closing their eyes and putting hot compresses over them; having the first
drink or two of happy, idle, or attitude adjustment hour (short of intoxi-
cation/addiction); submitting to the drowsy nirvana-and-sleep-inducing

drone of the lulling train or car ride; rocking in a rocking chair or hammock; being lulled by monotonous music; performing repetitive activities like crocheting or knitting; indulging in repetitive rituals like personal or religious compulsions or telling familiar stories over and over again; and reading escape literature that takes them away to the cold north, or out West, to the lone prairie, camping alone under the stars. If they suffer at all they suffer not from their isolation but from the social pressures that make them feel guilty about being as isolated as they really want to be. They want to eat, live, and play alone, but a critical world makes them ashamed of feeling the way they do, and of wanting what they want.

A married writer felt, "I would like to retreat from the world, line my room with cork like Proust, and write, write, write, alone, all day long." Then he did essentially just that: he purchased a house trailer which he parked in the driveway of his home and worked there, "to avoid having my family disturb my concentration." Eventually he moved from California to New York, leaving his wife and children behind, commuting on weekends. He acted not out of a fear of closeness but out of a desire for separateness in the belief, later proved correct, that distance would lend enchantment both to his work and to his relationship with his wife.

Avoidance can also be healthy because it the *bright side of an otherwise pathological state.* The bright side of pathological *grief* is that it permits an individual to be alone with his or her nostalgia, with his or her faded clippings and reminiscences, dwelling on a pleasurable past to deny an intolerable present, indulging in better days, if-only fantasy. One patient after the death of her husband arranged and rearranged her old photos and the sympathy cards she got when her husband died, doing so in order to keep him alive, in turn to avoid perceiving the pain of life without him. A man after losing his wife stayed in the large house they once occupied together just to be surrounded by all the pleasant memories there, even though the house was too large for his needs, too difficult for him to keep up, and in the suburbs although all of his activities were in the city. The bright side of Social Phobia is that it provides welcome escape from turmoil. For example, normals can escape their sadistic impulses by avoiding wild kingdom animal shows that rub their noses in the laws of the jungle, and avoid facing their sexual desires by avoiding R-rated/X-rated movies, doing so less for moral reasons than because the close-up anatomical view revives unintegrated/unmanageable primal-scene experiences or otherwise quiescent traumatic sexual molestations out of the past. Finally, the bright side of *obsessive-compulsive* procrastination is that it allows one time to think and gives pause, permitting internal conflicts and difficult real-life situations to resolve on their own.

Avoidance can also be healthy when it is *part of normal development.* For example, it is wise for adolescents to rebel against parents who try to keep them down by discouraging their growing up and going out on their own. It can also be healthy when it is an *appropriate response to circumstances.* Children *should* avoid parents who discourage them from ever leaving home, parents *should* avoid children who by refusing to grow up and go out on their own make it difficult for them to live their own lives, and lovers *should* avoid partners who do not reciprocate and offer love back. It is reasonable to avoid those who torture us by nagging us or involving us in prolonged time-consuming unnecessary struggles such as those about which direction to install rolls of toilet tissue, who are prejudiced against us, actually reject us, threaten to harm us emotionally or physically, or who revive unmanageable traumatic interpersonal agony. There is no sense in being a hero with wild, potentially dangerous paranoids having a fight that wins points but costs lives. (When brushing against a paranoid it can be well to say not, "You were in my way, you ass" but "I was in your way, mea culpa, I'm the ass, I will keep out of your way in the future, and I'm sorry.")

One artist reacted to criticisms from the *New York Times* with the thought, "They criticize with such conviction and knowledge that they must be right." He spent his early years depressed, hoping "for the big reward, more important than the Tonys and the Oscars—having the *New York Times* say something nice about me." His mental state improved when instead of trying to get the *Times* to reverse its position, he developed a healthy disdain for their opinion and went about his business, closing the eye formerly always open to what "daddy thinks of me."

A doctor's megalomaniac colleague continually put him down. For example, once he confessed to this colleague, "I don't like this person," only to be told, "I happen to know that the feeling is mutual." This colleague put the doctor down no matter how clever the doctor's formulations. Indeed, the cleverer they were, the more he put him down. The doctor felt that his ideas were being stomped to death while they were still fresh, young, and in their prime. For a while he kept trying, and kept failing to impress. Each night, after his failure to impress, he would go home feeling stupid and depressed, his self-esteem lower than the night before, and each morning he would go back for more, trying to get his depression to lift by bringing things around so that he could feel accepted instead of attacked, humiliated, and rejected. Finally, he realized the hopeless nature of the interaction and sensibly simply stopped talking to the colleague—beyond a curt good morning and a discussion of any business that had to be transacted. His therapist, in agreeing with this plan, added, "Don't think you are supposed to get along with someone just because you work with him." The doctor's self-esteem improved, his depression lifted, and his creativity and cleverness returned.

I call people who create healthy avoidance in others by forcing others into having limited or no contact with them, giving others the choice of being unhappy with, or happy without, them, avoidogenics. They represent one exception to Rapee's (1998) rule that "our feelings and emotions are not directly caused by the things going on outside us. Our feelings and emotions are directly caused by our thoughts, attitudes, and beliefs—in other words, by what goes on inside our heads" (p. 24). Not surprisingly, these avoidogenics are often avoidants themselves. Many are exceedingly cruel critics, particularly destructive to people who have a fluid sense of self associated with a tendency to believe what others tell them; to people who are passive for any reason, but especially because of previous abuse; and to people who are realistically dependent on them. However, avoidogenics are not always the obviously mean, unloving, critical and cruel villains familiar from melodrama. They also come from the ranks of the much admired—including psychoanalysts who sometimes criticize and reject their patients by disapproving of their behavior and humiliating them for the manifestations of their symptoms.

People proximate to poisonous avoidogenics would do well to consider the geographical solution as a way to leave actively before they are left passively, or otherwise injured. For such potential or actual victims their $E = MC^2$ is the equation, "avoidance $= 1/$avoidogenic proximity." This simply means that neurosis improves in direct proportion to the distance between an avoidogenic and his or her victim. Although pundits generally dismiss the geographical solution with the warning, "You will take your problems along with you," geographical solutions are constructive, creative, and effective when the people in one's current orbit make a significant contribution to one's difficulties, and/or a specific location is a significant force in the creation of one's suffering.

To illustrate how people blossom in simpatico surroundings. I note that there are many places where it is unwise for a borderline to go to live. As a consequence, very few "healthy" borderlines actually go there. Manhattan, for example, has proportionately more borderlines than the outer boroughs of New York City because the outer boroughs/bedroom communities are not tolerant of the borderline style of unpredictability and hysterical excess, and have little to nothing there to keep the borderline happy. They offer the borderline comparatively few single people to meet and to merge with, then excoriate and emerge from; and little art, theatre, ballet, and fine restaurants to alternatively wax ecstatic over (perfection itself!) and totally condemn (a complete disappointment!). (If you are a borderline yourself, or a person drawn to borderlines, and you do not function well in the outer reaches, you might consider getting out and moving to the central city.) Conversely, obsessionals ridden with guilt might look for a place where natural instincts are suppressed "for the greater good," and where the community brooks little deviation from a supposed "moral norm." As one patient put it, referring to her desire to leave Manhattan, "because I find the concept of original sin appealing/correct, the outer boroughs are for me."

Many severe avoidants are more isolated than they would otherwise be because, in addition to being chronically avoidant from within, they are cowed from without by a devouring mother or critical father. Such patients often blossom after a therapeutic removal from their poisonous avoidogenics.

In order to escape his schizophrenogenic parents, one child regularly fled upstairs to an honorary aunt for a second opinion about his parents' unhealthy attitude. The aunt, by offering the child a new reality that was healthier than his parents' distorted reality, essentially saved the boy from developing a serious mental illness. In contrast, a brother stayed at home, remained embroiled with the family, and, perhaps as a consequence, grew up somewhat emotionally disturbed.

Sometimes what is needed is a hospitalization that puts a wedge between patient and family. (Patients who need hospitalization for this reason are in particular need of a therapist who will plant both feet at the door when the parents, as they expectedly will, appear on the doorstep to remove the child from the hospital in order to re-infantilize him or her. Of course, should the patient then turn against the therapist and toward the family, nothing further, beyond more appeals to reason, can be offered.)

Of course, this is not a suggestion to abandon one's family. Even difficult family interactions have their bright sides. They can bring out/abreact and so resolve problems within the family, keeping these problems from spreading to and contaminating outside relationships. Or they can be pleasurable on their own as when, as often happens, members of one's family are inherently as or more interesting and loving as anyone outside of the family.

The following is an example of a three-way avoidant triangle where the healthiest response would have been for all concerned to put some distance among themselves.

A woman picked a married man to be her lover and then, when he threatened to become available, discouraged him from divorcing his wife—first by dissociating (not hearing his proposal, or, hearing it, passing it off as an aberration of the moment, not to be taken seriously), and then by becoming personally unappealing, just enough to create sufficient doubt in the man's mind to make him hesitate to take the final step.

The man, to ease his guilt about having an affair, selected this woman in the first place knowing that her need to have an affair with a married man meant that it was likely that she would lose interest in him should he actually threaten to become single again, get a divorce, and propose marriage. He sensed that because of her need to be the interloper and her all-too-apparent fear of success, she would be intolerant of real intimacy.

The man's wife knew that her husband was cheating on her from evidence that would have convinced the most trusting and innocent of people. But, because she, being an avoidant herself, unconsciously needed to permit and encourage the affair, she failed to recognize the obvious, then (when she could no longer fool herself) refrained from confronting him and having a showdown, giving the affair her imprimatur by being complicit in its neglect.

Finally, avoidance can be healthy when it is an *interim, transitional goal of psychotherapy*. Therapy works in part by enhancing healthy avoidance—by offering the avoidant a temporary sanctuary: the opportunity to become more avoidant now, in preparation for becoming less avoidant in the future.

CHAPTER 6

Avoidant People

This chapter describes avoidants as they appear to us on an everyday basis, in our everyday lives.

AVOIDANT PARENTS

Avoidant parents provoke their children to abandon them, then claim to be innocent victims, hurt and abandoned by their children.

A mother, convinced her son would abandon her when she grew old, deliberately set about to rile him so that his anger would give her reason to disown him before she died. She called him by her brother's name then blamed it on aging, although his was the only name she got wrong. She forgot how to call him on the phone, although she could still remember how to call the rest of her family. Then instead of apologizing, she replied to his justified anger by seizing the occasion of a festive country dinner to list the things she wasn't going to leave him in her will, and the occasion of a festive town dinner to leak the contents of the completed document. Then she completely disowned him in her will without telling him that she did so, joyously contemplating how he would not discover he was disowned until after she died, when it was too late for him to protest/repair the damage.

AVOIDANT ADOLESCENTS

A typical avoidant adolescent builds his or her self-esteem out of cruelty to others, developing a worthwhile person identity by making other people feel less worthy. For example, some adolescents develop a non-homosexual or straight identity by joining forces with other adolescents to ride around in cars hurling antigay epithets at passersby, while others develop an independent identity by becoming as different from, and presumably superior to, their defective parents as they possibly can be.

A second-generation child of an immigrant family longing to become as Americanized as possible became as unlike his parents as he possibly could, criticizing them in the process for what they were. In disapproving of them (and of those who later in life came to represent or substitute for them) based on such relatively unimportant things as their bad grammar, foreign accent, peasant-like behaviors, and improper attire, he failed to take into account such of their good qualities as their intelligence, practical sense, and capacity for warmth and love.

When the parents are conformists, rebellious adolescents may become antisocial beings unwilling to live according to the rules of society simply because their parents espoused these rules. But when the parents are nonconformists, rebellious adolescents may instead become hypermoral, oversubmissive compliers—however much they submit and comply resentfully. Parents cannot prevent this distractive adolescent behavior simply by acting in a way that makes their children proud of them because the need for most children to rebel against and counteridentify with their parents is too strong and too ingrained/automatic/biological to be so easily influenced.

AVOIDANT MIDDLE-AGED INDIVIDUALS

Middle-age avoidants deal with their midlife crises and the often intense fear of rejection and loss associated with these crises in two ways: by becoming old before their time or by becoming young after their time. Those who become old before their time get so involved with death that they become disinvolved with life. They might try to defeat death by accumulating money, based on the idea that rich equals powerful and that powerful equals immortal. They might spend an excessive amount of time writing their own obituaries or building and inscribing their own mausoleums, thinking that this will make them as permanent as stone. Or they might become rigid in attitude and behavior, believing that all change is the equivalent of progression, and that all progression is the equivalent of the progression from youth to death.

Those who become young after their time avoid stable people who would be good for them but who, on account of their stability, remind them of getting older. Instead, they seek unstable people whose instability gives them the illusion of perpetual movement, with perpetual movement in turn giving them the illusion of youth/the illusion that death has been conquered. They indulge in age-inappropriate, frantically gregarious, hypomanic roué behaviors meant to deny aging. These behaviors are often based on the following idea: young people are active; hypomanics are active; therefore hypomanics are young. They have superfluous face-lifts, lose too much weight, spend money excessively, become generally pro-miscuous, or specifically seek out situations of controlled promiscuity such as the ménage à trois, or threesome, relationship, which they con-vince themselves they have for healthy variety when, in fact, they do so not because they like what they are doing but to fool themselves that they are still capable of doing it—of being as sexually active, interested, and interesting as they were in their twenties. Some have threesomes with people their own age, while others have them with youths, some of whom are little more than passing strangers picked up in bars or hitchhiking, invited home without first being checked out. In this way they deliberately toy with fatal illness/being murdered to convince themselves that they are too strong to get a fatal illness and too invulnerable to be killed.

Another self-destructive behavior of middle-aged avoidants is to antic-ipate the unexpected loss of their parents by actively creating that loss. That is, they pull back from their parents now so that they can get used to what it will be like when their parents die later, unexpectedly. Their parents, mystified by the resultant remoteness, die with a sense that they have been abandoned, leaving the child feeling guilty and depressed be-cause now it is too late to make amends. Middle-aged avoidants some-times display destructive behavior with their children for essentially the same reason: to anticipate their unexpected loss as they grow up. Typically they condemn their children for normal adolescent rebellion. Not only do they thereby dampen the child's healthy spirits, but they also reject the child, effectively making him or her more rebellious.

Therapists should not routinely egg middle-aged avoidants in the midst of midlife crises onward and upward to change under the aegis of pro-moting healthy development. All satisfactory lots in life involve a degree of compromise, and many times peaceful acceptance of and adaptation to the way things are now, or to the inevitable, is a wiser course than attempts at self-improvement that involve illusory gains made for their own sake or, as with masochists, as a guise for making things worse.

AVOIDANT ELDERLY

Elderly avoidants deny they have personality problems by blaming iso-lation, which is actually the result of past and present avoidances, entirely on their age. They are alone not because people don't like older people, the reason they give to themselves, but because they rejected family and friends over the years, going through what is for everyone a finite pool of irreplaceable relationships formed in the early years, best kept for a lifetime, never to be made again. Also, they continue to reject family and friends in the here-and-now. Often a paranoid streak leads them to imagine rejections, which causes them to get angry over having been rejected, which leads them to behave in a way that causes others to actually reject them. Often too a depressive streak leads them to put people off, say, by feeling sorry for themselves in public. For example, one elderly avoidant could do no better than to loudly proclaim to all within hearing range, "Don't get old if you can help it. Old age isn't the golden time of life they tell you it is. One look at me and you will see why."

AVOIDANT WORKERS

Characterological Problems

Some avoidant workers are love-dependent people who take a job not for the salary or for the opportunity for professional satisfaction/advancement but for personal approval, that is, for acceptance by their coworkers. Even after they realize they work in a bureaucracy noted for making hard work its own reward by giving accolades and promotions not to the deserving but to the friends of the people in power, they continue to expect that they will be personally loved and promoted for the hard work that they do. When, as is predictable, no such satisfaction is forthcoming, they complain that their job is just a job, find it difficult to do their work, and develop burnout.

Other avoidant workers are selfish people who use their job to gratify their own needs and slake their own passions while entirely overlooking their part in the implicit bargain they struck when they were hired—that is, that in accepting a job they were agreeing to do it. Some are faultfinding individuals who bite the hand that feeds them as they complain about everything and everybody at work. Some are unfriendly isolated people who, instead of being warm and cooperative with bosses, coworkers, and underlings, act destructively testy, on edge, sullen, uncooperative, and stubborn, deliberately abandoning the traditional roles or unconsciously corrupting them with transference anger, like the nurse who actually said, "I don't come to work to get along with people." Here are some examples. (I assume, possibly incorrectly, that in the following instances the customer is right, that is, innocent of avoidogenic provocation.)

A salesman in a well-known haberdashery proclaimed a worthy sentiment that, however, should not have been expressed, as it was, within earshot of customers: "The management here sits on its collective duffs instead of helping out with the sales. Fourteen of them are upstairs doing nothing, while downstairs customers are waiting, and complaining."

A client who called to sell stock reached a vice president taking calls in the temporary absence of the client's broker. When he asked the question, "Can a vice president help me as much as my broker?" the vice president responded not to the request for information/reassurance contained in the question but to what she believed was an implied attack, and counterattacked with, "Of course I can, I'm better than a broker, after all, I'm a vice president who has been here 11 years, so I ought to know what I'm doing."

A worker in an antique shop was asked, "Can you tell me about this lamp?" Believing that she was being accused of selling a fake, she defensively replied, "No," reminding us that a characteristic for many avoidants is that "no" is the first word out of their mouths. When she went on to qualify the no, to say that she meant she "didn't have any information about the lamp beyond that it was an unsigned turn of the century object not made by a famous artisan," it was too late to correct the initial uncooperative impression, and the sale was lost. Another time when asked, "What is the nature of this delightful sofa?" she replied, believing that she was being patronized, and hating stupid people, "If you have to ask what it is then you probably can't afford to buy it." This exquisite piece of illogic lost her, and her company, the sale, because instead of helpful cooperation the customer got a clever crack, a sophisticated comeback, a "You should have seen his face when I got him" zinger. (Her behavior, more suitable for an insult comic than for an antiques salesperson, put her in the class of so many avoidants who do right by one job though, unfortunately, they hold another.) Finally, in another example of self-indulgence replacing positive accomplishment, she replied to a customer who asked the question, "Can you do any better on the price?" by saying, "Yes, I can. I can increase it. That way I will do better—by me." Later she revealed that, though she knew it was customary to bargain, she viewed bargaining as an assault on her ability to set fair prices, a threat to her sense of control, an attempt to deprive her of some of her needed commission, and an offensive expression of what "I most detest in some people: wanting to get something for nothing."

When such things happen in the private practice of medicine or dentistry, the result is as predictably masochistic as it is sadistic:

A patient told his dentist that Novocain shots made him anxious, whereupon the unsympathetic dentist became secretly angered at having to deal with a nervous patient, thinking, "My real skills lie in working on teeth, not coddling neurotics." He expressed his anger by making a little joke: "If you should die, I'll put you back in the waiting room facing forward, so it looks like you died there, before getting into the chair, and I had nothing to do with your demise." Then, escalating matters, he proceeded to make the patient more anxious by telling him of times he did have to call the ambulance for patients who fainted, and even once for a patient who actually developed a cardiac arrhythmia after his shot.

Affective Problems

Depression

Avoidant workers who are also depressed often cannot do their job well because of their excessive need for support and their inability to accept supervision due to a tendency to perceive constructive criticism as de-structive criticism. Rightly or wrongly, few people can, want to, or have the time or interest to coddle and cajole these people into doing the work they should be undertaking under their own steam.

One supply room worker resented his boss for not giving him the sympathy and support he felt he deserved, and his customers because a few in the past had complained about him to the authorities. So he wouldn't do anything unless any request being made was sugarcoated enough to appear to be supportive. He re-acted particularly well to an advance apology, like, "I am sorry for having harassed you." Even then "no" was usually the first word out of his mouth. This "no" had then to be met not with anger but by humoring him. If he said, "Supplies are only given out on odd days and today is even," one got supplies not by replying, "Only stupid people follow stupid systems" but by saying, "I will be happy to come back tomorrow, when it is an odd day." Then, and only then, would he melt and give you all the supplies you wanted, today.

Hypomania

Avoidant workers who are hypomanic antagonize customers by their overenthusiasms rather than by their underenthusiasms. As salesmen they annoy by pushing too hard, by refusing to take "no" for an answer, and by being quick to anger when crossed or otherwise thwarted. This often happens when a customer asks a lot of questions, and then doesn't buy anything.

A customer told a salesman he was interested in seeing more of the salesman's wares. In reply the salesman asked him, "Are you going to buy or just going to look?" then added, "Because if you are going to buy I'll show you more in the back room, but if you are just going to look, then don't waste my time. After all, looking doesn't pay the rent."

AVOIDANT BOSSES

I categorize avoidant bosses according to how and why they strike fear into (rather than instill confidence in) the hearts of their workers.

Demotivating

Demotivating bosses stifle their workers by placing them on a straight salary without incentives like commissions or stock in the company. Or they deliberately arrange to leave their workers on the level at which they first entered the company. In one case a boss, intending to let dust settle over his workers, told them, "I'll neither fire nor promote you, even if you stay here for the rest of your life."

Unempathic/Inconsiderate

Unempathic/inconsiderate bosses create resentment by their fixation on getting the job done, without concern for the workers who have to do that job. The assignment is the only important thing, and the individual counts for little or nothing. One boss shifted his workers from post to post without regard for their personal development. Another boss, priding himself on being an efficiency expert, did not allow the staff to use the clinic's refrigerators to store their lunch, although there was no cafeteria on the premises, then gave them only half an hour for lunch, although it was a fifteen-minute drive in each direction to the nearest restaurant. The same boss told workers he hired to work 9 to 5, "The job has to get done, no matter how late you have to stay to do it," a rule he made so that he did not have to hire more help or pay his workers overtime.

In the armed services bad experiences with unempathic and inconsiderate commanding officers can be as much the cause of Posttraumatic Stress Disorder (PTSD) as the combat experiences usually cited. Sometimes a veteran's PTSD symptoms, upon analysis, turn out to originate less in actual physically or emotionally traumatic battle experiences with the enemy than in emotionally traumatic experiences with the friendly fire of their immediate superiors. Veterans' continuing anger over how they were mishandled ("treated like cannon fodder," one said) can take the form of flashbacks and nightmares of combat that are little more than expressions of murderous fantasies directed toward authority displaced and projected outward and couched in the symbolism of fighting. We see the same process in civilian life where job fatigue or burnout is the equivalent of combat fatigue, here due to repeated bad experiences with the boss. This kind of job fatigue can resemble PTSD, taking the form of recurrent nightmares and job flashbacks consisting of an inability to put the job aside on weekends or while on vacation. We also see somatic disorders such as carpal tunnel syndrome, which in one case was partly a physical expression of the emotional conflict between the wish to use the hand for work and the forbidden wish to use it to strike out, to kill the boss.

Sadistic

Sadistic bosses initiate and maintain demoralizing, counterproductive, ultimately self-destructive, vicious cycles of hostility and counterhostility between themselves and their workers.

A man in charge of repairing computers was not doing his job properly for easily correctable reasons. But the boss, instead of finding out why and offering assistance, responded by withholding the man's merit raise. For spite, the man erased important data. Told to resign, or be fired and be prosecuted, he resigned, but the boss decided to prosecute him anyway. So the repairman went on the lam, changing his identity and disappearing, taking with him all the warranty cards so that the company had a difficult time getting free factory-covered repairs.

Sadistic bosses quash talented people because they perceive them to be the competition. They quash them by promoting incompetents over competents; by setting competents up to make mistakes by making impossible demands on them, or by issuing undoable assignments to them, or by giving out orders contrary to those already given by themselves or by another boss; or by inducing guilt by being overly critical and failing to temper their criticism with congratulations.

Inflexible

Inflexible I-am-the-boss bosses set a course at the beginning, then stick with it in spite of legitimate complaints or changing circumstances.

Too Easygoing/Friendly

Too easygoing/friendly bosses fail to discipline when discipline is indicated or desirable. They don't give the confused and anxious employee the firm, impersonal hand he or she needs. However, it would be a mistake to think that the easygoing, friendly approach is necessarily incompatible with discipline, is inimical to effective supervision, and predictably breeds contempt. The friendly boss governs well if he or she teaches instead of ordering, asks instead of demanding, or gives pat-on-the-back positive instead of terrifying negative feedback that reminds the worker of a distant mother or bloodying father. Indeed, failure to give compliments is perhaps a boss's most serious avoidant blunder. We hear, "They always tell you when you do something wrong, but never when you do something right." At best, the worker who is only criticized and never complimented says and does as little as possible and sticks with the tried and true to be safe rather than sorry. At worst he or she becomes withdrawn and depressed as a way to say, "When faced with the choice between doing a good job for you and sparing myself pain, I'll take the latter anytime."

Hypomanic

Hypomanic bosses are impatient people who strike fear into their workers by displaying tantrums and by flaring when things aren't done as quickly as they would like or in the way that they would like. They are often very critical people who say things like, "Doesn't anyone around here do any work but me?" They also overextend themselves, and hence their employees, as did one surgeon who forged associations between his hospital and at least 10 others, sending his workers to all corners of two states to do work assignments that really belonged to the staffs of the other institutions. Then, just when his empire building seemed complete, he went into partnership with another surgeon and opened up a penny arcade on the local boardwalk.

INTERACTION BETWEEN WORKERS AND BOSSES

An avoidant bureaucracy can be defined as one consisting of careless/ burned-out bosses tolerating/encouraging careless/burned-out workers in the hope that no one from inside will have to do any work, and that no one from outside will find out about it.

CHAPTER 7

Sociocultural Manifestations

Avoidant societies are organized like avoidant individuals—according to the premise that relationships come last, after God, country, money, things, and self. Sociocultural manifestations of avoidance within these societies include religious practices like shunning/excommunicating/dispensing symbolic death; political avoidances like deliberately voting for a president and Congress from different parties in hopes of watching a good fight or paralyzing the nation; economic avoidances like a monetarist's resolute inflation-fighting unconsciously intended to cause mass personal despair; literary avoidances like satire/ridicule that is really bigotry in disguise rescued from legal and personal consequences by such disclaimers as, "I was only kidding" or "I'm entitled to my opinion/freedom of speech"; and musical avoidances like the nose-thumbing works of Les Six, the moonlit remote works of Gabriel Fauré, the taciturn works of Anton Webern, the quirky schizoid works of John Cage, and the sometimes deliberately incomprehensible works of the serialists, one of whom was misquoted (though the misquote fit) as saying, "Who cares if they listen?"

Less lofty sociocultural avoidances are those of the bar-bouncer who waves nonconformists out as nonbelongers; the all-men's club maitre d' who years ago dismissed women with a summary, Germanic *Heraus*; the golf club with its exclusionary entry requirements; the small but nevertheless effective sign on the resort hotel that says, "No vacancy" when it really means no members of a certain race, color or creed; the New Yorker who dismisses people from the outer boroughs and New Jersey as "the bridge and tunnel set;" the people from New Jersey who will not go to New York because it is dangerous, unfriendly, and too full of people too close to each other; the tote bag carrier who haughtily proclaims to the world, "I like refined things, not the crude things you like"; and the owner of the bumper sticker that reads, "The worst day fishing is better than the best day working." Many of these avoidants are bigots who define flaws and virtues in simple, black and white, arbitrary terms that are justified as rational and satisfy an emotional need to ridicule. In fact it is irrational, originating in presumed but actually nonexistent imperfections, actual but insignificant imperfections, or imperfections for which there is a good, sensible explanation, as when an author grows a shaggy beard because he is too preoccupied with work to shave, an artist gets paint on his clothes because he is painting in them, or a landscaper gets dirt under his finger-nails because he is tilling the earth.

Bigotry is in fact the ultimate in avoidance, being harmful not only to the victim but also to the bigot him- or herself—by distancing the bigot from large numbers of people by defining them as "Those I don't have to, or want to, relate to."

A lonely avoidant homophobic single woman's bigotry isolated her from a large segment of the men in New York, thereby reducing her chances for developing an extended family from which a likely romantic prospect could emerge.

A bigot harshly criticized almost everybody as not "perfectly clean, pristine pure, beautifully mannered, from the right background, socially above reproach, and flawless in etiquette." For him the only acceptable woman was the fashion model, and the only acceptable man the WASP. Both were viewed as superior to ordinary mortals because they, when compared to the primitive races, were perfection it-self—not a statue made in the image of man, but man made in the image of a statue.

The double-standard/hypocrisy of the bigot is often as off-putting as the bigotry itself.

One woman was critical of homosexuals—that is, unless and until they served her immediate purposes. Thus she pulled out from the fire, Phoenix-like, a musically talented priest, whom she formerly viewed as the enemy of God, the pariah-designate, the apotheosis of sin, to be excluded and banished, shunned and ig-nored, cast out and consumed in flames, to reincarnate him just so that, as her critics complained, she could use him for a promotional poster for an arts group in which she was active.

CHAPTER 8

Course

Some patients with AvPD improve over time without treatment. Other patients with AvPD get worse over time without treatment. They become progressively more avoidant, and even more agoraphobic and depressed. AvPD gets worse when it becomes modified and elaborated by the development of vicious cycling, described below.

THE DEVELOPMENT OF VICIOUS CYCLING

In a typical vicious cycle, an avoidant's display of unreasonable fearful timidity and shyness soon creates plenty about which he or she can be reasonably fearfully timid and shy. This happens because avoidants put others off by withdrawing from them. Others react negatively because they do not like being avoided, thinking not "He is afraid of me," but "He doesn't like me," or even, "She hates me." They also react negatively because they do not like being reminded of their own potential for loneliness and isolation, and because the avoidant's sensitivity to rejection gives him or her an air of vulnerability that provokes sadists, most of whom become even more sadistic when they sense people are already in pain, knowing that people already in pain when tweaked jump that much higher. As a result, others reject the patient, the patient's fear of rejection is realized, and that prompts further withdrawal and further retaliation from others. Millon's (1981) example describes such vicious cycling as follows: "The patient's discontent, outbursts, and moodiness frequently evoke humiliating reactions from others, and these rebuffs only serve to reinforce his self-protective withdrawal.... He often precipitates disillusionment

through obstructive and negative behaviors [then] reports feeling misunderstood, unappreciated, and demeaned by others" (p. 313).

THE APPEARANCE OF SECOND-LINE DEFENSES

As time goes by, second-line defenses develop, increasing the avoidance
by bolstering the first-line defense of protective remoteness. These second-
line defenses include, in addition to the defensive misanthropy, hypomania, inertia (a striving for familiarity and sameness), and defensive
acting-out discussed in Chapter 1, those described below.

Rationalization

As discussed in Chapter 5 on healthy avoidance, some avoidants truly
want to be alone. They claim that they are not troubled by their avoidance.
They basically believe that their avoidance is not pathological but a matter
of preference, taste, wisdom, or necessity. Other avoidants make the same
claim, but they make it not because they really like being alone but because they fear the alternative—connecting. Their claim is, in other words,
a rationalization. Rationalizations can be identified by the tendency to
protest too much. For example, many avoidants protest too much about
the wonders of splendid isolation, insisting (not quite convincingly, because of the modest gratification to be obtained from the advantages
listed) that, "I like being alone because at least my apartment stays
straight, I can sleep through without a lover's snoring, no one stains my
upholstery and wall-to-wall rug, and for companionship I have what I
need—my two delightful, loving cats."

The most common rationalizations I hear are:

"I don't have the time to meet people." This excuse was given by one
man who placed a personals ad and then, making it look like his work
left him no room for pleasure, arranged to always be too busy to respond
to any takers.

"I'm not ready, I want to play the field a while longer." Some field
players are commitment phobics, while others are neophiliacs who act
either like impulsive children who abandon old toys for new ones due to
a tendency to tire too quickly of what they already have, or like thrill-
seeking impulsive adults whose pursuit of the unfamiliar reflects their
constant need for stimulation through variety. Neophiles are described
further in Chapters 4 and 12.

"The world is a terrible place, full of terrible people." Examples of this
rationalization are, "I have nothing but bad luck," "I never meet anyone
any good," or, in extremely unfavorable cases, "There aren't any people
where I live worthy of me." A sample uninsightful/cruel statement made
by a woman in a singles bar on why she would never place a personals

ad: "The creeps in here are bad enough; imagine what you'd find if you put in an ad."

A patient had several ways to rationalize his desire not to relate. He announced, "Relationships are really not that important or essential." He dwelled philosophically on the meaninglessness of everything interpersonal until, as he later suggested, he became so "preoccupied with the sound of one hand clapping that I can't erupt into spontaneous applause." He constantly reminded himself, "What's the use, because we are all going to die anyway" and of how the world was a terrible place because of life's little sardonic twists, such as, "You can't get a job unless you have experience, and you can't get experience unless you have a job." (The possibility of starting small and working his way up gradually eluded him entirely). When all else failed he convinced himself that he should go into removal by making a connection between two entirely unconnected themes: "What kind of a world is it where we can send men to the moon, but we can't rid our faithful dogs of fleas?"

"I can't help myself. It's not my fault." It is true that some avoidants are in fact so anxious and fearful that they cannot help but retreat when faced with the possibility of a relationship. But others, whose anxiety and fear are relative, not absolute, could, if they would, struggle against their anxiety, try to relate, and do so successfully. However, they choose not to use willpower to fight their anxiety. Then, out of shame or guilt, they say not "I choose not to," but "I can't."

The grapes are sour. One patient afraid of women thought instead, "Who wants one?" and gave as his reason, "After all, insides beneath that lovely exterior make a woman nothing but a well-packaged bag of dirt."

A caveat is that it is necessary to distinguish rationalization from its opposite—guilt about self-expression. In rationalization things that are feared are turned into matters of natural preference. In guilt about self-expression, matters of natural preference are turned into things that are feared. This was the case for one woman who wanted to remain single but was embarrassed to say so, so said instead, "I am too fearful to even try to connect."

Denial/Counterphobia

Avoidants in denial mask their fear of rejection by assuming a breezy, devil-may-care attitude about the possibility or actuality of rejection. Some, in an outburst of poor judgment that can lead to problems down the line, do not admit of the possibility of rejection by falling in love at first sight and pressing to get married before they and the other person change their minds. Others accomplish essentially the same thing by flitting from one person to another to give the lie to their fear of closeness. Still others mask their fear of rejection by hardening themselves to rejection. Hardening gives them a protective shell, a defensive insensitivity that replaces their former hypersensitivity. Their plan is to fail to perceive rejections even when they are deliberately intended and clearly conveyed. So they refuse to take the hint that they might not be wanted. Or, if they do take the hint that they are not wanted, they insist, "Who cares" and act as if rejection doesn't matter.

A worker persisted in pestering his colleagues each morning before the workday began with a rehash of what he heard on the financial news the day before—old news to his audience, and an intrusion on those who wanted to do their work. To make their point that he was bothering them they actually had to insult him. But he didn't care, thinking, "This is not a rehash, but a creative synthesis," and, "In time, should I stop, they'll realize what they are missing."

A patient, new to train travel, noted that his seatmate on the train either didn't respond with appropriate annoyance to the overly loud loudspeaker announcements overhead or, if he did, kept his response to himself. Although the patient held his ears in pain, looked at the other in hopefully shared dismay, and made sounds and faces meant to indicate a desire for mutual recognition of shared agony, the other sat determinedly impassive throughout, either trying not to let the patient catch his eye, or, if he caught it, refusing to acknowledge their common plight. When later the patient, screwing up his courage, asked him the reason for his stoic impassivity, he replied, "I've given up complaining to other people on trains. I'd rather be ignored completely than made out to be a fool."

Hard shells should logically make things better. In fact they actually make things worse. First, the individual comes to look not fearful but remote, unfeeling, and uncaring. Second, being underresponsive requires a constant expenditure of energy, sapping energy that could otherwise be made available for relating, diverting it into denying and binding one's natural instincts.

On the job, avoidants in denial may become the office clown—the person who doesn't take anything seriously enough to be bothered by it. Or they may become workaholics who are not as productive as they look because they are devoted not to quality but to quantity, to frantic effort (that gets them the praise they desperately need) over actual results (that gets the work done).

Depression

Avoidants who use the depressive defense too quickly give up on relationships, thinking, "I'm not good enough for him or her" and retreat into protective inertness and self-abuse. Sometimes disuse atrophy sets in, making the avoidance semi-permanent. Masochistic defenses that are often simultaneously present incline the avoidant to court abuse for the satisfaction involved in suffering.

A gay patient met someone he really liked. They had a first date but the patient, thinking that he messed up by saying the wrong thing, decided it was futile to pursue the relationship. His new friend called him several times but each time the patient told him that he was busy. He then promised to call back soon but never did because "I can never handle anyone right anyway." In a gay gym a man asked him if he wouldn't mind moving a little so that the first man could get into his locker. Even though he was lonely and looking for companionship, instead of smiling in a friendly fashion and starting a productive conversation, he closed off further productive interaction by taking himself to task, whining, "You are right; I am sitting here like a lump. Actually, I am a lump."

Once he accidentally left a bottle on a bus he was riding on. A week later (he only took the bus once a week and at the same time each week) the bus driver complained that last week that very bottle had rolled on the floor, "creating havoc," at least that's the way the bus driver put it. The bus driver was so angry with him that he almost didn't stop to pick him up—indeed, for a moment he seemed instead to be actually trying to run him down. Instead of reporting the bus driver to the authorities, he worried, "I am dependent on this man for my weekly ride, he could pass me by if I say anything." So instead of complaining to the driver directly about his rudeness and dangerous behavior he thanked him profusely for the ride each time he got onto and off the bus, and ultimately apologized for leaving the bottle behind as if he were admitting to, and grieving over having committed, a serious crime. The bus driver, thinking this man did not mind being abused, allowed himself to get even madder, and to become even more threatening.

Identification with the Aggressor

This defense (involving a degree of paranoia) relies for its effect on the good offense, rejecting others first as a way to defend oneself against being rejected by others. The idea is to put others down before they can do the same thing to you. Overlooked in the quest for immediate gratification is how, in the long run, putting others down makes one's own life more difficult. Some avoidants identify with the aggressor quite subtly and passive-aggressively. One individual, a physician, put his colleagues down by repeating the negative remarks patients made about them behind their backs. A second put his wife down by telling her of his dreams, whose motive and meaning were clear even though his wife was psychologically unsophisticated and even though in the dream, as he reported it, he disguised his desire to reject her as a fear of being rejected by her: "you are leaving me" instead of "I am leaving you." A third put people down with the pregnant association (the anti-Freudian remark quoted in Chapter 3). A fourth put people down by obvious displays of chronic dissatisfaction, boredom, listlessness, moodiness, despair, and burnout to get back in kind at those he believed to be uninterested in him. A fifth put others down for sexually harassing her as her way to cope with her own fear that she might want to seduce others, and others to seduce her.

Misattribution and Projection

Avoidants often maintain their self-esteem by convincing themselves that the world is to blame for their isolation and loneliness. They weave the threads of pathological fantasy, cognitive error, and the self-fulfilling prophecy of provocative individual behavior into the cloth of external stress, blame their inner anxiety on external fear, then avoid as the only possible response to what they imagine to be difficult or impossible external circumstances. A familiar example is the single man or woman blaming his or her loneliness entirely on the absence of likely partners where he or she lives, when in reality the lack of suitable and eligible partners is due mainly to his or her avoidance of anyone suitable and eligible. This was the case for a picky woman who could do no better than to treat an otherwise desirable partner as "geographically undesirable" because seeing him would mean changing subway trains on the way to his house. Beck's (1990, 1999) cognitive treatment devotes itself in large measure to reality-testing the projective errors of thinking that contribute to such essentially paranoid errors of perception, errors that lead avoidants to view the world as a place full of frightening potential adversaries.

Although Beck presses his patient, Audrey, to recognize that her provocative behavior contributes to others' hostility toward her, and finally gets her to admit that her landlord responds more favorably to her requests when she presents them in a calm instead of in an angry fashion, she essentially persists, in spite of his suggestions to the contrary, in her belief that she is an innocent victim who in no way has contributed to her own rejections, and she continues to protest that others' hostility to her has no basis whatsoever in her being hostile to them.

Dependency (Codependency)

Many avoidants seek safety in numbers by becoming dependent on groups of like-minded avoidants. On the positive side, these groups give avoidants the high self-esteem that can come from a sense of belonging—of being wanted and involved. On the negative side, these groups possess avoidants and keep them isolated as the group becomes deliberately antagonistic to members outside the group in order to enhance pathological intragroup attachments.

A group that sets out en masse to go to singles bars to cruise soon began instead to collectively giggle at and humiliate everyone who approached an individual group member. Mutual jealousy, mutual interdependence, and latent intragroup homosexual attraction were some of the causative factors in their collective attempt to defeat any group member who showed interest in anyone outside of the group, and anyone outside of the group who showed interest in any group member. Often the group egged an individual member on when they sensed that he or she was uninterested in someone outside of the group, but disrupted things when they sensed that he or she was interested—say by making the sign of the devil (two fingers extended as a "V" to resemble horns) behind a head, by making obscene gestures meant to crack everyone up, or by aping and caricaturing, within vision/hearing, any potential suitor's behavior/speech until, feeling entirely unwelcome, he or she fled.

Type IV avoidants become defensively dependent, or codependent, by regressing on their family, a close friend, or a lover, surrounding themselves with a protective "you-can-all go-to-hell" shell in order to hide out from a world that they perceive to be threatening and rejecting.

Doing and Undoing—Mixed Approach/Avoidance

Fearful avoidants sometimes deal defensively with their fears of others in the same way that fearful swimmers deal defensively with their fears of the water—by putting in one toe and then taking it out, or by wading in without actually swimming. Such avoidants alternate between interest and detachment to the point that they resemble borderlines who merge and emerge. They play Berne's (1964) game of Kiss Off (p. 126), beckoning others to come, only to change their minds at the last moment when they arrive. Potential lovers find their unpredictability confusing, and leave, if only so that they will at least know where they stand. When these fearful individuals eventually marry—as some of them do—they often become Type III avoidants whose marriages are marred by a similar ambivalence.

One Type III avoidant married an attractive woman because his association with her gave him confidence. But then he divorced her because her beauty showed up his all too plain looks. Then he married an unattractive woman, inspired by the belief that he could be as hostile to her as he liked and she would need him too much to care. Then he found her too plain to be worthy of him, and filed for a divorce.

Undoing positive feelings with negative ones, and vice versa, often spills over into the professional sphere.

A reviewer's inability to become intimate with anyone in his personal life was reflected in his withholding the rave review, however merited it might be, to show his audience that he wasn't getting too fond, really, too close. In every review he wrote he forced himself to say something bad even about a good book so that he could undo everything positive he had already said. Yet he said the bad things in the next to last paragraph so that he could still leave himself space to undo again, taking back his penultimate negative remarks with a final, positive, conclusion, the familiar, reconciliatory, "Overall, however . . ."

Dissociation

Dissociation is a flight from the possibility or actuality of either rejection or acceptance. For successophobics, dissociation is particularly suitable for acceptance emergencies when by chance, bad luck, or in a moment of weakness they find themselves in a relationship they were unable to foresee, and to avoid. In a typical case of dissociation, avoidants fail to respond to positive gestures. They laugh off a serious approach or seduction that comes their way, so that any work they have done until now to promote relationships comes to naught.

One homosexual who dissociated when the big moment arrived—not registering it or, registering it, denying it—still remembers an incident 40 years ago when a handsome sailor made it clear he wanted him, but instead of replying in kind he ignored him, sloughed him off, to use his words, "laughed off the approach like a silly girl." He doesn't know why he did it, but he suspected he did it because he was anxious. Forty years later he was still bothered by his tactical error, still had fantasies of making it with the sailor, and still brooded, "Was the pleasure dangerous—the pain desirable? Did I perceive danger though there was none, see risk in the absence of a reason for concern?" His only consolation, which he ceaselessly repeated to himself for reassurance, was that had he gone with this sailor he wouldn't have gone with the other man he met that night, and it was through this other man that ultimately he was to meet his lifetime lover.

Aloofness to others is a fixed, ongoing protective dissociation become the bad habit of reflexively squelching and submerging feelings perceived to be dangerous or forbidden by distancing oneself from others who elicit these feelings.

A doctor wanted to give up his practice but didn't have the heart to expel his last patient—a wealthy borderline who seemed unable to handle the separation. So he agreed to continue to work with her as long as she would pay his entire (not very considerable) practice expenses. Soon he became inexplicably angry with her for forcing him to do something he didn't want to do, and, because he was merely meeting expenses but not making a profit, for costing him money. So one day, without warning, he became remote and detached from her as part of a plan to provoke her to leave treatment on her own. A self-analysis of his behavior indicated that his conscious anger with her hid an unconscious anger with himself, on two levels. He was angry with himself for being a "sucker for every one who needs you," and also, but more importantly, he was angry with himself for liking

her enough to want to help her even though it meant inconveniencing himself—
an admirable trait for which instead of congratulating himself (for being kind and
empathic) he condemned himself (for being soft and weak).

Aloofness is often associated with protective boredom, one form of
identification with the aggressor that in effect says not "I am afraid you
find me uninteresting and reject me," but "I find you uninteresting and
reject you." Boredom is off-putting partly because the victim feels rejected,
partly because the victim correctly perceives the narcissism and grandiosity in the avoidant's belief that he or she is in a position to be bored by
others; partly because the attitude that "You are so boring" usually leads
the hearer to the unassailable conclusion that "only bores are bored"; and
partly because so often boredom comes across as snobbery. For example,
an avoidant individual who presented to the casual observer as the snob
who never said anything to anyone because he was "bored with the whole
scene" was in fact not a snob but a fearful man protecting himself from
rejection by becoming defensively detached.

Protective aloofness to others almost always filters down from personal
to impersonal pursuits and affects choice of profession, or choice of job
within that profession. As a general finding, with plenty of individual
exceptions, serious avoidants tend to become physicists rather than
doctors, and, within the medical profession, surgeons rather than
psychiatrists.

Aloofness to oneself is a way to deal with strong feelings deemed threatening and forbidden:

A patient couldn't bear attending art exhibits because the art was too beautiful.
For example, when he tried to view the crayon drawings of Hans Hoffman he was
so overtaken with intense pleasure, deemed intolerable because excessive, that he
had to leave after a few seconds, as he said, "because this is too much for me to
bear." He also could not watch *Star Trek* because after overidentifying with the
characters he felt himself in danger throughout. His position that he hated opera
and his refusal to go because he was bored were in fact a cover-up for his over-
involvement with the characters and his perception of the music as too intense.
He fell asleep during opera not because he did not understand it (the reason he
gave to himself and to his wife) but to defend himself from it. The fear, "I might
faint during the performance," in fact represented a secret wish to "pass out to
get away."

Dissociation in Type II avoidants was also discussed in Chapters 4 and
6, and will be discussed further in Chapter 10.

Passive-Aggression

Defensive passive-aggression is a way to antagonize others subtly. Its
goal is to avoid the strong feelings associated with being close by pro-

voking a negative response in others that lessens the possibility that intimacy will actually occur.

THE FAILURE OF DEFENSES ALREADY IN PLACE

Defenses can fail when they handle anxiety inadequately. Now we see panic, excessive anger, increased self-monitoring where fear of making a mistake breaks one's stride, breakthrough depression, and ultimately even behavioral regression. Breakthrough depression appears when avoidance can no longer delay or eliminate the possibility of negative evaluation by others and keep the avoidant's own guilty sexual and angry feelings in check. It also appears after avoidant defenses create new, depressing problems that are a product of the immediate and long-term difficulties bound to occur in the lives of individuals who are isolated from, and antagonistic to, others.

CHAPTER 9

Comorbid Disorders: Comorbidity with Schizotypal, Schizoid, and Affective Disorders

The first section of this chapter describes avoidant traits in other disorders, for example, avoidant traits that occur in depression. The next, much larger section of this chapter and the entirety of the next two chapters describe the clinical picture that appears when Avoidant Personality Disorder is comorbid with another personality disorder. This is an extremely common occurrence. As the *DSM-IV* says, Avoidant Personality Disorder is often diagnosed with "Social Phobia of the Generalized Type . . . with Dependent Personality Disorder . . . with Borderline Personality Disorder and with the Cluster A Personality Disorders (i.e. Paranoid Schizoid or Schizotypal Personality Disorder)" (p. 663). Therefore, in real life, Avoidant Personality Disorder is rarely pure and the classic presentation of the shy, withdrawn, shrinking, isolated, fearful person rarely seen clinically.

AVOIDANT TRAITS IN DISORDERS OTHER THAN AVOIDANT PERSONALITY DISORDER

A perusal of the *DSM-IV* reveals the following "avoidant" traits in disorders other than AvPD. This list can also serve as a guide to differential diagnosis between Avoidant Personality Disorder and other major disorders with avoidant traits.

1. Schizophrenia: dysfunction of interpersonal relations (p. 285); restrictions in the range and intensity of emotional expression (p. 275). Schizophrenia, catatonic type: extreme negativism (p. 289). Schizophrenia, paranoid type: argumentativeness, superior and patronizing manner (p. 287).

2. Delusional Disorder, Jealous Type: delusion . . . that [a] spouse or lover is unfaithful . . . based on incorrect inferences (p. 297).

3. Manic or Hypomanic episode: [moderate] impairment in social or occupational functioning (p. 338), excessive involvement in pleasurable activities that have a high potential for painful consequences (p. 338), irritable mood (p. 335).

4. Major Depressive Episode: markedly diminished interest in pleasure in all, or almost all, activities most of the day (p. 327).

5. Dysthymic Disorder: low self-esteem, prominent . . . self-criticism (p. 345).

6. Panic Disorder with Agoraphobia: anxiety about being in places or situations from which escape might be difficult (or embarrassing) (p. 396), fear of being outside of the home alone (p. 396) . . . and of traveling (p. 396).

7. Social Phobia (Social Anxiety Disorder): fear of one or more social or performance situations in which the person is exposed to unfamiliar people or to possible scrutiny by others. The individual fears that he or she will act in a way (or show anxiety symptoms) that will be humiliating or embarrassing (p. 416). The avoidance [and the] anxious anticipation interferes significantly with the person's normal routine (p. 417).

8. Specific Phobia: fear that is excessive or unreasonable, cued by the presence or anticipation of a specific object or situation (p. 410).

9. Obsessive-Compulsive Disorder: obsessions or compulsions . . . that are severe enough to be time consuming . . . or cause marked distress or significant impairment (p. 417).

10. Posttraumatic Stress Disorder: efforts to avoid activities, places, or people that arouse recollections of the trauma (p. 428).

11. Generalized Anxiety Disorder: the individual finds it difficult to control the worry [which is] far out of proportion to the actual likelihood or impact of the feared event (p. 433).

12. Somatoform Disorders: (a) Somatization Disorder: antisocial behavior . . . and marital discord (p. 446); (b) Conversion Disorder: dependency and the adoption of a sick role (p. 454); (c) Hypochondriasis: concern about the feared illness often becomes a central feature of the individual's self-image, [and] topic of social discourse, deterioration in doctor-patient relationships, with frustration and anger on both sides, family life may become disturbed as it becomes centered around the individual's physical well-being (p. 463), miss[es]time from work (p. 464).

13. Dissociative Disorders: (a) Dissociative Amnesia: Impairment in work and interpersonal relationships (p. 478); (b) Dissociative Fugue: sudden, unexpected, travel away from home or one's customary place of daily activities (p. 481), clinically significant . . . impairment in social, occupational, or other important areas of functioning (p. 481); (c) Dissociative Identity Disorder: a primary identity [that is] passive, dependent, guilty, and depressed (p. 484) and alternate identities that are hostile, controlling, and self-destructive (p. 484); (d) Depersonalization Disorder: feeling of detachment or estrangement from one's self (p. 488).

14. Paraphilias: imagery . . . acted out with a nonconsenting partner in a way that may be injurious to the partner (p. 523), behavior, sexual urges or fantasies [that] cause clinically significant . . . impairment in social, occupational, or other important areas of functioning (p. 523), social and sexual relationships may suffer (p. 523), impairment in the capacity for reciprocal, affectionate sexual activity (p. 524).

15. Sexual Dysfunctions: disturbance in sexual drive [that] cause interpersonal difficulty (p. 493).

16. Personality Disorders: impairment of social, occupational, or other important areas of functioning (p. 630).

THE CLINICAL PICTURES THAT PRESENT WHEN AVOIDANT PERSONALITY DISORDER IS FOUND IN ASSOCIATION WITH OTHER DISORDERS

AvPD is often found in association with other Axis I disorders (Clinical Disorders) and with other Axis II disorders (Personality Disorders). These comorbid disorders alter the clinical presentation, the dynamics, and the treatment of AvPD. For example, in the realm of treatment, comorbid disorders often determine the kind of resistances that will appear and impede progress. Thus, avoidants who are also *paranoid* tend to be resistant due to a distrustful and disdainful streak that makes them reluctant to expose themselves to having relationships with others just on the therapist's say so. Avoidants who are also *depressed* tend to be resistant because they see anything other than pure encouragement on the part of the therapist as nonsupport. Avoidants who are also *masochistic* tend to be resistant because they respond to getting better by feeling worse, a negative therapeutic reaction that if not recognized and managed correctly from the start can lead to therapeutic failure. Avoidants who are also *obsessive-compulsive* tend to be resistant due to being volatile, unpredictable and stubborn individuals who respond to treatment by taking one step backward for every step forward.

In the remainder of this chapter and in the following two chapters I discuss the various clinical pictures we see when Avoidant Personality Disorder is comorbid with Axis I disorders (Clinical Disorders) such as Major Depression and other comorbid Axis II disorders (Personality Disorders) such as Obsessive-Compulsive Personality Disorder. Chapter 9 describes the clinical pictures that present when Avoidant Personality Disorder is comorbid with schizotypal, schizoid and affective disorder. Chapter 10 describes the clinical pictures that present when Avoidant Personality Disorder is comorbid with such neurotic-spectrum disorders as Obsessive-Compulsive Disorder, and Chapter 11 describes the clinical pictures that present when Avoidant Personality Disorder is comorbid with personality disorders other than AvPD, for example, with Borderline Personality Disorder.

AVOIDANT PERSONALITY DISORDER AND
SCHIZOTYPAL PERSONALITY DISORDER

In the following discussion I separate schizotypal and schizoid personality disorder from the other personality disorders to emphasize the almost schizophrenic-like severity of the withdrawal found in many of these patients.

Patients who simultaneously present with Avoidant and Schizotypal Personality Disorder are highly impaired in their ability to relate to others. But their impairment is relative, not as some observers would have it, absolute, that is, it is due to anxiety, not to a basic incapacity for interpersonal relationships. These individuals remain capable of intense relationships but they withdraw from them defensively, to an extreme. As an example of one such patient's ability to retain relationships, a severely schizotypal and possibly even schizophrenic patient, convinced that enemies were writing warnings on the bottom of his feet, stroked my hand seductively to illustrate how.

A homeless man who was diagnosed both with Avoidant Personality Disorder and Schizotypal Personality Disorder complained that the shelters for the homeless were so bad that he preferred to live out on the streets. An analysis of his complaints revealed a typical avoidant wish to relate to others in conflict with a fear of relating. His wish to relate to others could be inferred from his distinct preference for lively populated areas, like streets in the busiest neighborhoods and populated railroad terminals, over isolated areas, like railroad yards; and in his desire to locate his cardboard slab in such a way that it touched the slabs of others, not only because space was at a premium but also because he wanted to interact with people. His fear of relating could be inferred from an analysis of his complaints that conditions were bad in the shelters. He was actually complaining that in there things were too close for comfort. When he complained that his bunkmates in the shelters were dangerous, he was in fact complaining that they were rejecting him. That inspired him, as it might inspire anyone else, to retreat to the streets to stay away from people who might disappoint him in love and to seek out others who might salve the wounds of previous rejections. On the streets his anger at being turned down when he begged for money was similarly motivated by a need for love. In cursing people when they refused him a handout, he acted less like a deprived beggar who only wanted money, and more like a rejected lover who also wanted a relationship.

A schizotypal avoidant only occasionally spoke to others, and then spoke a few words only. He also grew a long beard, and rarely bathed. He selected a town path of precisely two and a half miles and walked it precisely four times a day. That his behavior was interpersonally motivated by a forbidden wish to get close to me became clear when I discovered that his walk took him on a path right past my home, thence to the clinic where I was treating him.

An in-depth study of his private fantasy life revealed a "secret relatedness" embedded in what at first looked merely like an impersonal "stereo fetish." What seemed to be little more than a lonely desire to amass impersonal sound-generating equipment in fact turned out to be a lining up of audio pieces that symbolized parents and siblings, his way to make "an electronic family."

So often the obscurantism found in schizotypal avoidant individuals is not only a hostile heaping of disdain in the form of mysteriousness and incomprehensibility intended to confuse and befuddle those who are detested, but also a heaping of retribution on those believed to have hurt and rejected the patient.

A patient when asked, "Do you have any friends?" replied, "I have exactly thirty-eight of them," first to deliberately perplex the examiner as a way to retaliate for the examiner's not scheduling sessions frequently enough, and second to test the waters with a toe in anticipation of pulling out his foot should the temperature prove to be too low. Thus, his first presentation was obscure. But if a listener were interested and asked, "What do you mean?" the patient, pleased he was being heard and sensing the listener's desire to understand him, would clear up his thinking as a consequence and reward—by explaining that there were "thirty-eight friendly staff members" on the rolls of the clinic the patient was attending.

Schizotypal avoidants, like many other avoidants, are least avoidant when they feel wanted and needed. Many psychiatrists are familiar with the remote isolated patient who becomes nonavoidant long enough to rescue someone in trouble, for example, a hospital staff member being attacked by another patient, only to immediately once again retreat into a self-contained world. In addition, when these individuals feel wanted and needed, they can make their eccentricities appealing instead of un-appealing. They can change an off-putting seediness into a pleasing, even creative quirkiness, eliminating the element of shock-and-annoy to become instead quite charming.

AVOIDANT PERSONALITY DISORDER AND SCHIZOID PERSONALITY DISORDER

Avoidants also diagnosed with schizoid personality disorder tend to be shy and withdrawn to the extreme. Some observers are thus led to conclude that they have a primary deficit in their ability to relate. Others conclude that, as with schizotypal patients, their lack of relatedness is secondary, that is, due to anxiety.

AVOIDANT PERSONALITY DISORDER AND PARANOID PERSONALITY DISORDER

In these paranoid avoidants the classic fire of sensitivity to the possibility of criticism, humiliation, and rejection is fueled by an inability to trust others. Paranoid avoidants lose their ability to trust others because they question others' motives based on incorrect assumptions they make about what others are thinking. Many of these incorrect assumptions originate with defensive projection that amounts to attributing their own negative thoughts to others. As a result, paranoid avoidants conclude that others disdain them the same way they disdain themselves, and that others dislike them the same way they dislike others. They then withdraw after becoming wrongly convinced that others hate them—a withdrawal they secretly planned all along. Some even take the next step and treat others dismally in order to provoke them to give them the stress, bad luck, or nebulous incompatibility they need to have the excuse they want to keep to themselves, and even to have the fight they were seeking to give themselves the rationale to make the break they long desired. Paranoid avoidants are all too eager to view cancellation of a date due to sudden illness as a personal rejection; an ogling look from a stranger not as a cruise but as a hostile stare; an offer of friendship or love as sexual harassment; an intimate's platonic relationships with others as cheating; a personals ad not as an offer to meet but as a pack of lies designed to ensnare; a potential partner's request to have an exclusive relationship as an attempt to control; an offer to match-make as a humiliation of those who are so desperate that they need to be fixed up; and the best-intentioned advice, including that from a concerned therapist, as either criticism for prior wrongdoing or as an attempt at control for the personal gain of the advisor.

For one patient any sign of another's self-interest meant a complete uninterest in her. She demanded to see a psychiatrist immediately, and was obliged. However, the psychiatrist was just finishing an apple that was part of his lunch. The psychiatrist, who accepted having his lunch hour interrupted but not letting a good morsel go bad, took his apple into the interview and continued eating it. The patient, wanting the psychiatrist's full attention and wanting it now, viewed the apple-eating as a sign of full—rather than minor and partial—uninterest, and stormed out of the interview saying, "Obviously you are too completely self-preoccupied to be of any use to me at all."

AVOIDANT PERSONALITY DISORDER AND AFFECTIVE DISORDER

Avoidant Personality Disorder and Depression

Self-Destructiveness

Avoidants who are not depressed often try to get over being avoidant by developing their old and finding new relationships. To this end, instead of allowing their appearance and behavior to deteriorate, they take special pains to maintain and improve their interpersonal appeal in the hope that they will meet new people who will be part of their recovery. In contrast, avoidants who are simultaneously depressed enhance their avoidance by staying stuck in the mire of their depression, deliberately failing to make repairs so that they *can* stay unappealing to others, even setting out to antagonize or horrify others just so that they can make disappointment, rage, grief, and hypersensitivity the orders of their day, and the cry, "I fear no one will love me" their hopeful prediction.

Hypersensitivity

Depressed avoidants take everything much too seriously and imagine that they are being rejected when they are not. For example, they get angry even at a little joke that is in any way at their expense, or misinterpret positive gestures as negative.

A customer was asking a salesperson in an upscale food store many details about the merchandise. The salesperson patiently explained his wares to her, and then said, meaning it as a compliment, "I have never spent so much time with a customer before." She took this as his criticizing her for taking up his whole afternoon, refused to return to the store, and complained to management that she had been sassed.

An emergency patient severely castigated members of the Department of Psychiatry for referring to her as a "walk-in," a status she believed inferior to the status possessed by "those who have an appointment." Later in the interview, when discussing real estate holdings (the source of her current depression), her examiner merely asked her, "How many properties do you own?" To this she replied that the questioner was putting her down by criticizing her for being so stupid as to be overinvolved in real estate in a down market.

Selfishness

Depressed avoidants tend to be selfish people who act as if they are the only ones with feelings and needs. For example, one such depressed avoidant never attended funerals because "death bothers me," knowing that he would, and actually hoping to, antagonize family and friends also bothered by death.

Anger

Depressed avoidants, like other depressives, are angry people but instead of internalizing their anger, hoping to keep it to themselves to spare others' feelings, they express it freely, then excuse themselves with a convenient rationalization such as "I am undergoing assertiveness training," or "I feel better once I have cleared the air." How you feel is of no consequence to them whatsoever.

Low Self-Esteem

Depressed avoidants develop low self-esteem that leads to an increased need for approval from others. This increases the likelihood that they will interpret any sign that they are not fully accepted as evidence that they have been rejected. As a result they constantly feel criticized, humiliated, rejected, and abandoned, and require full reassurance that they will be accepted before they can even think about relating. What many require is a "parental" stamp of approval before starting or pursuing a relationship. For example, a gay doctor wanted to move in with her lover until her father told her that living with another woman would ruin her reputation and so her professional career. So, instead, she and her lover decided to rent separate apartments. As a result their relationship languished.

Depressed avoidants use their low self-esteem to hold others off or drive them away. Their low self-esteem takes on a critical quality toward others as they attack others with their self-criticisms. For example, when they say, "I am not good enough," they really mean, "I envy you for having all the things that I don't have." When they say, "I don't see how a wonderful person like you could possibly like a low-down person like me," they really mean, "if you like me, there must be something wrong with you." When they say, "I am not good enough for you," they really mean, "You are not good enough for me." They also use the guilty conscience behind their low self-esteem to hold others off or to drive them away. For them, sex is immoral, and they don't mind saying so. They note that those who approach them sexually are an example of the immorality of which they speak, and view even a legitimate sexual approach as a sexual harassment. When they demean themselves it is not in the hope that others will disagree with their own negative self-assessment and say, "There, there," but in the hope that others will first agree with them and second, instead of loving them for their imperfections, reject them on that account. Instead of looking for a second opinion from someone more positive about them than they are about themselves, they stew in their own self-denigration and then give up, thinking, "No one could ever love me." They then too readily conclude, as planned all along, "What's the use of trying to relate, no one will love me anyway because I am not loveable."

Very soon a vicious cycle begins: relationships don't work out. This intensifies their self-critical tendencies and with it their low self-esteem, leaving them even more hypersensitive to criticism. As a result their low self-esteem drops even lower.

Apathy and Boredom

In depressed avoidants apathy and boredom is a way to send the off-putting message to present company that "you are not worth my time and attention." The message is either sent in words alone or nonverbally in behavior via a certain restlessness whose message is "you are too dull and too boring to hold my attention for long."

Anxiety/Panic

Instead of suppressing panic for the greater good, depressed avoidants encourage it in themselves in the hope that it will become contagious, just so that they can give their misery some company.

A depressed alarmist when insightful described himself, in essence, as follows. "I am like the local television news show. If you listen to me, you think the world is coming to an end, so much do I elaborate ordinary events into the crisis of the day, or week. I assign every occurrence a wind-chill factor, making a '30 degree day' into a 'minus 10 experience.' I claim fire when there is only smoke, and rarely tire of annoying people by telling them the different ways my world can conceivably come to an end."

Grief

For the depressed avoidant, grief is an opportunity to live in the past as a way to tell others in the present that they don't match up to former friends and lovers. During the difficult transitional period after a loss, instead of grieving for old relationships because they are gone, and instead of grieving to maintain old relationships, if only in fantasy, depressed avoidants grieve predominantly in order to make a retrospective positive distortion of a partly or entirely negative relationship so that they can treat any new relationship as inferior, and as an infidelity, to an old one. For example, a woman who just lost her husband decided to have a few friends over for dinner, only to later feel unbearably guilty for using her dead husband's house to have the fun by herself that they used to have together. Whereas for grieving nonavoidants every new relationship is a fresh sign of hope, for grieving avoidants every new relationship, by recalling the old relationship lost, becomes a fresh reason for despair.

Avoidant Personality Disorder and Hypomania

Compulsive Sexual Behavior

Eli Coleman (1992) in his article "Is Your Patient Suffering From Compulsive Sexual Behavior?" describes what he calls "nonparaphilic compulsive sexual behavior" (p. 321), which is "normative sexual behavior taken to a compulsive extreme" (p. 321). I classify nonparaphilic compulsive sexual behavior as affective to emphasize how this behavior is primarily a hypomanic defense against depression. Hypomanic avoidants often act out sexually, doing so in one of the five ways Coleman delineates: compulsive cruising and multiple partners, where cruising is ritualistic and trance inducing; compulsive fixation on an unattainable partner; compulsive autoeroticism; compulsive multiple love relationships; and compulsive sexuality in a relationship. As Coleman notes, these are not "sexual addictions" (p. 321) but "anxiety-reduction mechanisms" (p. 321) used to maintain self-esteem. He states that one of these subtypes, compulsive autoeroticism, is comorbid with Avoidant Personality Disorder (but notes that all types of compulsive sexual behavior are associated with "relationship discord" [p. 322], one manifestation of which is numerous love relationships that are short-lived, intense, and unfulfilling).

Superficial Euphoric Franticness

Hypomanic superficial euphoric franticness is a way for avoidants to relate poorly while simultaneously fooling themselves and others into thinking that they are relating well. They relate to large numbers of people in order not to have to relate to one significant other or even to a few intimates. While actually keeping people at bay, they maintain the illusion of making/having meaningful relationships via a hyperrelatedness that serves the purpose of denying their remoteness and isolation to themselves. Some relate to an anonymous them, as did the avoidant who had a relationship with his fan club to avoid having a relationship with a personal fan. Others accomplish essentially the same thing by relating strictly to other people's superficial qualities—picking others on the basis of such ectodermal" attributes as looks or possessions, in effect substituting impersonal for personal relationships by relating to attributes instead of to people. Still others compulsively plan for, but never actually proceed with, a seduction, as did the individual who decorated and redecorated his apartment so that "women will yield when they see my beautiful place"—though he never actually invited women up to visit.

A hypomanic avoidant, an alcoholic gambler, preferred accolades from drinking and gambling buddies to love from family and close friends. He lived for the congratulations his buddies heaped on him for being able to hold a large amount of liquor and for being able to beat impossible odds at the gaming tables.

A familiar Greenwich Village pedophile cruised for young boys in part so that he could brag "how many I have had this year" within earshot of passersby, as a way of "impressing" the anonymous hordes.

An actor when asked, "And how are you doing these days?" instead of saying, "Fine, thank you," and then inquiring about the well-being of others, responded by reciting his recent roles in theatrical productions, along with excerpts from his latest favorable reviews. Once when asked his consuming interests he listed, in no particular order: late-night disco-dancing; taking euphoriant drugs/alcohol; the fabulous ultrasophisticated tea dance and Sunday brunch; decorating with plastic plants ("because they require no light they can be strategically placed away from windows to a spot where they look best") and recessing wires on stereos and lamps to avoid "the ugly tangles"; wearing leather and blue collar drag; hanging out with homosexual "sisters"; traveling to exotic places to bring home pictures to impress friends; playing the role of the entertainer who makes people laugh wherever he goes; searching for and finding the perfect pun and double entendre that would confer upon him the status of "life of the party"; being the best looking person at the party with the most perfect body; picking up the best looking person at the party with the most perfect body; falling in love at first sight, often for no better reason than an attractive deposition of body hair; rubbing elbows with important people ranging from the owner of a shop famous for its "beautiful and sophisticated bathroom fixtures" to the celebrities he saw walking down New York streets; bragging of a "personal relationship" with the bartender of the currently most famous gay bar in the city based on the friendly greeting the bartender gave him when they met by accident during the day (especially potent when the greeting was given within earshot of admiring friends and acquaintances); and living in a town that is "where it's at" because the bars stay open later than the bars in the provinces (breathlessly he bragged, "Imagine, on New Year's Eve they are open all night long!").

A summer homeowner in a fey country resort preferred having a busy house to having a meaningful relationship. He abandoned close friends and family for guests who came around at vacation time, but at no other time. Once he bragged, "When winter is on the wane and the sun stays up after 5:00 P.M. (leading the radio announcer to say, "Spring is on its way"), that's when I feel good all over, because that's when my many friends start to call me up to make plans to stay with me for the summer." A favorite activity when summer came was sophisticated discussions with cognoscenti/enthusiasts/quintessentialists about the increase in the number of "illiterati"/dullards/philistines these days, with particular emphasis given to the current dearth of good, snappy, fey formulations/comebacks/withering repartee. That is, his was an overconcern with what played well in the cocktail lounge, and an underconcern with what played well in the living room and bedroom. A favorite story, which he told and retold, involved a clever quip made on the beach by a minor movie star. Many years later he still chortled when he recalled to anyone who would listen how he heard this man distinguish "Love" from "True Love" from "Undying Love" from "Transcendental Love" on the grounds that "Love was a relationship on the beach at night, True Love a relationship in a hotel room overnight, Undying Love a relationship in a private apartment overnight, and Transcendental Love the second date."

A man formed relationships with good looking, considerably younger women, only to lose interest in them when he felt the bloom was off, which for him meant the appearance of the slightest flaw—the first sign of coarsening facial features, the appearance of skin nodules, or the hint of undesirable body fat. Now he disrupted relationships that worked with people he knew for relationships that might not work with people he hardly knew. Although he instinctively perceived that as he grew older leaving the familiar to try out the new was a dangerous way to live, he often moved on just to tempt fate, only to later become depressed, and wildly lament his future prospects, saying, "I feel nothing works out for me; I feel too sad to look for a new partner and look too sad to get one." After some months of analyzing his self-defeating behaviors, I asked him, "Why don't you find a woman of your own age for companionship and love?" To this he atavistically replied, "No matter how nice her personality, I wouldn't be interested in someone my age. Too many wrinkles."

A man preferring peer-group approval to loving and being loved formed relationships just so he could brag about them to his buddies. He wanted people to say, "Look at him, isn't he lucky, look at what he got." He so needed approval that he would even break up with suitable partners for the accolades forthcoming from his *schadenfreude*-loving friends who were egging him on to do just that simply so that they could watch him fall flat on his face. Later in life, he became depressed because he realized when he looked back and around, that no amount of applause could gloss over the essential poverty even of his positive accomplishments, and because, older now, he was to discover a painful truth—as he put it, "As you get on in years, it's easier and better to keep old love than it is to get new congratulations."

Grandiosity and Narcissism

Grandiose narcissistic hypomanic avoidants are selfish people who recognize their own but not others' needs, give only in anticipation of getting, have a "what did you do for me lately" attitude that makes others only as good as their latest contributions, and develop an undue comfort about exacting greater and greater tribute while feeling neither beholden to those who give it nor the need to pay them back. The following cases illustrate how the distinctly negative interpersonal consequences of the narcissism and grandiosity associated with hypomania contribute to avoidance:

A hypomanic man displayed his disregard of other people in an impatience to score that he himself compared to banging stuck jars to get them open, in a rush breaking them instead, and in his belief that the end was the only worthwhile thing and the means to the end an encumbrance. Instead of doing things gradually, progressively nurturing and developing relationships, he asked for sex on the first date as repayment for footing the dinner bill—of course destroying any possibility of furthering the relationship.

A hypomanic woman attended every opera and concert performance she could, though money was tight and her husband felt abandoned because he felt she did not want to stay home with him. She countered his complaints with, "The theatre is the most important thing in my life, and if I can't go, then what is life all about, and what is our marriage worth?" He got the message and countered with a "most important thing" of his own—a relationship with another woman.

Two guests, as they later admitted, had the "chutzpah" to turn their host's home into, "an Inn for Bed and Breakfast, and Lunch and Dinner Too." Once they appeared at the door for an extended stay announcing that they had spent all their money on liquor and that they would be bored and starve all week unless their host would graciously consent to pay for their groceries and entertainment.

A self-preoccupied hypomanic doctor wrote a letter to a colleague after the two squabbled: "I choose neither to speak to you nor to see you again, but should we meet at a convention, for appearances' sake and for professional reasons important to me, you will continue to show me cordiality and act as if nothing happened."

A man who early in his career had become used to being in lofty administrative positions, where he was in charge, had to settle later in his career for front-line work. Instead of cheerfully adapting to his new role, he continued to administrate and supervise his colleagues, haughtily treating them as underlings, say, by demanding that they do him little favors. For example, each morning when he came to work he knocked on a colleague's ground floor office window to in effect order him to open a side door, caring little that the man asked him not to use him as a doorman and begged him not to startle him in this way.

A single man at the beginning of the evening complained to his date, "I had to interview 90 women just to get you," and at the end of the evening, "I've dated women with small breasts, and I've dated women with large breasts, but no matter how hard I try I can't seem to find a woman whose breasts are exactly the right size."

Hostility

Hostility is the opposite side of the coin of hypomanic hail-fellow-well-met hyperrelatedness.

A hypomanic secretary in a psychiatric clinic prided herself on "how well I get along with the patients because they like to be kidded," though in fact her humor was cruel and insulting. For example, asked by a patient's wife if the records indicated her husband was cheating on her, she replied, with a hearty laugh, "Not to worry about his being unfaithful. If he says he's having an affair, he's lying. He's too ugly for anyone to find him interesting."

CHAPTER 10

Comorbid Disorders: Comorbidity with "Neurotic" Spectrum Disorders

AVOIDANT PERSONALITY DISORDER AND SOMATOFORM DISORDER

Most of the following comments on the picture presented by somatizing avoidants are speculative because most patients who somatize, being unable or unwilling to share what they are thinking, are in effect silent about their dynamics, and even choose somatic patterns of expression so that they *can* distance nonverbally, that is, without actually putting what they are doing to themselves and to others into words.

Somatizing avoidances include those who suffer from the familiar "not tonight dear" headache; some cases of Epstein-Barr chronic fatigue (mentioned further below); palpitations of the heart (when used for purposes of anxious withdrawal); hypoglycemic-like symptoms (pressed into service to render one too weak to relate); lactose intolerance and colitis (the latter also mentioned below, used to render one too gassy to relate or unpleasant to be related to); a genital itch (when announced in untimely fashion to render oneself sexually unappealing); and sexual dysfunctions (when intended to express a general disinterest in sex or a general interpersonal joylessness). (That avoidants with sexual problems like impotence or dyspareunia often don't try other kinds of sex, using a flimsy moral excuse, suggests that much of what we call sexual inhibition should instead be called "avoidant" inhibition.)

Some avoidants use obesity to distort their body in order to avoid worldly pleasures. They surround themselves with protective, off-putting folds of fat intended to keep others figuratively and literally at bay. In one case a patient complained, "They don't like me because I am fat," and "They stare at me as if I am a freak"—even though fatness and freakishness were precisely what he intended in order to see to it that others would not like him, and would stay away. Nonavoidant obese individuals view their eating as a compulsion that keeps them from relating. In contrast, obese avoidant individuals view their relationships as a compulsion that keeps them from eating.

Bulimic avoidants, when closeness threatens, may overeat to become obese as a way to distance; then, when loneliness threatens, go on to restitutive vomiting to lose weight to make themselves look better, with avoidant overeating resumed as soon as the promise (really threat) of a relationship appears. Some avoidant bulimics and anorexics deliberately arrange to look thin, wan, and cachectic to ward off potential suitors. It was in character that a bulimic refused to wear gym outfits consisting of shorts and sneakers when working out, instead favoring street clothes and sandals, even though the latter were specifically prohibited by the gym rules. Some anorexics even hope for the amenorrhea that can be associated with anorexia nervosa because it assures them that "I can't get married because I can't have children."

Avoidants who stutter can be attempting to remain silent in the guise of trying to talk. Or they can be attempting to spit hatefully at others, both figuratively and literally. The avoidant intent can sometimes be inferred from the effect of the behavior on others: the rather unfortunate temptation to make fun of stutterers (and mimic them, as one mimics people with tics, my next subject).

A possible purpose of physical and verbal tics in the avoidant is to annoy others and drive them away. A patient himself understood that behind his shoulder-shrugging tic was his impatience with others for "invading my space," with his tic a way to "shrug off people who got too close." It was in character that a patient with a facial twitch that resembled a grimace developed a reputation around the gym she attended for pushing people who were in her way out of her way. Nail-biters are often caught up in a vicious cycle. When, as unconsciously intended, others reject them because of their habit they become more anxious, and their habit intensifies, as does, on that account, others' rejection of them.

Hypochondriacal avoidants use worrisome complaints to drive others away. Again, the reaction of others to these avoidants is a good measure of how these avoidants intend to provoke the people with whom they come in contact. A typical victim response might be, "I can't stand any more of his whining and complaining about imaginary illnesses." Conversion hysteria avoidants express an avoidant desire in body language. However symbolic the expression, the avoidant intent is not completely lost on the observer. This was the case for a patient with a scissors gait who when walking kept her knees and thighs together and navigated only with her lower legs and feet outstretched in the shape of an upside-down "V" in order to "discourage all suitors from scoring."

Factitial dermatitis in avoidants can be a method to deform the skin to make oneself unappealing. An example is the off-putting ravaged cuticle syndrome caused by picking at the skin of the thumb.

In one case a "pimple on prom night" went nicely with a general anxiety over coming of age, and a specific desire to repulse a date. In this case one furuncle was squeezed just moments before the social contact took place and another shortly after it was initiated, the manifest reason being, "To look better," with the actual results, of course, just the opposite.

Acne rosacea in avoidants can have a hostile component in those patients where the flush appears when others get too close emotionally. Gaseousness/colitis in avoidants can express a secret wish to distance. At least this seems to be the case in those patients who say, "I know I shouldn't have eaten that but I did anyway," a revelation of how they secretly wish to aggravate their gaseousness by improper diet/drinking/smoking in order to make unpleasant, off-putting oral/anal sounds. For example, one patient admitted, "My belches are a way to complain to the world and the people in it that they nauseate me."

The complaints of symptoms of chronic fatigue in avoidants (Epstein-Barr avoidance) such as, "I am tired all the time" can be code for, "Don't bother me, I prefer to stay asleep." The attack (so often heard) on the treating professional takes the form of, "You say this is psychological but it's really physical." In true chronic fatigue, this attack is a legitimate questioning of the diagnosis. In chronic fatigue in avoidants this attack is an in-character sign that the patient wants to hurt another person, as is his or her style, simply because this other person tries to get close, and offer help.

AVOIDANT PERSONALITY DISORDER AND SOCIAL PHOBIA

In the following section I depart somewhat from the *DSM-IV* definition of Social Phobia to use the term as most cognitive therapists (for example, Anthony and Swinson) use it. Some patients with symptoms of Social Phobia have concurrent symptoms of AvPD, or the other way around, as in the following case example:

In his romantic life one Social Phobic expressed his fear of driving to his lover's home as a fear of driving through green lights and over bridges. On those occasions when he was able to reach his lover and have sex, during sex he expressed his fear of commitment indirectly as a severe ejaculatio retardata, and directly by telling his lover that his inability to have an orgasm made it necessary for him to finally give up on sex entirely, because it "is more trouble than it's worth." In his social life he expressed his fear of people as an isolating telephonophobia that began with his installing an answering machine not to receive but to screen messages, and ended with his neither answering the phone nor returning the messages that people left for him.

Other patients either have symptoms of Social Phobia or symptoms of AvPD, but not both. They fear public speaking yet they have normal or close-to-normal relationships with significant others, or they are shy but have little trouble speaking in public—and, as is the case with some actors, their shyness even lifts completely when they are on stage, only to return when the play is over.

As previously mentioned in Chapters 1 and 4, I make a distinction between Social Phobia and Avoidant Personality Disorder both on dynamic and on descriptive-clinical grounds, distinguishing Social Phobia from AvPD both on the basis of the dynamic reasons for and on the basis of the mode of expression of the social/relationship anxiety (from now on just called "social anxiety") that underlies the two clinical syndromes.

The dynamic reasons for social anxiety are discussed throughout. In social phobics the social anxiety tends to be mainly called up by a fear of criticism and rejection, as cited in the *DSM-IV*. In patients with AvPD the social anxiety tends to be called up by a much broader and comprehensive spectrum of fears—not only fears of criticism and rejection, but also fears of flooding, depletion, and acceptance.

In the realm of the mode of expression of the social anxiety, patients with a Social Phobia express their social anxiety not directly but indirectly, that is, symbolically. They pour it into interpersonal terror that appears strictly in response to specific trivial social cues. Social phobics do not withdraw from interpersonal *relationships* so much as they withdraw from interpersonal *situations*—from discrete trivial prompts that symbolize interpersonal relationships—neatly packaged, tangible happenings that are stand-ins for interpersonal upheavals. These upheavals are condensed and externalized to become outwardly expressed holographic representations of intense inner conflict. For example, a patient who fears urinating in public or a patient who fears signing her name to a check while others watch is expressing what are *dynamically* deep interpersonal fears of criticism and rejection *clinically* in a condensed and displaced fashion. Examples of social phobias each with their underlying meaning follow: A phobia of blushing that signifies being criticized for turning red hot; a phobia of eating in public that signifies being criticized for using the mouth in situations where observed; a phobia of speaking in public that signifies being exposed and vulnerable to humiliation; a phobia of urinating in a public men's room that signifies exposing one's genitals to the man standing in the next urinal, in turn signifying vulnerability and castration anxiety; and a phobia of signing one's name to a check while others watch and wait in eager anticipation that signifies a fear of cooperating and thus of being called submissive. In short, social phobics wall off and contain their interpersonal fears of criticism and humiliation, in effect relegating them to short-lived pseudointerpersonal encounters that simultaneously refer to, and obscure, the real thing.

I believe that social phobics do this for a specific reason and purpose. Unconsciously they make a choice to be less interpersonally shy, remote, and withdrawn than avoidants, that is, to remain more interpersonally outgoing and related than patients with AvPD. They desire and hope to keep their whole personality out of it. So they involve only part of their personality, doing so intentionally in order to leave the rest of the personality intact. As a result, unlike many patients with AvPD, social phobics are by nature outgoing, and able to form close and lasting relationships, and even to do so easily. They tend to be happily and permanently attached or married to someone, and they are often professionally quite successful. Their problems tend to consist merely of troublesome islets of panicky withdrawal. This insular expression of social anxiety in turn spares the rest of their lives, permitting full and satisfactory relationships to take place on the mainland.

In contrast, patients with AvPD wear their faint avoidant hearts on their sleeves. They present clinically with mild to severe generalized relationship difficulties. They fear closeness and intimacy and commitment itself, not a substitute, stand-in, or replacement for these. As a result, avoidants are clinically more socially anxious and withdrawn than they are phobic, that is, they present not with an encapsulated fear on the order of a fear of public speaking but either with a generalized shyness that consists of difficulty meeting people, or with an ambivalence about relationships that consists of difficulty in sustaining relationships with people they have already met. As a consequence, they are either painfully tentative about seeking out relationships in the first place or, if not tentative, then ambivalent about the relationships they find, so that they start relationships only to then pull back from them. Now they become not withdrawn fearful wallflowers but mingles or seven year itch avoidants who cannot make up their minds about a given relationship and about relationships in general. They get engaged, then cannot decide whether or not to get married; decide to get married but never go through with it and afterwards break off the engagement; propose but leave their brides or grooms at the altar; or marry, then develop a seven year itch and file for divorce because "I cannot stand that person any longer." Alternatively, right from the start they flee from a world that is too much with them, not into shyness, remoteness, or ambivalence, but into the protective arms and engulfing bosom of a mother-figure, relating to him or her in order to avoid having to relate to everyone else.

This said, as Benjamin (1996) carefully notes, "the differential diagnosis between Social Phobia and AvPD is difficult when Social Phobia generalizes" (p. 190). This was the case for a socially phobic adolescent afraid of going to school because of a painful startle reaction to the loud school bell. This child soon became so fearful of all street noise that she was unable to leave the house at all without her mother. Eventually as an adult she stayed home with her mother all day long, her phobia having spread so that the only meaningful relationships, besides the one with her mother, were the ones she had with her cats.

A careful history can help distinguish patients with generalized Social Phobia from patients with AvPD. Historically, at least in my experience, patients with AvPD as children are more likely to be withdrawn and to otherwise have impaired interpersonal relationships. In comparison, patients with a Social Phobia are historically less shy with their peers, less likely to be picked on and criticized by them, and more likely to have relationships outside of their family, yet also more likely to have circumscribed childhood phobias, such as school phobias, symptoms that limit their movement more than they limit their basic interpersonal abilities.

Making the distinction between Social Phobia and AvPD is important because certain therapeutic approaches indicated for the one are not as helpful for the other. The following distinction is relative, not absolute: Social phobics who become anxious in relationship to specific trivial prompts like public speaking or urinating in public places, and avoidants who are mainly shy, tend to respond to a therapeutic approach that emphasizes cognitive insight into the symptom ("you fear public speaking, or saying hello, because you feel that if you make a minor mistake than all will be lost"). They also tend to respond to behavior therapy that offers the patient tasks of graded difficulty geared to overcoming the specific behavioral inhibition involved, and possibly to pharmacotherapy meant to reduce anxiety. In contrast, patients who present with distancing due to relationship volatility, seven year itch problems, or removal via dependent immersion tend to need and respond to insight into the nature and meaning of the interactive problems that keep them from becoming, and remaining, intimate with significant others. Conversely, common sense tells us that cognitive-behavior techniques useful for a fear of public speaking and shyness, particularly techniques of graduated exposure, will not be quite so helpful for treating an ongoing fear of commitment, closeness, and intimacy. While a patient afraid of public speaking can ask him- or herself, in a reassuring manner, "What is the worst that can happen?" then expose himself or herself to the feared situation to prove he or she is safe, and while avoidants who are shy can use exposure to help them overcome their fear of meeting new people, avoidants afraid of intimacy and commitment cannot use exposure therapeutically to get close because getting over their dating anxiety would require trial intimacies and commitments, which, if at all possible, would be selfish and cruel to others in the extreme.

AVOIDANT PERSONALITY DISORDER AND OBSESSIVE-COMPULSIVE DISORDER

Perfectionism

Obsessive avoidants become perfectionistic not as a way to improve their relationships but as a way to destroy them. Matters of correctness, honor, propriety, and etiquette become reasons to deselect, that is, to overlook, ignore, and remove oneself from, others. There is no consideration for extenuating circumstances like others' bad days or pressing personal problems, and there is no desire to compromise and forgive for the sake of the big picture, the forest for the trees. Fyodor Dostoyevsky might be describing such perfectionistic avoidants in *The Idiot* (1969 edition) when he says, "If you have a wart on your forehead or your nose it always seems that no one has a thing in the world to do but look at your wart, make fun of it, and condemn you for it, though you might be the discoverer of America" (p. 348).

Instead of using the occasion of a grammatical error as an opportunity to make both a helpful correction and a delightful friend, one individual instead destroyed a nascent relationship by arguing if it were correct to say, "So and so was born on the same day I was born" or "on the same date." She also deselected and rejected people entirely on the basis of their interests, using a simple, elegant, but entirely inaccurate formula of her own devising to determine, "Is he, or is he not, what I want in a man?" According to her, an appreciation for ballet was civilized and acceptable, while a love for baseball and fishing was uncivilized and unacceptable.

Perfectionistic avoidants are also worriers who hurt their relationships by subjecting them to constant questioning, always asking "Can he or she be the only right one for me?" and answering the question as "maybe," then remaining somewhat aloof in a relationship due to "not knowing the answer." They might become serial dating men or women always looking for that perfect partner yet finding everyone who comes their way wanting in some (often realistically unimportant) respect. As married men or women with the seven year itch, they question the value of a present relationship, look for something better, and start affairs. Then, after attempting to use a new lover as their bridge out of their present relationship, they think twice about leaving the comfortable old relationship and abandon the second lover because the new relationship is not as perfect as they had fantasized.

Ritualism/Brooding

Obsessive avoidants employ rituals less to maintain inner control of sexuality/hostility and to keep it from showing and more to annoy and attack others. Contrast the hand-washer in private with bedtime rituals done when alone with the man who approaches and reapproaches his victims to ask them, "Did I bump you?" until he finally manages to bump them, then sidles up to apologize, only to bump them again so that he can ask them again, "Did I bump you?" Also contrast the lover who worries constantly but in silence when his lover is ill with the lover that disguises his annoyance with his companion's illness as a nonstop concern about the other's health, asking her many times a day how she feels and if she is feeling better, really telling her to "get well, because your being sick is inconveniencing me."

Argumentativeness

Argumentative avoidants intend not to be right but to be annoying. That is why they do not give up their arguing in time to rescue and maintain their relationships. Instead, they know when they have reached the limit, and then deliberately take the next step, over the edge.

They develop a facility for taking either side in a debate. Thus, a realtor, who secretly envied anyone who was propertied, told all clients who had an empty apartment for sale to furnish it, "because accomplishment sells better than potential." But it was the other way around when the apartment was furnished. Then the cry was that "the empty place is more desirable because it allows the individual buyer's fantasy to flourish."

Instead of quietly brooding over imponderables, such as, "Why does a chair have four legs, not three," they start discussions over matters that cannot be settled, particularly those of the half full, half empty variety. Theirs are totally gratuitous distinction arguments characterized by a concreteness of thinking, a tendency to split hairs, and a loss of perspective that overlooks the importance of the grand sweep and with it the enjoyment, pleasures, and rewards of magnificent, deliberate, inexactness. An example, particularly apt for our present concerns, is the ongoing debate—as passionate as it would seem to be irresolvable—about whether Social Phobia is condensed AvPD, or AvPD is generalized Social Phobia.

A butcher, when asked for boneless chicken breasts, just to be contentious said he didn't have any—but as an alternative offered the customer chicken breasts that were boned. His counterpart, a counterperson in a pastry shop, when asked if she had "cheese bacon biscuits" said no, but allowed that she had "bacon biscuits with cheese." Their counterpart, a man guarding the entrance to a town recycling center, became annoyed when a customer told him that he was entering in order to "throw some sticks away." Before he would let the customer in he made him admit that what he should have said was not "sticks," but brush.

A man told a friend how much his brake job was going to cost. When the friend questioned such a large amount, the man replied that it was because the master cylinder was shot. The friend then reformulated the problem as, "Then it's not your brakes that need repairing, it's your master cylinder." This was a totally gratuitous distinction, since the master cylinder is in fact a part of the braking system.

A man who bragged, "I don't pay for heat in my New York cooperative apartment" was reminded of what he knew, that, while he didn't pay for it directly, he paid for it indirectly, in the maintenance. Along similar lines, an appliance buff found he could annoy the man by asking him to distinguish between a guarantee and a warranty.

A health worker stymied progress with her need to distinguish goals from objectives and with her need to decide in advance of each team meeting whether the meeting should have an agenda. She stymied progress even more with her eventual preoccupation with whether to include the preoccupation itself in the agenda.

One cooperative apartment building got its reputation, to quote one of the people who lived there, as a "nonhello kind of place" for its mean-spirited battles less notable for their light than for their heat, a place where the management dwelled on rule-making about such things as how often one could barbecue on terraces, whether one could use woks in kitchens or whether they caused intolerable odors to be emitted into the halls, and what should be the exact interval for painting the walls and changing the carpets in the common areas.

Ambivalence (Doing and Undoing)

Obsessive avoidants do and undo not only as a way to express and resolve conflicting emotions, relieving sexual and angry desire temporarily with guilt, then expressing them again out of persistent desire, but also, like Type II mingles avoidants, as a way to grate on others' nerves by being annoyingly erratic and unpredictable. Determined to keep others in suspense as to where they and their victims stand, they keep one foot in and one foot out of relationships. Now they drive people away, now they pull them back, now they do both simultaneously. Now they complain of fear of rejection, and now they complain of fear of being closed in. If married, they alternate between being abusive to their spouses and demanding a divorce, and guiltily regretting their anger and pleading for a second chance. Or they do both simultaneously, expressing undying love on the one hand while cruising wildly with their eyes on the other, getting drunk and telling not their lovers but their waitresses, or the people at the next table, how much they love them, or calling out another's name during sex, or during a dream, giving the game away in their ecstasy, or in their sleep.

One man put ads in the personals columns, then did not reply to the people who wrote to him, or what was worse, replied in essence, "I'm a young, virile guy longing to meet you, rich and famous, and I'm sure we can get along because you sound just right for me, but I'm so busy now that I just can't take the time to meet someone as wonderful as you seem to be, but I will get back to you as soon as I can, but meanwhile feel free to meet other men, though I hope you will wait, because I will call, if you will only be patient."

A single man who consciously feared he would never have a lover nevertheless abruptly arose in the middle of a date with a new, rather exciting, adoring partner to leave for home because he couldn't wait until tomorrow to play his new compact disc recording of Sibelius' Fifth Symphony. At another time, under similar circumstances, he abandoned a partner to go home to check to see if he had left his sound equipment on—saying he was afraid it would overheat and start a fire. Still another time under similar circumstances he left to check to see if, by playing a CD on a damaged machine, he had scratched and ruined it.

A common method of doing and undoing found both in the personal (sexual) and professional sphere is teasing and disappointing—first seducing, literally or figuratively, then abandoning.

A man in singles bars dressed to look alluring, stood in alluring poses and gave others come-hither looks. Then at the first sign of interest, he removed himself to become aloof and disdainful, even though he was the one who had first extended the invitation. In ongoing relationships he said, "We must get together sometime," but he never made a date, or, making one, broke it, reassuring the victim that this was the very last time it would happen, just so that he could make it happen again. In his sexual behavior premature withdrawal was the order of the day—not to prevent conception, but to first tempt and excite, then to frustrate by stopping short of fulfillment.

Two obsessives in concert came within $2,000 of consummating a large real estate deal, then refused to budge not because of real financial issues but because each was angry with the other, even though each was in fact getting what he wanted. The buyer was angry because he felt deprived of his money, and the seller was angry because he felt deprived of his home.

An obsessive-compulsive patient demonstrated her uncertainty equally in her symptoms and in her personal relationships. When driving she believed any thump meant, "I have run someone over." At first she drove off thinking, "I did it but he deserved it," but then she thought better of it and returned to check to make sure there was no innocent victim in the road needing help. The extra trip, however, created more thumps, more of the same worries, and so forth. In her personal life she married to get away from home, but feeling unfaithful to her mother, divorced her husband so that she could go home again, only to complain about the singles life, about her inability to tolerate living with her mother, and about the difficulty divorced women have in getting remarried.

A priest left his religious order to become a pagan poet, going overnight, as he himself put it, "from the cloth to the blacklist." On the blacklist he married, and then slept with his brother's wife in circumstances that made discovery likely, hoping to force a divorce from his own wife so that he could consider renouncing worldly pleasures and becoming, once again, an abstinent pastor.

One patient worked every weekend and every holiday, taking days off only on nonholiday weekdays. Her apologies to her family about having to work on holidays were a way to hide how she had volunteered for holiday duty. Similarly, her protestations that she hated being assigned on the holidays were meant to obscure her desire to not be with her family. When she arranged "lovely family dinners," they were late in the evening of her day off, which predictably was late in the eve of a workday for the rest of her family. Scheduled to work late on the evening of Christmas day, she invited her family over "just for a gift-exchange" on Christmas morning. Then, though everyone had made other arrangements for later that day, she brought out a full dinner, served it, and kept it coming, deaf to their pleas that they had to go because, at her suggestion, they had made other plans.

Because avoidant obsessives undo their positive feelings with the same zeal as their negative feelings, we see a streak of uninterest and remoteness superimposed on their ambivalence. If positive feelings are expressed at all, they are expressed paradoxically, that is, when they are no longer anticipated, or indirectly, for example, to a person other than the one who is the actual recipient of those feelings.

When in the presence of a suitor, one man gave a negative response to every positive gesture, reserving a positive response for when the gesture had been withdrawn. Or, instead of responding positively to a suitor's attentions directly, he told his friends of his favorable reaction, hoping (and not hoping) it would get back. The only time he offered warmth and friendship face to face was when he was certain it wouldn't or couldn't be accepted.

Through resolute neutrality at times of crisis, obsessive avoidants use indecisiveness and remoteness to make themselves persona non grata. Thus, one man, trying to make everyone happy, sympathized and agreed with everybody in a general way, suggested to everyone that there was another side to every story, and concluded that all arguments were merely cases of "locking horns," that is, two parties always had equally justified positions, and rarely, if ever, was one position clearly more justified than the other.

Hypermorality

The tendency obsessives have to express guilt symptomatically, that is, intrapersonally, for example, in the self-castigation implied in their ongoing rituals, becomes in the obsessive avoidant guilt expressed interpersonally, for example, by criticizing others for being immoral. They reserve the most intense criticism for those who think or do the same thing that they themselves think or do, and criticize in themselves.

A father, himself a guilty latent homosexual, refused to have his homosexual son and his lover over for family dinners because he believed his son's homosexuality was both immoral and a negative reflection on him (the father).

A man expressed guilt about his own sexual excitement by becoming simultaneously heterophobic and homophobic. He condemned both heterosexuals and homosexuals for having a "filthy mouth, mind, and body, and doing filthy things," reserving his sharpest criticisms for mutual masturbation, oral sex, and performers acting in the pornography he eagerly watched. He was opposed to abortion not for itself but as a way to condemn the sexual basis of pregnancy. His preferences in people ran to those believed "pristine pure, unlike me." This began with a natural enough favoring of people with good hygiene, and then progressed to a search for the person who "didn't have a body." Solid, workable relationships were abandoned with increasing familiarity because with familiarity he could no longer ignore evidence of another's bodily functions. As he put it, "For me, ecstatic love becomes impossible in the absence of inaccurate perception." Like more people than care to admit, he actually held the belief—which he deemed crazy, though it maintained a hold nevertheless—that some people in the world "don't excrete," or at least he would have liked to have thought so. Perfect dress and stunning good looks were demanded not only because they were appealing for themselves, but also because they held out the possibility of the flawless body beneath, the person without insides.

Excessive Shame

In obsessive avoidants shame is more than a typical handmaiden of guilt. It is also at least partly motivated by a desire to retreat and retire from an active social and professional life.

One patient gave up his career as a concert pianist though in fact he played well and others enjoyed listening. He gave up his career because he couldn't tolerate all the adulation he received when he played the piano in public. For him playing in public was a shamefully exhibitionistic form of showing off, with "crescendos, moderatos, and other expressions of feeling one step removed from having sex in public." To bolster his decision to retreat from public performance he convinced himself that his audiences might not love him: "If I play I will make a fool of myself, and then everyone will snicker."

Perseveration

In avoidant obsessives perseveration serves a dual purpose. Like any other obsessive, avoidant obsessives have private rituals, like the patient who wore the same outfit every day and hardly ever washed his underwear because "I don't do anything to dirty it." In obsessive avoidants perseveration is also meant to pin another to the wall, as one patient put it, "to machine-gun them to death."

A haranguer condemned a friend for liking Rachmaninoff, saying, in essence, "Rachmaninoff is too much to bear, especially when he wears his heart on his sleeve, and he doesn't stop, but does it over and over, repetitively, in all of his works, until you can't stand it one more time, until you think you can never listen to his music again because of his prolixity, verbosity, and tendency to reiterate the same theme, over and over again."

Parsimoniousness

Obsessive avoidants are not parsimonious strictly because they are anally retentive (the classic view). They also use parsimoniousness to be hostile, off-putting, impossible people.

One woman fed her guests generic ice cream while serving herself an expensive brand. In the cooperative apartment in which she lived she was one of eight tenants attempting to form consensus on how to decorate the common area outside of their homes. In spite of being voted down several times, she persisted in her suggestion that they save money on a hall table by resurrecting the base of an old sewing machine she kept in the storeroom, covering it with glass, and using it for a table lamp and resurrecting a vase she also had in storage, saving even more money by filling the vase with reeds she herself cut down and dried in the sun.

The owners of a superette made their store unappetizing by turning off the air-conditioning and many of the lights. Patrons bought the minimum and got out, with the losses greater than the actual savings. The only time the store was busy was when the son, a cheerful young fellow with more regard for people than for pennies, turned on the lights, air conditioning and the radio, and sold merchandise by creating one positive total experience (incidentally, more than covering his extra expenses).

One patient went to the extreme of deliberately losing what money he had so that he didn't have to spend it on others. For many years he saved his money, in part by never having a date. (He once took a girl out but never repeated the experience because he became intensely angry when she ordered something other than the cheapest item on the menu.) Then, after he saved two million dollars, he thought "It's time," and fell in love. But now he found himself making bad investments in the stock market, thinking, "Better to lose it honestly than to have it taken away from you by some gold-digger."

A patient ordered an inexpensive item on an on-line auction site, paying $3.50 for it, plus shipping. He then demanded that the sender insure it at the sender's expense. The sender refused, saying that that would cost far more than he was making from the sale. Graciously, the purchaser agreed to pay for the (relatively considerable) insurance costs, leading the sender to wryly note that the purchaser was in effect buying a lottery ticket for one dollar when the prize was fifty cents.

Stubbornness

Obsessive avoidants favor responding to another's legitimate needs by foot-dragging or by outright refusals. One salesperson when asked, "Do you have one of these in my size?" replied, "I will look." He then, resenting what he believed to be an order to behave in a certain way, took so much time looking that the customer lost interest. Another salesman, instead of even bothering to look replied, "If you don't see it on the rack then it isn't in the store," without offering to search stock or to order the item from another branch, and without suggesting alternatives (such as "there is a sweater in the next department that is just as nice").

AVOIDANT PERSONALITY DISORDER AND HYSTERICAL NEUROSIS (HISTRIONIC PERSONALITY DISORDER)

Histrionic avoidants make up a large portion of those Type II avoidants who distance primarily out of a fear of closeness, intimacy and commitment.

As one gay man put it, speaking of a new potential lover, "He's handsome, funny, very presentable, and I like how he deals with me, especially how he listens and remembers what I have to say. But it's really confusing. I see him one time, I like him; I see him the next time, I don't like him. He really wants me. I gave him my card and he called me right back. But I just cannot commit to him. I hear my mother's voice going around in my head, saying, "What are you holding out for, someone who will treat you like a piece of crap?" It's the old story; you want the ones who don't want you, you don't want the ones who do. Anyway, he's not my body type. He doesn't have any body hair, and his legs are too short, a shock when you see him naked for the first time. So I started telling him the negative things about me: how after all I am not perfect and how right now I'm not going to object if he pushes for a relationship, but I'm not going to encourage him either.

The final choice for this man: an anti-Semitic partner who criticized him for being a "Jewish" stereotype because he saved money by using in-store coupons, "something they just don't do in my family."

Like this man, histrionic avoidants ignore the likely in favor of the impossible, react positively in negative situations and negatively in positive situations, form strong attractions where the possibility of fulfillment is weak, and vice versa, and are turned off by those who are warm, yielding, permissive, and available, and on by those who are distant, unfeeling, forbidden, and unavailable. In their pursuit of negative situations and unavailable people they sometimes become enamored of movie stars to the point of stalking them. Or they favor oedipal triangular situations, pursuing people who are already involved with and committed to someone else, such as almost divorced lovers who promise to leave their husbands and wives and marry them, but never actually do. This pursuit of unavailable distant people has oedipal roots. They are replaying a scenario of taking mother away from father, or father away from mother. Next, fearing the consequences, they make certain that they fail at the attempt.

Once in a relationship, they continue the oedipal theme. Fearing closeness because of its incestuous overtones, they reestablish distance by acting jealous, or by cruising compulsively, prowling for new people to meet just because the old people have become available. They also become competitive individuals who focus on status and identity to the detriment of a relationship, thereby turning what could have been a cooperative into an adversarial relationship.

A competitive histrionic single man's first dates were never followed by second dates because of his need to prove his manhood in every relationship with a woman. For example, he had to be the one to decide where to go to dinner or which movie to see because he was "the daddy in this affair." The same need to always be one up appeared in his daily life—even in his relationships with strangers. Thus, he was unable to tolerate his car running out of gas because as he waited for his car to be refilled he thought only of how all the other cars were going somewhere while he was stuck in place. (When driving from Maine to New York, because he wanted to set records more than to get there comfortably, he permitted his passengers one, and only one, rest stop, and told them to avoid fluids for a few hours before the trip so that they wouldn't have to use the bathroom on the way. A number of times he humiliated a companion by telling her before they left a social gathering, in a loud enough voice for everyone to hear, "Use the bathroom before we go so that you don't have to do the usual and pee a hundred times on the way." He compulsively topped every story he heard, so that when told of how another made a great deal of money in stocks, he related how he made even more money in bonds—less to brag to improve his own low self-esteem and more to throw cold water in the face of anyone who dared stand erect before him. When a neighbor who was selling an apartment identical to the one he was selling but on another floor asked him, "How much are you charging for yours?" he refused to say to avoid giving a rival helpful information, preferring instead to start a round of counterproductive price cuts between the two sellers, just so that he could be the one to sell his apartment first.

Histrionic avoidants are also "hysterical" in the lay sense of the term, meaning that they are prone to exaggerate. In particular they exaggerate the intensity and importance of others' negativity to them. As a result, a cancelled dinner date becomes a signal that the whole relationship is troubled. They also exaggerate the negative features of closeness. As a result, closeness becomes commitment, commitment becomes entrapment, and entrapment becomes fatal smothering. Now we hear, "freedom is *completely* out of the question within the bounds of a close, loving relationship; freedom is what I want in life; I want to be me as well as free, so that I can go home where, in a state of splendid isolation, I can be surrounded by the things I love, able to come and go as I please, beholden to no one, to no one *at all*."

AVOIDANT PERSONALITY DISORDER AND THE DISSOCIATIVE DISORDERS

The dissociative mechanisms in the patient with a nonavoidant dissociative disorder are a way to distance oneself from/suppress one's own forbidden instincts and passions. For example, the primary purpose of the dissociative mechanisms used by patients with Dissociative Identity Disorder (Multiple Personality Disorder) is to develop a new identity in order to disavow forbidden feelings that are part of the old, dominant identity. In contrast, in dissociative avoidants, the same mechanisms are used for a different purpose: flight from the familiar to a distant, remote, unfamiliar, foreign, strange, terra incognita where what are perceived to be the discomforts, harassments, and fears of the old world of relationships, or of a specific relationship, no longer exist. Dissociative avoidants intend to send other people in their lives the message: "Corner me and I will disappear," pull the curtains around "me," exclude "you," and retreat into a minifugue that "takes me away from the dangers I associate with closeness and commitment."

A paradigm of such an avoidant minifugue is the true fugue of a man who reacted to a terrorist attack in New York City by taking his daughter out of New York City and running off with her to Buffalo, New York, even though he had never been to Buffalo before and knew no one there. When he arrived he rented an apartment in a gated community and stayed put for three weeks, without a car. (In any event, a car would have been of no use to him, because he was unable to drive.) He only left the house he was holed-up in three times a day, to take his daughter across the road for fast food. He told no one in his family where he was. After three weeks he "awoke" from his fugue, called his by now frantic family, and agreed to come home—but had difficulty returning because he could not take public transportation due to his fear of bioterrorism.

The parallel minifugues of dissociative avoidants consist of detached, trancelike, and confused states where they view a relationship as a terrorist attack, then float off emotionally to a new place with new people that threaten them less. They mutter about needing to take a break from a relationship, or actually call for a hiatus or break an engagement. Or, if a bride or groom, they get last minute cold feet and do not appear for the wedding. Later, when they calm down and become rational again, they become painfully aware of the opportunity missed. Now we hear recriminations about how they utterly ruined their lives. Unfortunately, past regrets usually do not translate into improved future performance.

A wistful depressive homosexual responded to those who tried to get close to him by calling himself by girls' names, like "Mary" or "Jane," or by announcing his future plans to live his life by himself, camped alone under the stars, in an adobe in the Arizona desert, on a farm with only the animals for companions, or on an island off the coast of Maine. The following two dreams recurred regularly during his childhood:

He dreamt he was running down a long corridor to escape an unknown danger. At the end of the corridor an object variously described as the tassels of a riding crop, the straws of a broom, and the feathered tail of a rooster appeared through the wall and shook at him, tracing an up and down trajectory. The sight of this terrified him, though he did not know why. He remained terrified until he progressed further along the corridor when he saw a sign that read, "Safe to the left, danger to the right," whereupon he ran to the left, and felt safe. In the dream's aftermath he wet his bed and awoke. In association to his dream, he recalled how one day after playing doctor with a childhood sweetheart his grandmother whipped him, then took him aside and showed him a picture from a bible book: a harp whose pillar was carved in the shape of a nude body of a man, genitals absent. The grandmother suggested that he would become that man if he continued to play such games. The shaking tassels/straws/rooster tail then both represented the whip and his being whipped and with it the threatened castration, and reassurance that his phallus was still intact. The running in the dream was both a running away from being whipped and castrated, and a running to a place of safety.

In a second dream there was a park "over there" with skyscrapers arising intact from an excavation pit. The above-mentioned childhood sweetheart lived on the street next to the park. He wanted to go there but was afraid, and couldn't find his way. In his associations to this dream, he described himself as a distant and lonely avoidant preoccupied with searching for new people he would like better and for new places where he would be happier. Thus, in later life he fled from city to city looking for a relationship, even when he had satisfactory relationships in the old city. On one occasion he moved for no better reason than that the new city's skyscrapers were bigger than the old. The old city without skyscrapers referred to being devalued, punished, and castrated for his sexuality. Fleeing to the new city, the "park with skyscrapers," represented a restitutive attempt to avoid/ undo castration and become physically intact once again. Fleeing also represented safety, because a bigger city was "more anonymous, a place where no one would know who I am, and hurt and abuse me for what I do."

Finally, the following rule helps distinguish nonavoidant amnesiacs from amnesiac avoidants: while nonavoidant amnesiacs conveniently forget bad things about themselves, amnesiac avoidants conveniently forget good things about others.

AVOIDANT PERSONALITY DISORDER AND POSTTRAUMATIC STRESS DISORDER

Avoidants who also suffer from Posttraumatic Stress Disorder (PTSD) do not try to live around their flashbacks and nightmares so that these will interfere only minimally with their lives and relationships. These individuals actually encourage their PTSD so that it *can* interfere with their lives and relationships. In the most serious cases, they gainfully live in the past to avoid the present and present relationships. In order to isolate themselves they deliberately (if unconsciously) confuse new people they might love or who might love them with old people who once traumatized and hurt them. If in a relationship, they gleefully torture their partners with their symptoms, as they include friends and family in, or make no effort to exclude friends and family from, the prompts that reawaken earlier traumatic experiences. Instead of viewing their own abuse in the past as a reason to spare others similar abuse in the present, they make uninvolved present company scapegoats for their bad early experiences, even though present company has no connection to, and no responsibility for, these experiences. Exasperated and annoyed wives and lovers are part of the retinue of such patients. They typically complain that they perceive something in everyone that relights their trauma, and they correctly perceive the motivation to be a need to distance already in place, here expressed in the language of posttraumatic stress.

One PTSD avoidant patient was, according to his own self-description, a "cry-baby" who damped his friends' festive occasions by complaining that he could not get over his illness, that it only got worse in time, and that as a consequence he had no life to speak of. He frequently and with very little prompting announced that he remembered the sirens during the World War II blackouts, huddling in bed holding his radio close to comfort him, and resenting those sirens as an intrusion on his privacy and as an interference with his sleep. In later life he lived in a town that used sirens to summon the volunteer fire and ambulance squad. Each time such a siren sounded it woke him up. But instead of going back to sleep, he woke his wife up to complain, bemoan his fate, and suggest the possibility of selling the house and moving—a conversation he knew to be as unsuitable for the early morning hours as the siren itself.

A patient, whenever his wife unwittingly approached him from behind and startled him, told her to "get lost because you remind me of how I was jumped from behind by the enemy in Vietnam." He demanded she sleep in another room so that she would not roll over on him, "like dead bodies did in the trenches." Whenever she asked for anything for herself or for the household, he called her requests "demands" and said her demands reminded him of his being drafted against his will, of how his commanding officer unfeelingly sent him into battle without his assent, and of how the army treated him not as an individual but as "just a number, part of a human wave, nothing but a piece of cannon fodder."

AVOIDANT PERSONALITY DISORDER AND THE PARAPHILIAS

By themselves paraphilias interfere with the ability to love because the attractive (paraphiliac) object or situation is part, but *only* part, of normative arousal/activity patterns, for example, a nonhuman object, or a partner's humiliation. For paraphiliac avoidants the attraction to the part, instead of to the whole, is primary, intended, and intended specifically for the purpose of distancing oneself from the whole object.

One fetishist drove a foreign car in a summer resort to distance himself from the bourgeoisie—specifically, the working class who lived there year round. (The "bourgeoisie" in turn fought back with a fetish of their own—the open pickup truck with a black Labrador retriever in back.) In his sexual relationships he said, "I relate to things below the ankle (a foot) so that I don't have to relate to anything above—like heart, or genitals." In locker rooms he first shifted his gaze from an attractive man to his attractive foot, then shifted his mindset from a sexual attraction to an aesthetic appreciation of the structurally perfect appendage. He was also preoccupied with seduction scenes instead of with the goal of seduction. His consuming interest in overdecorating his apartment and summer home to make it a place where he could get men to yield was both a substitute for having close relationships and a way to break up close relationships already formed. As he once said, speaking of how he wanted to kick his present companion out, "I long to get my delightful apartment back, to get rid of that schmutzy man, to have the place to myself so that I can keep it clean and neat, stop all the breakage, and redecorate it the way I want."

Paraphiliac avoidants are both attracted to relationships that have a nonreciprocal, nonaffectionate quality and experience a decrease in arousal when the object promises (actually threatens) to approach. A friction queen frotteurist, who preferred rubbing over penetration, rubbed in the subway because he was only attracted to partners whom he sensed did not share his paraphilia, and because there a complete relationship was out of the question. In like manner, Don Juan paraphiliacs serial date as a way to relate to others sexually so that they do not have to relate to them affectionately.

The attraction to danger that exists in some of these individuals is partly based on the equation, Dangerous = Unavailable. With this equation in mind, some paraphiliacs pick up strangers in bars and take them home before getting to know them, cruise places in spite of, or even because of, a rash of murders known to occur there, expose themselves in public houses known to harbor undercover police, or pick up prostitutes who might have a disease or, if a prostitute, pick up johns who might kill.

For leather and chains fetishists the mechanism of distancing involves expressing a sadistic attitude toward the world and the people in it by dressing not to relate but to shock, appall, and repel. Such fetishistic avoidants may actually use whips and bondage; or they might water their sadism down to become a sadistic derivative, such as a perverse contrarianism used to hold at arms length, erect walls, humiliate, and drive off. Some male transvestites sadistically desexualize others by reducing them to a mere appreciative audience for their costumery, while some threesome paraphiliacs sadistically humble their partners. What they rationalize as an attempt to "expand our world of experience and intensify our sexual pleasure" is often at bottom a wish to humiliate and denigrate a partner by making him or her observe his or her lover take pleasure in the body of another.

AVOIDANT PERSONALITY DISORDER AND THE IMPULSE DISORDERS—GAMBLING AND OTHER ADDICTIONS

While nonavoidant gamblers, alcoholics, and drug addicts also enjoy the interpersonal aspects of the casino, the bar, and the shared needle as much as the game, the drink, and the drug, respectively, gambling, alcoholic, drug-addicted avoidants in contrast substitute the activity for the people associated with the activity. They drink, gamble, and take drugs not to be involved with, but to retreat from, the world and the people in it, by entering, figuratively as well as literally, the fantasy world of the casino.

A man gambled in Atlantic City to get away from his wife. He fancied himself a guest of the owner, as if the owner wanted not his money but him personally, and he viewed the casino as the perfect home with the perfect people, to contrast it with "my own shabby surroundings and impossible home life."

In especially unfavorable cases, avoidant gamblers, alcoholics, and drug addicts use their illness to mistreat others guilt-free. Even though they know their gambling, drinking or drug taking is ruining the lives of their loved-ones, they continue to squander money meant for the necessities of life, and otherwise harm others who depend on them financially and emotionally. Then they excuse their behavior on the grounds that they have a disease, to avoid the sensible reflection that "This disease, c'est moi."

AVOIDANT PERSONALITY DISORDER AND BISEXUALITY

Bisexual avoidants behave homosexually to avoid heterosexuality, and the other way around. They both deal with the fear of rejection by one sex by finding solace with the other, and go to one sex to reject the other. Of course, the fear of rejection/need to reject returns with the new partner, and the cycle begins again. (Some choose an alternative to cycling: they have one or more lovers simultaneously, but in different ports.) The following is a case history of a bisexual avoidant man.

A professionally successful and wealthy man simultaneously "married" a woman of a different religion and "married" a man of a different race—spiritually, if not legally, compounding bisexuality with bigamy.

A dream that he had in the beginning of therapy illustrated his conflict between homosexuality and heterosexuality. In the dream he was in a heterosexual singles group house in a well-known summer resort. But he was bored with the dull, pedestrian, straight people there, and desperately longed for his homosexual soirees where he could be himself again, dressed in expensive stylish clothes, his sense of self-worth increasing in direct proportion to their elegance, admired not for such of his personal qualities as kindness and love, but for his clever opening and exit lines and the sophisticated badinage in between. He missed his male lover and feared he would never see him again. He made a phone call to this lover, saying, "Come rescue me from all this." Then he dreamt he had gotten together with this lover, then had broken up with him and gone back to his wife. He thought, in the dream, "If there is any further question about the wisdom of giving up my lover for my wife, read the obituaries and see that some of the world's most successful homosexuals seem to have died alone." He next saw himself applying, with his wife, for membership in a straight health club. But no one was there to take his application, and he didn't really want to apply because the club was duller and more boring than the gay health club around the corner. But then he saw the image of the gay health club, merged into another image, one previously seen on television, of people swimming in a pool in a retirement community, which he interpreted (while still dreaming) as referring to "growing old gay without children."

As he saw it, his shifting sexual preferences were due to fears that could be traced to the following developmental events. First, there was humiliation by peers. As a child he was at first heterosexually oriented. But, as he recalled, "I threw a baseball underhanded, my friends humiliated and abandoned me, and my self-esteem fell." As an adult, bisexuality protected him from rejection and consequent loss of self-esteem by allowing him to surround himself with "two different kinds of people in case one kind humiliated me."

Next there was overattachment to and identification with his mother. He believed his homosexual fantasies took strength from his attachment, really overattachment, to his mother. From what was the result of this overattachment or his identification with her, he first acted toward male companions in a way that reproduced his mother's seductive behavior toward him, then fled from homosexual relationships because he felt too much like a woman. He also firmly believed that his mother's unwelcome infantilizing and engulfing him turned him away from all women. In addition he felt that he turned from women because his mother and her friends squelched his earliest romantic interests and experiments in infantile heterosexuality by saying, "It's silly, and shameful, to be interested in girls at your tender age." As he also believed, he reacted to his wife as if she were his mother. Every time his wife was unpleasant to him she "sent him to men" because she reminded him of his hostile mother, while every time she was warm/seductive toward him she "sent him to men" because she aroused an oedipal/incestuous anxiety due to "my mother-fixation."

Finally there was disrespect for his father. He felt that a damper on his heterosexuality was his inability to identify with/a need to counteridentify with a father whose appearance he disliked and whose behavior he believed shameful on account of a number of what he considered to be revolting personal habits. He believed the resultant counteridentification with this "slobbish" father accounted for his fetishistic attraction to clean, well-turned-out men, men who were Adonislike, that is, as unlike his father as possible. Yet a continuing love for his father was to account for his paradoxical, Pygmalion-like, never-ending search for an imperfect man whom he could make over into an ideal father.

When pursuing the perfect Adonis-like man he was involved with such trappings of sophisticated life as theatre and fine restaurants—when the goal of life became not the solid, monogamous, reciprocal relationship but the hard table in the trendy eatery and being seen in all the right places by all the right people. Soon he gave that up as being superficial in the extreme. Then he began pursuing the imperfect man to make over. But now he felt uncomfortable being associated with people from a lower socioeconomic class and their relatives, people whom he condemned as "low rent" and whom, after an initial honeymoon (when he thoroughly enjoyed their refreshing crudity), he began to humiliate for their pedestrian attitudes and low-life behaviors. Finally, with supreme gall, after driving them away, he announced, when they left, that they had missed a tremendous opportunity to participate in a joint endeavor with him to "get them out of their personal ghetto."

Throughout, he rejected overtures from all suitable people, men and women, plain, simple lovers who were really interested in him. Referring to their need to settle down and set up housekeeping, he criticized them for demanding that he "walk out of *New York Magazine* and into *Working Woman.*" Indeed, whenever a suitable person of either sex approached, he felt mysteriously drawn elsewhere, and began to dissociate and fugue, not only in fantasy, but in reality as well. Once, for example, after moving from New York to San Francisco to get away from a woman to be with a special man, he suddenly returned to New York and to the woman on a flimsy pretext—really because the man in San Francisco suggested they get an apartment together and settle down for life. As he concluded, "I use my bisexuality to serve two masters so that I never have to call one place home."

AVOIDANT PERSONALITY DISORDER AND BIGOTRY

In general, bigoted avoidants, of which homophobes (my next topic) are one type, hate in order to avoid having to relate. In addition to homophobes, classic examples of bigoted avoidants are xenophobic, anti-Semitic, and racist avoidants whose prejudices are installed, at least in part, as a way to suppress forbidden, often forbidden positive, sexual, impulses towards foreigners, Jews, and blacks, respectively.

AVOIDANT PERSONALITY DISORDER AND HOMOPHOBIA

False Homophobic Avoidance

False homophobic avoidance is the depressive/paranoid avoidant tendency to see true homophobia everywhere, overlooking how some people care not if one is a homosexual, but only if one is nasty, or crude, as in the following case:

A mental health worker deliberately stirred up the community's wrath by acting "the role of a whore," incessantly talking about sex in the most lurid of terms and seducing inappropriate people in entirely inappropriate circumstances—such as at weddings of members of his family and in the clinic where he worked, approaching clinic patients on clinic time, on clinic grounds, behind clinic closed doors, asking select patients not, "How do you feel today?" but "What shall we try today?" Although he complained that his behavior created what he called "irrational personal animosity," the animosity was in fact rational—directed, however, not to his sexual preferences but to the way, manner, and circumstances under which these preferences were expressed.

True Homophobic Avoidance

Because "homophobias" are only sometimes true phobias, there is a differential diagnosis of avoidant homophobia distinguished according to the specific hate patterns, as follows. In *paranoid* homophobia, perhaps the most common variety, homophobia is a way to destroy on the outside what threatens on the inside. It is a self-cleansing, a self-vindication.

A man told his neighbor, "Get out of here, you faggot, and go back where you came from—and where you belong—to New York—everybody agrees, all the neighbors think so too." The ideas "you must go" and "everyone agrees" were a way to reassure himself that he didn't want the neighbor to stay. In turn, he was denying a hidden wish to be closer than he dared recognize.

A patient, himself a latent homosexual, wanted to leave treatment because he suspected his psychiatrist of being a homosexual and was "deeply concerned that you are one of them." When his internist, whom he had not previously suspected of being a homosexual, died of AIDS, the patient became even more suspicious, thinking that, "Your doctor can fool you—his training makes him clever enough to do so." To keep tabs on his psychiatrist, the patient moved a few blocks down the road and then began eating at a restaurant on the same block as the block where his psychiatrist lived. Even after the psychiatrist moved away, the patient believed that he had spotted him wandering about in suspicious places on more than one occasion.

In *depressive* homophobia a self-directed homophobia is a response to any hint of homosexual desire. In many such cases the homosexual thought and desire elicit as much self-hate as the homosexual action. Many such individuals even condemn themselves for run-of-the-mill homosexual fantasies just so that they can torture themselves with the possibility that they may be overtly homosexual. Next the hypercritical self-assessment spills over to become a negative assessment of others, that is, a homophobic attack on others that extends the homophobic attack on the self.

In *masochistic* homophobia the homophobia is also self-directed. The masochistic self-homophobic individual, desiring love more than absolution, makes a plea for love from others via a self put-down meant to please others, an identification with one's enemies that proclaims, "Love me because I hate homosexuals just as you do."

In *obsessive* homophobia, hatred for homosexuals, as with depressives and masochists, starts as a self-hatred for homosexual desire. Hatred of others does not spill over to others so much as it is deliberately installed to prove to the conscience that "I am not really one of them." Often, obsessional homophobia represents merely one instance of other instances of a dislike for anything sexual.

An obsessive man found transvestites attractive because they allowed him to have heterosexual fantasy during homosexual activity. However, after sex he regularly became assaultive to his transvestite partner—less because he felt cheated/fooled when he discovered that the partner was a man (the reason experts assessing assaulters of transvestites often give for the assault) and more because of a mix of heterosexual and homosexual guilt elicited by the general sexual nature of the transaction, with the guilt handled by an assault on the presumed cause of that guilt.

Some obsessive homophobes dislike homosexuality and homosexuals not because they view it and them as morally wrong, but because they view it and them as dirty and diseased. In such cases the homophobia offers an opportunity to express thoughts and fears already in place less about sexuality than about contamination.

Passive-aggressive homophobia refers less to the animosity directed to homosexuals than to the way that that animosity is expressed. Instead of physical or mental gay bashing, we see condemnation of gays and lesbians by inaction (say, by a refusal to vote for antibias laws), often rationalized on moral/religious grounds.

Hysterical (histrionic) homophobia originates less in a criticism of the homosexual behavior itself than in an envy of what is perceived to be the competition. A woman might dislike a homosexual man because he competes with her for men, and a man might envy the unfair competition from what he calls "dinks"—homosexual couples who have "double income no kids."

In *dependent* homophobia, we see gay bashing as a way to gain approval from a peer group or from the world. Groups in danger of dissolving might use the homosexual as an external, organizing enemy to shore up the fragmenting organization.

In *antisocial/psychopathic* homophobia, the gay bashing is excused with a clever trick of logic that in essence says, "I do it not to hurt, not for evil, but for good." As in all antisocial/psychopathic personality activity there is an expectation of a palpable return—perhaps a political reward for advocacy of "family values."

Finally, in *sadistic* homophobia another's homosexuality is a ready-made excuse to express hateful/violent desires already in place. (A complete discussion of the pathological aspects of homophobia is to be found in my [1998] book *Homophobia: Description, Development, and Dynamics of Gay Bashing.*)

CHAPTER 11

Comorbid Disorders: Comorbidity with Other Personality Disorders

AVOIDANT PERSONALITY DISORDER AND NARCISSISTIC PERSONALITY DISORDER

Selfishness, Self-Preoccupation, and Self-Importance

Nonavoidant narcissists use people for personal gain to some extent, but at least they try to reconcile their self-interest with an ongoing concern for others. They sugarcoat their narcissism, holding back on excessive displays of selfishness and petulance to avoid antagonizing others completely. If at first they do not get what they want, instead of flying into a selfish rage they intensify their efforts to get it. Instead of giving up on possible sources of gratification they attempt to bring others around to gratify them. After getting something they give something back, if only so that they can get some more. In contrast, narcissistic avoidants are thoroughly selfish people who make little or no attempt to take others' feelings and needs into consideration. They not only use people, they use them up. They plan all along to discard them when they are done. When any particular well runs dry, they simply move on to look for another.

One narcissistic avoidant completely antagonized a psychologist friend with his display of selfishness. Seeking help for his bulimic daughter, he invited the psychologist over for cocktails then, after drinks were served, brought his daughter in on cue, saying, "Mary, introduce yourself to the doctor, tell him why you regurgitate everything you eat, and ask him what you can do to keep your food down."

A narcissistic avoidant, a student in dental school, called a medical school colleague once or twice a day to unload his serious emotional problems on him. After several months of this the dental school student suddenly stopped calling. Concerned, the medical school student called him up to ask what was wrong. To that question the dental school student replied, "I can no longer speak to you. I just got an important sensitive academic position and I cannot even let on that I know you. You know much too much about me for that."

A narcissistic avoidant greatly antagonized people by putting them on hold until something better came along. He made dates, then broke them when it suited his convenience and purpose. When visiting his psychiatrist, either he came two hours early for an appointment, silting up the small waiting room, or two hours late, demanding nevertheless to be seen as soon as he arrived. Or he came without making an appointment at all—falsely declaring a life or death emergency. Or he said he made an appointment when he had not, hoping that the secretary would think that she had made the mistake and allow him to see the doctor anyway. He said he lost his benzodiazepine prescriptions so that he could get more drugs than prescribed, and he had more than one doctor for the same purpose. He demanded notes from his medical doctors after the fact to excuse him medically from being absent from work on the grounds of an illness the doctor had no opportunity to observe, flew into rages at the first sign that he might be refused, and to back up his demands, threatened to report the doctor to the medical society on various trumped-up charges. When the Department of Veterans Affairs opened a clinic in his area specifically geared to serving veterans, they refused to continue to pay for his therapy with his private psychiatrist. Now he appealed, demanding that he be allowed to continue to see his private doctor, and his VA therapist supported his appeal. Then, when the VA, rather unexpectedly, agreed to continue to pay, he wrote letters accusing his VA therapist of rejecting him and of trying to throw him out of therapy.

A woman invited guests for a July 4th barbecue, saying that July 5th was the rain date. Then, after putting her guests on hold for weeks so that she would have company for the holiday no matter what, she left them high and dry, calling them a week before the holiday to cancel the entire arrangement because something better came up—the opportunity to earn a little extra money at work by covering another (less avoidant) employee, one who wanted to be home for the holidays.

A man dropped all his friends each time he had a love affair, then tried to get them back each time he broke up with his lover. He relegated his friends to the category of, "okay to know when I am alone but an embarrassment to know when I am with someone." After he graduated from medical school he divorced his wife, saying of her, "She was good enough to support me through medical school, but she is not good enough for me now that I am a doctor." Then he remarried, only later, when he became famous, to divorce his second wife, saying that "she might have been good enough to be with when I was a big nobody, but now that I'm a somebody, she's not important enough for me to bother with."

When attending family functions with her husband, a woman insisted that they go in separate cars just so that she could make an appearance, then leave half an hour after she arrived. One day, attending a party for a man whose novel had just been made into a successful movie, she was warm and friendly to everyone—just so that they would ignore him and pay attention to her and to the flyers she was passing out hawking a play that she had recently written.

While nonavoidant narcissists remain attuned to others, that is, they remain empathic if only the better to manipulate them, avoidant narcissists disrupt relationships by being so self-centered that they become remote from, and oblivious and unresponsive to, others. Notable is their self-preoccupied maddening failure to be interested in and impressed by others' achievements. For example, a patient's father never once in 20 years actually asked his son what or how he was doing professionally. When his son gave him a copy of a book he had just written, he put it away in his bookcase, literally shelving it, unceremoniously, without so much as giving it a second glance. Like this father, such narcissists give others little recognition no matter how clever the formulation, how great the accomplishment, or how intense the love. If they give anything back under any circumstances it is in the form of a derivative, wet-rag response. They substitute chagrin for disappointment, concern for fear, and interest for love, proffering the limp hand for the congratulatory handshake, the limp self for the personal relationship, the limp joyless genital for sex.

When contemplating starting a relationship, they don't ask themselves, "Am I the right one for him?" only, "Is he the right one for me?" Once in a relationship, sooner rather than later they push the person they are involved with aside to look for someone better, someone they believe to be more suitable for their lofty self-worth, someone who will give them the complete acceptance and love they feel entitled to receive. They do not care if they hurt others by abandoning them. They ask, "Should I or should I not leave this relationship?" not, "Will you feel uncomfortable when I declare that this relationship is over?"

A jealously guarded identity of which they are inordinately fond keeps them from getting close to and maintaining relationships with others. They refuse to give up "being me" so that they can "be us." "Who I am" (*my* masculinity, *my* identity as a woman, *my* identity as a gay man) becomes more important than "Whom I am with." They stand on principle even though that means standing alone.

When brought up short, instead of the healing regrets favored by the nonavoidant narcissist, we get further off-putting, self-serving justifications supported by nice tricks of logic, or even white lies. A canceled appointment is excused on the grounds of a transcendent professional responsibility that in fact could have been postponed, or an irregular work performance is excused on grounds of car trouble or a nonexistent or exaggerated relapsing illness. Frequently, charm is employed in the belief, which unfortunately tends to be accurate, that good manners divert from bad intentions.

AVOIDANT PERSONALITY DISORDER AND PASSIVE-AGGRESSIVE PERSONALITY DISORDER

Both the following statements are true: avoidance is a form of passive-aggression, and passive-aggression is a form of avoidance. By definition passive-aggressives are avoidant because they are excessively angry people. However, they are less avoidant than they might be if they expressed their anger directly rather than indirectly. By expressing anger indirectly—in the form of a passive-aggressive compromise formation—they can both retain relationships out of love and destroy them out of hate.

A delayed reaction is characteristic of the victim response to passive-aggression. This reaction is called-forth by the passive-aggressive method of inflicting wounds. The paradigm for this method is the mosquito bite—initially painless, swelling and itching only later after it is too late to smack the perpetrator, who has by now flown off. The victim's delayed reaction consists of a typical victim biphasic double take, that "I wonder what he meant by that?" response with which most of us are familiar from our own experiences with the passive-aggressives in our lives.

The following are some specific techniques passive-aggressive avoidants use to express their anger indirectly.

Making Snide Remarks

One guest wrote a thank-you note to a hostess who had him over for dinner, a note that reminded her how with some people no good deed goes unpunished. It read, "I just wanted to take another opportunity to thank you for such a wonderful dinner and such a lovely evening. Anyway, I've been sick since Sunday night with the flu. How is your flu? I don't know if you are to blame for mine, but in case you aren't, something is certainly going around." Another time under similar circumstances he wrote the following note: "We had a wonderful night last night, except that you had to leave so early." Still another time he complained that a new lover, who was busy serving the meal, did not immediately sit down to eat with the rest of the crowd. Then he went on to complain that the lover took too long to serve dinner. As he put it, "If I had to wait one more minute for dinner we would have not dessert for dinner but dinner for dessert."

Defying Social Convention in Dress and Comportment

To drive people off, some passive-aggressive avoidants become motorcycle-gang avoidants whose pleasure from revving up the engine comes from knowing that others hate the noise. Others cultivate being personally unappealing for the same reason. One man dressed inappropriately and sloppily, did not get a needed haircut, and fixed his hair trying to hide his baldness in ineffective and often bizarre ways that, if we assume that motivation can be inferred by response, must have been, at least unconsciously, intended to displease and horrify.

Being Subtly Annoying

A passive-aggressive avoidant spoke so softly that no one could hear him, forcing others to ask him to speak up and repeat himself, giving him the excuse he needed to lose patience with them.

Neglecting to Respond

Some passive-aggressive avoidants express their hostility by failing to respond to others who hope for a reaction, or by failing to help others in need:

The lover of a passive-aggressive man dreamt: "I looked out of the window of our house and there were all these children, some of them little savages, playing on our property. Then the construction crew came and tore up our property and left garbage all over the place. They kept trying to get into our house, and I was afraid they would let the cat out, and I begged them not to come in. But you made no attempt to stop them. Instead you just sat by passively, saying that you can clean up after them, and who cares about the cat."

This dream occurred after the patient and his lover met one of the lover's co-workers in a shopping mall. The co-worker spent 30 minutes forcing both men to listen to a nonstop attack on her boss, until the lover lost patience. Later the lover complained that the patient just stood there, making no attempt to break off the conversation and move on. "You are putting me last," the lover complained, "sacrificing my comfort out of concern that you might somehow offend her." Then the lover said, "Instead of affirming me all you did was yes me to death by saying 'exactly,' not in its evaluative but in its dismissive sense."

Failure of Empathy

More aware of their own sensitivities than those of their victims, passive-aggressive avoidants go through life unconcerned about how others feel. As avoidants they overlook that withdrawing from others is a disdainful act that predictably sends the message, "I don't want you." When brought up short, they actually seem surprised to learn of the negative effects their withdrawal has on those from whom they withdraw.

One passive-aggressive physician complained throughout his career that no one referred patients to him, although he thought himself a brilliant man. He was completely unaware that he arranged his fate by snubbing his associates. For example, he stayed away from medical conventions and dinners, giving multiple excuses like "I don't want to work nights and weekends," and "There is no one gay there for me to meet; I'd rather cruise the bars and try to connect with a lover." Others remarked, "He seems to prefer the possibility of meeting new strangers to the probability of improving old relationships."

Being Brutally Honest

The above-mentioned physician thoroughly prided himself on being a "brutally honest person," one who told helpful truths even though they hurt. To quote him: "I refuse to kiss up to people, to not tell them how I feel when the things I have to say are for their own good. If they don't like it, then that's their problem." He disagreed when his therapist said, "In fact, no one likes brutal honesty, being hurt for a noble cause." To this he replied, "They may not like me now, but they will thank me in the future, long after I'm gone" (really, long after they are gone—because he destroyed the relationship).

Ridiculing

The above-mentioned physician did poorly in medical school not only because he constantly challenged his teachers on theoretical grounds, but also because he made fun of them personally. For one thing, he turned all their names into pun-filled travesties, like "dorky" for "Dorothy," which he unfailingly communicated to them. For another, he openly laughed behind their backs while they lectured, or went to their lectures just so that he could protest their content by deliberately stalking out of the room shortly after the lecture had begun.

Setting Overly Harsh Limits

Later in his career, the above-mentioned physician began to resent expending time and effort in his clinical work with patients. He saw each patient visit as a burden that kept him from thinking about and mulling over such "pleasant, rewarding things as his finances and love affairs." One way he expressed this resentment was by setting excessively harsh limits on clinic patients who came early and stayed late attempting to make a social occasion out of their visit to his clinic. He couched his hostility as a meant-to-be helpful, "You wouldn't have to come here early if you had more important things to do with your life, so let's work on that problem." This was really a way to condemn them instead of tolerating, pitying, and helping them precisely because they had such constricted lives. (In contrast, another doctor's less avoidant formulation was, "Let them have a home away from home. That's what people need when they feel lonely and unloved.")

At home he began a movement to deprive absentees in his cooperative apartment of their right to vote by proxy, giving as his reason what he believed to be a sensible reflection: "They shouldn't vote because they aren't around to hear both sides of the story," as if hearing both sides of the story required a constant presence. He was completely unconcerned that the absentees were neighbors and potential, or actual, friends of his. As he coolly replied when they reproached him (although they were really trying to make personal repairs and hoping to get close), "After all, business is business."

Keeping 'Em Guessing

To create a painful, "not knowing where you stand" response, passive-aggressive avoidants merely hint at the negative things that they are thinking, without coming out with them, blowing up, clearing the air, or even offering an apology.

A head of a Department of Psychiatry expressed his hostility indirectly by wondering aloud, for many years, "Who should be leader of the treatment team?" All along he never intended to answer the question or to appoint the leader. His behavior was a way to tell each person, "Maybe you're not up to it," to keep them "stewing in their own low self-esteem," and to keep them wondering if someone with less training and experience would be promoted over them.

Giving the Backhanded Compliment

The victim's response to the backhanded compliment is a good illustration of the just-mentioned biphasic or, for the more obsessional among us, triphasic response to the provocation of passive-aggressive avoidants.

After great sex a young man told his older partner, "I've never enjoyed it so much with a man your age." The victim's first response was, "How wonderful to think, though older, I'm still great." But by the next morning his sense of humiliation and anger was fully aroused as he interpreted the statement to mean, "Most men of your age don't do it very well." Now he began to scratch the man's name out of his address book. But then he thought twice: "After all," he said to himself, "he did compliment me, and he did say how great the sex was. Perhaps I am just being oversensitive."

Asking the Hostile Question

After passive-aggressive avoidants ask hostile questions they dismiss the question's hostile intent by saying, "It was only a question."

A New Yorker visiting her psychiatrist after he moved to a small town reported the following incident during her session: "On the way to your office I asked directions of a motorist, a Lincoln look-alike carved from a rocky crag. He did not respond, like most New Yorkers would, with helpful overkill, but instead asked succinctly, actually rudely, "Do people who walk instead of drive ever learn how to get anywhere on their own?"

A nurse, when told that a respiratory therapist would cover for neonatal emergencies, asked the respiratory therapist, "Are people with your license actually permitted to take care of patients?"

A woman, aware of needing friends to ease her loneliness, complained, "I am all alone—no husband, no family, no friends, except the few I have on the job. If I ever lose this job I would be completely alone—finished—finished!" Yet the next morning she greeted a coworker as follows: "Boy, do you look tired today. Are you getting too old for this job?" (When confronted, she denied her hostility, instead insisting that her question merely reflected her concern that her coworker's busy schedule was keeping her from being as good to herself as she should be, and possibly ruining her health.)

A homophobic passive-aggressive was fascinated by the strange man who gave his coworker a ride every morning and picked him up every evening. He suspected, with justification, that the man was the co-worker's lover. His questions were all seemingly idle curiosity, but not the less hostile for that: "He looks just like you, is he your cousin?" "Boy, are you lucky to have a chauffeur, where did you get one? Where can I get one too?"

Withholding

Passive-aggressive avoidants use familiar withholding techniques to express anger. They might make an appointment, then come late or cancel at the last minute, or send "belated birthday cards" (with the additional element of a narcissistic shift in focus from "Your birthday" to "My having forgotten your birthday").

The son whose father never paid him any attention invited his parents over for Memorial Day. They agreed to come at 1:00 P.M. The mother then called at 1:00 P.M. to say she would be there at 2:00 P.M., and then actually arrived at 3:10 P.M. The father called at 2:00 P.M. to announce that the mother had not told him that they were supposed to come down for the holiday, and since he just found out about it he would be late, too. Then he arrived at 4:30 P.M.

Other methods of withholding are leaving incomplete messages, ominous in their incompleteness, such as, "I have to talk to you—when can we discuss a matter of some importance?" or, the boss's favorite, torture by the creation of unbearable suspense, as in, "I have a bone to pick with you, let's get together, that is, when I have time—say, next week."

Related to withholding is giving others the opposite of whatever it is that they want:

An avoidant aware of a colleague's need to be recognized as an important person instead deliberately put him down, talking him up only when he sensed he wished to remain in the shadows. When he did encourage him onward and upward, he said, in essence, "Your God is too small." Instead of supporting his colleague when he needed support, he criticized him; and when criticism was desired, as when the other was really pleading to have limits set, he offered sympathy, pity, and an "understanding of your plight." Under other circumstances the positive gestures would have been an admirable try, but here they were merely a method to hurt and maim in the guise of doing good.

Throwing Out the Pregnant Implication

A man, when meeting a potential mate, waxed ecstatic about the joys of polygamy, not openly and directly, but by expressing his reservations about monogamy by telling a series of stories meant to illustrate how "all my monogamous friends have problems with their lovers and their sex lives." Also belonging to this technique is the roving, cross-cruising eye (excessive, compulsive flirting), either while initial contact is being established or after a relationship has formed. A homosexual man, when approached, before saying yes, checked out the rest of the room to see if there was anything better in it than what he already had. His comparison-shopping eye movements were invariably noticed, their correct meaning invariably perceived.

Damping Festive Occasions

While dining out, a guest complains aloud about the high cost of the meal and during the meal reminds everyone "we are all mortal." Another insists a partner shower before sex.

Doing Things behind the Back

Doing things behind the back is a particularly passive-aggressive avoidant mechanism when the things are deliberately done in such a way that they will get out later. This is clearly the motive when the backbiting is done to a close friend of the individual in question.

Refusing to Forgive

Long memories are among the passive-aggressive avoidant's frequently used weapons for starting feuds and keeping them alive.

Acting Out

An example of communicating anger by acting it out is announcing an impending divorce by moving out the furniture.

Being Clumsy

Nonavoidant clumsiness is confined to masochistic self-harm, like staining clothes, while passive-aggressive avoidant clumsiness is geared to have a precise effect on others. The passive-aggressive avoidant plays Berne's (1964) game of Schlemiel (pp. 114–116). He or she spills things on the rug, or knocks expensive vases over and breaks them, all the while saying "I'm sorry." Saying "I'm sorry" constitutes further provocation and attack, first, because it inevitably raises the answerable questions, "If you are so sorry, then why did you do it in the first place?" and, depending on circumstances, "to what extent is your sorrow appropriate given the magnitude of the actual harm you did?" and second, because it devilishly changes the victim's feeling from anger to guilt over being angry. Compounding all is the piteous cry, "Can't you overlook a little accident?"— a clever and often successful ploy to shift the blame from one's own bad behavior to another's failing to forgive that bad behavior.

Using Shyness and Fear of Rejection to Be Hostile

Shyness and fear of rejection to create discomfort and frustration in others is shyness and fear of rejection compounded by passive-aggressive attack. The passive-aggressively avoidant person of this ilk intends to be shy *and* to hang around watching the effect of the shyness. He or she intends not to pull back, at least immediately or completely. Rather he or she intends to watch others squirm, desperately trying to relate as he or she, the object of their affections, purposefully holds off, and eventually slips away.

Double-Binding

Passive-aggressive avoidants put people in a damned if you do, damned if you don't position.

The damned if you do and damned if you don't realtor originally described in

Chapter 10 as the realtor who first said it is better to sell an apartment furnished because it looks cozy and lived in, and second said buyers prefer apartments unfurnished because that way the buyer's fantasies flourish and grow, added something else for good measure. Whenever she tried to sell an apartment that was unfurnished, she said that that was no good because many buyers are depressed about the process of moving and people who are depressed like a ready-made home to move into because it reminds them of their old home and their childhood. Then whenever she tried to sell an apartment that was furnished, she claimed that that was no good because many buyers are narcissistic and most narcissists don't like to have their dreams tampered with by someone else's possessions.

Cheating Sexually

While the nonavoidant passive-aggressive cheats for the sexual gratification and tries to disguise his or her cheating afterwards, in contrast, the passive-aggressive avoidant cheats less for the sex than to send a message to a lover that something wrong is going on (while making sure that the lover can't get enough proof to actually have an air-clearing showdown that creates closure, one way or the other). When the passive-aggressive avoidant cheater is discovered, he or she is not so much caught as he or she is fulfilled.

AVOIDANT PERSONALITY DISORDER AND PASSIVE-DEPENDENT PERSONALITY DISORDER

Some passive-dependents are nonavoidant. They are nonavoidant when they suppress their hostility in order to maintain their dependency. They act kind when we would expect them to be unkind, say "It doesn't matter" when they should be setting limits, say "yes" when they should be saying "no," suppress their sexuality because they deem it troublesome to others, and generally behave in a self-sacrificial fashion—all in order to avoid offending, so that they may avoid being dismissed and rejected.

When Avoidant Personality Disorder is comorbid with Passive-Dependent Personality Disorder we get the typical Type IV avoidants who use their passive-dependent relationship with one to avoid having multiple healthy relationships with others. Such avoidants either become overly close to a parent to avoid having a lover (or to avoid having to go to work) or form an overly close codependent relationship with a partner in a womb-like arrangement that enables them to abandon everyone else. They are also avoidant when they are more passive than dependent—too passive to form or maintain relationships. One man from New Jersey desperate for, but unable to meet, a partner was advised to go to New York and try hanging around at a gay and lesbian center. In response, he could do no better than complain, "Too far, and every time I meet someone there they live another 40 miles away, on Long Island." As passives they might leave it entirely up to chance to determine if they will meet the Mr. or Ms. Right of their dreams. One such passive avoidant, afraid that being too active would lead to her being rejected, refused to follow her friends' advice to be more forward. She merely said goodbye back to a man she liked when he said goodbye to her, ignoring her friends' advice to instead say, "I won't let you go until I get your phone number." As with most avoidants, her passivity was partly the product of guilt and shame about her sexual needs. To her, simply acting interested in a man meant that she was proposing an illicit liaison.

Passive-dependent avoidants already in a troubled relationship make little or no active attempt to make repairs and rescue it. One way they do that is by not taking responsibility for the outcome of their relationship, and they do that by allowing everyone else to decide what it will be. For example, rather than looking for problems and coming up with solutions on their own they write letters to strangers who do not know them, such as newspaper columnists, asking "what do you think?" Or they find therapists who tell them whether to stay or go. They often select a columnist or therapist who they know intuitively or from previous experience will discourage them from continuing in the relationship. Then they lead the therapist or columnist on by censoring information that might make the case for them to stay.

AVOIDANT PERSONALITY DISORDER AND HISTRIONIC PERSONALITY DISORDER

Histrionic avoidants, also discussed in chapter 10, express their avoidance through off-putting theatrical mannerisms. They may exaggerate. Instead of being merely upset they are troubled and outraged. Or they cultivate a heavy-breathing feyness, as exemplified by the psychotherapist who, when asked what he did for a living, claimed that he was a coach. When asked, "Do you coach elementary school, high school, or college?" he replied, "None of those things. I coach adults." When asked, "What do you coach adults in? Baseball, football, tennis?" he replied, "None of those things, I coach people in how to feel alive."

AVOIDANT PERSONALITY DISORDER AND BORDERLINE PERSONALITY DISORDER

All borderlines are avoidant due to their ambivalence about interpersonal relationships. They both love too well and hate too intensely. They favor close ties, then abandon them with very little reason, seducing and then dropping others suddenly, without provocation or warning. They alternately close in and distance (merge and emerge) along the lines of Freud's quaint simile of porcupines who approach each other because they are cold and who then, pricking each other with their quills, move farther apart to relieve the discomfort, only to feel cold once again and move closer together. Part of borderline merging is overestimating others as all good, and part of borderline emerging is underestimating others as all bad. Now they assign individuals the qualities of savior, wise and honest one, and now they assign them the qualities of villain, fool, and cheat. Now they feel lonely, hunger for contact, and call and come over constantly, and now they remain aloof, refusing invitations to visit or be visited or refusing to return phone calls. Now they are relentless seekers for love and affection, and now they disrupt relationships offered or already in progress, rupturing those that promise to work, however much they unconsciously fear loneliness and abandonment. When they are involved in relationships, they dream of how wonderful it was to be alone, and they grouse vocally that others invade their space and get too close too fast. Then when they are alone they dream of how wonderful it was to be involved in relationships and complain that others do not get close enough. But when they are once again involved in relationships, they provoke others to provide the match that lights the fuse that explodes the tumescent bomb of a long-simmering avoidant fantasy. They even permit themselves to blow up over things that people concerned with relationship maintenance would at least try to tolerate—such as not replacing ice cubes after using them, not covering the cat food and allowing the food to dry out, or putting feet up on the sofa, even when the sofa is old and the feet are clean.

In the realm of rupturing relationships:

One borderline in the emerging phase had few friends/lovers because she criticized all acquaintances both for things beyond their control, like their looks and financial status, and for things within their control, but essentially unimportant, like wearing yesterday's clothes, or recommending and taking her to all the wrong places. For example, she was very close to a colleague for many years until that colleague got slightly depressed and needed someone to talk to, at which time she told her, "I am not interested in doing therapy with my friends" and refused to have anything more to do with her. She also criticized people for things that were no fault of theirs, or were her own fault. For example, she was utterly shattered over having missed a bus stop (though the next stop was only a few blocks away) and severely castigated the bus driver for not reminding her to get off—even though, assuming (incorrectly) he knew her from earlier trips, she had not told him the location of her stop. She often attacked innocent people just because they were around and available to be attacked. Sometimes it was the messenger, sometimes it was the next person to come along after the last person who troubled her, and sometimes it was the repairman who was trying to fix the problem. For example, she yelled at the bus driver of the bus that came (for there being so few buses) because she was angry at the driver of the bus that did not come. She yelled at an airline ticket agent when her luggage was lost although it was the person who handled the luggage, not the ticket agent, who, if any abuse were deserved, was the one who merited it. Finally, she often went back in time to tease out one thread from the skein of life's normal give-and-take, stretch the simple unremarkable strand, and weave it into a tapestry horrific-appearing enough to enable her to have negative feelings about potentially positive relationships. Thus, after 43 years of not seeing a childhood companion, she was reintroduced to him at a large party she gave, whereupon she recalled, loudly and unforgivingly to all those present, "Here's the boy who, when we were both two years old, threw dirt in my carriage."

A psychiatrist saw a patient without an appointment as an emergency, for a two-hour visit, and offered follow-up care the next day with both himself and a psychologist. At first the patient felt, "These people are wonderful—look how much time they spent with me." Then, in short order, she changed her mind to: "These people are dreadful—they are trying to overwhelm me, get too close, and press me to open up before I am ready. Besides, they are only doing it for the money."

Then, after rupturing relationships, they panic and long for what was lost.

After breaking up a relationship with a lover over his wearing a designer belt (as part of an attack skillfully geared to put the blame on him for his pseudosophistication instead of on her for her unrelatedness), a woman thought twice and called the lover constantly, begged him to give her one more chance, and added, as often as she could, "I really like designer belts and, most of all, the people who wear them."

AVOIDANT PERSONALITY DISORDER AND PSYCHOPATHIC/ANTISOCIAL PERSONALITY DISORDER

Psychopathic/antisocial avoidants use people mainly for their own selfish purposes. They are purely and simply out for supplies like money, power, or sexual favors.

A psychopathic avoidant assumed a false, more alluring identity for purposes of sexual conquest. Relying on his victims' desire to be associated with rich and famous people or to find a patron for their careers, he seduced young women by telling them he was the president of this, the big financier of that, "impressing them into bed," then leaving them feeling rejected and betrayed.

A psychopathic avoidant told the clinic staff that he wanted a prescription for a controlled substance to which he was addicted. When refused, he hinted broadly at what would happen if he were not given what he wanted. Clenching both his teeth and his fists, he said: "I have gone to jail for putting people in the hospital, and for a lot less."

Some are also out to get specific emotional rewards. For example, they desire to elevate their self-esteem by bringing others down just to give themselves a sense of greater power and control. If they care at all whom they hurt in the process, if they control their blind ambition, back stabbing, and throat-cutting in any way, they do so only a little—just enough to promote a relationship so that they can continue to manipulate and wring it dry.

AVOIDANT PERSONALITY DISORDER AND SADOMASOCHISTIC PERSONALITY DISORDER

Sadistic Avoidance

To nonmasochists all sadists are avoidant, because they prefer criticizing, humbling, humiliating and hurting people to loving them. Sadists accomplish their avoidant ends either directly or passive-aggressively. Those who are openly and directly sadistic might wound people for personal characteristics they can do nothing about, like wearing glasses (four-eyes), or their extreme youth, advanced age, high or low social standing (as the sadist perceives it), or their race, creed, or color. They typically view others' positive feelings toward them as a sign of weakness and vulnerability, and so a signal to attack.

A sadistic avoidant was late for an appointment. When he called up the woman he was to meet to tell her he would be delayed arriving, she reassured him that that was okay and told him how glad she would be to see him when he finally appeared. After he hung up the phone he turned to a buddy of his and complained that she was much too eager to get together with him. As he put it, "I am going to find someone else, someone completely different from that idiot who waits at home all day for me, with nothing better to do than to drool over me until I get there."

Those who are passive-aggressively sadistic might hurt others in the name of compassion. The doctor who puts human values last by refusing to give pain medication to terminally ill patients on the grounds that it is theoretically addicting (though the addiction has no practical implications or consequences), the government agency willing to remove a foster child who has lived for years with two gay men committed to each other "in order to spare the child from having two homosexual parents," and the advocate who allows a suicidal patient to hoist himself on his or her own petard of irresistible but transient suicidal impulses, going to his grave after killing him or herself, with his or her civil rights the only thing still intact, have as their counterpart the "tough-love" parent who abuses in the guise of disciplining; the romantic who abuses others "for their own benefit"—abandoning another for "positive reasons, out of love, with your best interests at heart"; the workaholic who deliberately takes a second job on nights and holidays ostensibly for the money but really to stay away from family and friends; and the selfish opportunist whose lofty aspirations lower the lofty aspirations of others—as happens when an untalented spouse makes the other spouse work at a menial job to support an ill-conceived, unsuccessful, and unprofitable artistic pursuit.

The following are some illustrative cases:

One avoidant sadist, instead of acting in a therapeutic fashion to bring others around, cast them off because of small and remediable imperfections. When his lover said she felt uncomfortable during the bedroom scenes of R-rated movies, instead of expressing sympathy and reassuring her that he would let nothing harm her, he humiliated her by calling her "square" and "crazy," saying, "Nobody reacts that way to sex any more."

A man told his wife, "I hate being married to you because we have nothing in common. We disagree about the importance of the theatre, politics, and giving to charity, and that's why our sex life is as dead as our relationship." He convinced his wife to attend sex therapy. Then he made sex therapy an occasion for treatment for his "complete loss of interest in sex, at least with you." When pressed by his therapist he admitted, "I'm sadistic," but his awareness was not the first step either in understanding himself or in mustering real regret. Rather, his "insight" was merely a way to confess to, in order to avoid actually having to change, his attitude and his behavior. (It is of interest that the sex therapist he chose revealed his general fascination for and identification with sadistic people. As his wife described it, "He liked her [his therapist] because she reminded him of mud wrestlers and tall, blond Swedish women with whips, and because she had a sign on her entrance door that said, "Trained in Judo.")

A homosexual, knowing "they were meant for each other," introduced two people—friends of his who had not previously met—and suggested that the three of them take a trip together. One evening when they were on the road, the two friends, almost predictably, said good-bye, left him behind, and went off for a long walk. To express his resentment at being left he disappeared into the night and took the bus home without leaving a note in the car explaining his absence. At the time, he convinced himself that he left because he wanted the friends to be alone together to consummate the affair, but actually he wanted them to worry. This would be his revenge for their excluding him. He contemplated how, instead of enjoying each other's company, they were wondering where he was and if he were still alive. He said later, "I knew of that big cliff on the beach and how they would think I fell off the edge, in the darkness."

A father who had a small business wanted his son to be a doctor "so that you can have a better life than I had." Yet when his son became the doctor he wanted him to be, he perceived the son as "rejecting me and everything I stand for" by not joining him in the family business, and, by competing with him, achieving an elevated position in life he, the father, had never been able to attain. The father would have his retaliation after death. During life he made himself as unloving as possible. Then, before he died, he left notes for the son labeled, "to be found after the funeral." The notes said, in essence, "How much I love you, something I couldn't tell you while I was alive" and added, for good measure, "I know you loved me too, even though you didn't act that way when I could have appreciated it, before I died." This left the son with a lifelong legacy of self-blame and guilt over not appreciating and loving the father before it was too late.

One doctor called his secretary the "enforcer, critic, peanut gallery, and torturer all rolled into one." She complained that patient care suffered because he took too much vacation time, and suggested that his clerical work was interfering with his patient contacts. (She couched her accusations all too patently in the guise of concern, as in, "I am concerned that I have to interrupt you to ask you to see patients instead of writing your medical notes.") To spare his patients long waits, she insisted that he take them in as soon as they arrived, not when their appointment time began. When he complained to her about her behavior, she first encouraged him to speak up to "clear the air," then cut him off, interrupting him in the middle of a sentence first to seize control of the conversation ("As I was saying") and next to condemn him for what he had to say. Many years later she admitted, "I knew I was making him mad, but still I did it because I liked him more than he liked me."

An organizer of an affair said, "Those who aren't going to volunteer may leave." Then, as they tried to get out of the door, even though she was the one who had given the permission to go, she, feeling rejected, harshly castigated them for refusing to help out.

A homosexual used satire to wound, the clever remark or zinger, to avoid getting close. He had moved to a blue-collar neighborhood to get away from phonies, but he came to hate his "pedestrian blue-collar" neighbors because they did not accept him. Soon his sadistic retaliatory fantasy life began to flourish, and he contemplated possible sophisticated put-downs. One way to get back at one neighbor particularly delighted him: "The neighbor's Labrador mix dog is called Coco. I want to purchase a French Poodle, paint its toenails blue, adorn it with ribbons and a diamond collar, and name it, so I can be heard calling out to it, in as sissified a fashion as I can muster, 'Rococo.'"

Masochistic Avoidance

While other avoidants do not relate well in order to *avoid* personal suffering, masochistic avoidants do not relate well in order to *induce* personal suffering. Some masochists do not attempt to relate at all. Most, however, attempt to relate, but to people who cannot or will not relate to them. Therefore, they deliberately extend themselves in situations where acceptance is unlikely. Unsinterested in people who overlook their flaws or see them as virtues and wanting most of all to get approval from someone who disapproves of them, they actively seek the very critical, humiliating, and rejecting people they say they fear. They seek them precisely because they already know that they will be unsuitable for, or will reject, them. Thus they become attracted to people who are too different from them to allow them into their lives, or to people who actually disdain them.

A masochistic bisexual found people the most fascinating when they were actually unpleasant, defective, hurtful, abusive, unclean, unwashed, or on a lower rung of the social ladder. Part of his masochism involved a special attraction to prostitutes. In the attraction to heterosexual prostitutes, the money transfer was avoidant because it convinced him, "I don't love, I buy." In the attraction to transvestite prostitutes, his need for someone with an unclear or hermaphroditic sexual identity was avoidant because it maintained distance via involvement in a situation where there was too much confusion for closeness. (For prostitutes themselves the avoidant attraction often is, "I do it with many people not for love but for money," an excuse which simultaneously precludes closeness and provides an opportunity for expression of hostility toward people who can't get it but have to buy it.) All the while he simultaneously shrank from people he sensed would accept and love him. For example, he placed ads in the personals, then did not reply to people who seemed interested in him, and he turned down introductions from friends and family who wanted to fix him up when he sensed things might work out, accepting introductions only when he sensed the stage was being set for the disappointment he eagerly sought.

Some masochistic avoidants actively seek out dangerous situations:

A masochistic homosexual, actually hoping to get caught, exposed himself in pornographic movie houses even though he heard all the up-to-date rumors that there were undercover agents present. He denied that he wanted to get caught. Instead he rationalized his gambling and tempting fate by thinking, like the man who plays Russian Roulette, that the bullet was for the next person, or by thinking, like Pollyanna, that "This is the undercover agent's night off," or by convincing himself that "he is on, and he will catch me, but then he will forgive me and let me go because in his heart of hearts he must recognize that it is a sin to be so cruel to one's fellow man, and over so little of real importance."

The following case illustrates the successophobic element in some self-defeating masochistic object choices:

A patient, drawing inspiration from a successophobic belief that what was bad for her was good for her, and the reverse, made such a masochistic choice when first she selected her husband. She herself said, "I avoided all the attractive men I met to instead marry one man I knew was unattractive, impotent, thin, reserved, self-preoccupied and mother-fixated." Her burgeoning successophobia was later illustrated in a dream "that my driving phobia"—a symptom of which she long complained in reality—had "lifted enough for me to be able to park a car, but in parking it I would swing it widely, and into traffic, bumping, hitting, and destroying other cars in the process." Later, after meeting her goal of marriage to an unattractive man, she was actually surprised, as if she were learning it for the first time, that they had nothing in common, or that, as she put it in more specific sexual terms, "his penis doesn't fit my vagina."

After seeking out they stick with unfulfilling relationships. They set about converting their harshest and most disdainful critics, the harsher and more critical the better. Many willingly become submissive pushovers who will do anything, even things that are not in their best interests, just to make these relationships work. For example, a man, too willing to tailor his own expectations to meet the expectations of his partner, humored his unartistic partner by denying he wanted a career in show business, and even entered the world of professional sports just because that was what his partner wanted him to do. They even excuse the most outrageous behavior in their partners. For example, one masochist excused a sadistic partner for cursing and reviling him in the foulest of terms on the basis of "anyone who hurts another like that must be in pain himself."

When reality fails to hurt and punish masochistic avoidants, they arrange to hurt and punish themselves. They imagine negativity in a neutral or positive relationship. A man might call and leave a message for someone on Friday and, forgetting about the weekend, imagine he was being rejected because the call was not returned until Monday. Many let a simple, resolvable personal flaw in others become a cause célèbre that mars an otherwise solid relationship, and make no effort to repair a relationship problem even when the relationship is solid and the problem solvable. Not surprisingly they often fail to give recognition and respond when a partner improves spontaneously or through therapy. Instead, in a headlong rush to a painful divorce, they continue to view a mate who has become interesting as still boring, who has learned to compliment them as still insufficiently positive for their liking, or who has changed from remote to close as someone who now threatens their valued freedom, independence, and identity.

After some years of treatment the patient who made a masochistic choice in selection of her husband learned to get along with him. "He is really not a bad guy," she finally admitted. But then a new symptom arose—her seven year itch. Unlike nonmasochists, where the seven year itch is a longing for variety originating partly in boredom, which can even have a basis in reality, her seven year itch appeared precisely in order to disrupt a relationship that was finally going well now that her remote, distant, uncaring, cruel unavailable husband took her by surprise and began to love her.

Masochists act out with place as much as with person. In the self-destructive geographical solution, they choose a place where they sense they are not wanted so that they can never be happy there. They have a civil right to be there, but a more important issue (at least for the practically oriented nonavoidant) is that (1) he or she does not fit in, so that (2) he or she would be far happier in a place where he or she had both a right and a reason to be. For example, sophisticated masochists pick a small town to live in, then complain of the small-town mentality and try, predictably without success, to get along in what is for them a hopelessly foreign culture.

A patient went to a working-class town to obtain relief from what he called the "oppressive sophistication" of places where people spend their entire lives waxing ecstatic over possessions. Predictably, he soon longed for the oppressive sophistication of the places he left behind. He most wanted to get away from "people who wait outside the bakery door at 6:00 A.M. so that they can be the first ones in to buy coffee and a doughnut, do little more than consult each other about where and when the fish are biting, and have nothing better to do than complain about, or admire, the latest baseball trade."

Masochists often come full circle by turning into sadists who use their masochism as a roundabout way to hurt others in addition to themselves. For example, one masochist not only put himself down but also did so repeatedly, proclaiming, "I am not worthy of you," until the other person both got the point, got tired of hearing it repeated, and wondered if what was really meant was "You are not worthy of me."

In therapy masochistic avoidants resist improvement. They find ways to keep their avoidance in order to keep on suffering. They vocally rationalize their loneliness as preferential, and attempt to convince their therapists of the same thing. They claim that privacy and independence are to be valued over all else, that "Marriage isn't right for everyone and it's not right for me," and that having regular sex is not all it is cracked up to be. In the words of one such avoidant: "Some of the best things in life are only available to the isolate, like being able to sleep without being awakened by my partner's snoring, being able to stay in bed as long as I like, dropping my clothes on the floor without anyone else complaining, not having to pay for a partner's financial excesses, and being able to travel without compromising my itinerary just to meet someone else's expectations."

Should therapy appear to be working, they defeat it in a masochistic triumph that consists of cutting off their noses to spite the therapist's face. This was the motivation of a single individual whose goal to meet people became secondary to her goal of proving to family, friends, and the therapist who was trying to help her that "No matter what you do, I still can't meet Mr. Right."

This masochistic single complained to her therapist: "I have searched the world and there is no one in it for me." The therapist suggested she ask her relatives, who knew many eligible bachelors, to fix her up with a blind date. They did and the dates were not bad. But to defeat her relatives and her therapist she announced, "Blind dates never work out," and refused to accept being fixed up in the future. (The reality is that blind dates can be as successful as the participants allow. The oft-drawn equivalent between being fixed up and being disappointed is usually little more than a statement of self-fulfilling prophecy. Put bluntly, blind dates get an undeservedly bad reputation because those who ask for them, need them, and get them are often, like this patient, masochistic avoidants who until now have seen to it that no relationship will develop, and continue their self- and other-destructive behavior into the blind date itself.)

In conclusion, rarely does AvPD exist in the absence of comorbid disorders. Mixed disorders such as paranoid/avoidant personality disorder are common. The clinical profile of and hence the required therapeutic approach to the resultant mixed disorder differ, sometimes markedly, from the profile and hence the therapeutic approach to pure AvPD. One-size-fits-all remedies, which fail to consider the different avoidant styles and subtypes of avoidance that are a product of comorbidity, can be ineffective or actually harmful. For example, while phobic avoidants need to focus on exposing and immersing themselves in relationships so that they can get close without becoming overly anxious or disruptive, paranoid avoidants need to take a first step before they attempt exposure. They need to focus on and master their tendency to project their low self-esteem and anger onto others to the point that they feel others are avoiding them. That is, while phobic avoidants have to expose themselves to the real world, paranoid avoidants have to rethink their fantasies about the real world to which they will soon be exposing themselves.

CHAPTER 12

Cause: An Overview

In this chapter I identify and briefly discuss the evolutionary, developmental, psychodynamic, cognitive-behavioral, interpersonal, and existential causes of AvPD.

EVOLUTIONARY CAUSES

Becoming Human

Becoming human entails a degree of loss of "animal" warmth and spontaneity. The cat that, knowing that its owner is aggrieved, sits on his or her foot to offer sympathy, companionship, and comfort, with evolutionary refinement becomes the human who responds to another's suffering with, "Grin and bear it," "Cut it out," or "Go get professional help."

The Incest Taboo

In 1913 in *Totem and Taboo*, Freud (1950) relates avoidance (in primitive peoples) to the horror of incest, which leads to the practice of forbidding any sexual relationship between members of the same clan, a complicated assurance against the possibility of committing incest. Thus, "a rule of avoidance [Freud's word] . . . among the A-kamba . . . of British East Africa [is that] a girl has to avoid her father between the age of puberty and the time of her marriage. If they meet in the road, she hides while he passes, and she may never go and sit near him." Freud goes on to suggest that in civilized peoples avoidances between near relations are protective measures against incest. He uses the man's relationship with his mother-in-law as an example. Freud believes that the mother-in-law serves as a mother substitute—that is, a man who "chose his mother as the object of his love, and perhaps his sister as well, before passing on to his final choice . . . because of the barrier that exists against incest" (p. 16), reflects his love "from the two figures on whom his affection was centred in his childhood on to an outside object that is modeled upon them. The place of his own and his sister's mother is taken by his mother-in-law" (p. 16). Now, because a "marriage between a man and his mother-in-law . . .[is] not theoretically impossible . . . a special guarantee against that possibility . . . [becomes] necessary" (p. 13). This guarantee originates from the ambivalence inherent in the relationship with the mother-in-law—that is, the relationship is "composed of conflicting affectionate and hostile impulses" (p. 14). "A streak of irritability and malevolence that is apt to be present in the medley of his feelings [toward his mother-in-law] leads us to suspect that she does in fact offer him a temptation to incest" (p. 16).

In 1913 in the "Theme of the Three Caskets," Freud (1957k) describes the three inevitable relations man has with women: the mother who bears him, the companion of his bed and board, and the destroyer (respectively, the mother herself, the beloved who is chosen after her pattern, and Mother Earth who receives man at the end). An intriguing idea, not pursued, is that avoidant men eschew the second (relationships with women) because women recall and remind them of the first (their mother) and/or the third (death). Another intriguing idea, also not pursued, is that the avoidant may even, due to a mother or father-fixation transferred onto strangers, *seek* rejection in order to protect him- or herself against the possibility of carrying out unconscious incestuous wishes.

The Death Instinct

Freud's "death instinct" can be thought of as describing an avoidant ego state. I speculate that for some avoidants their behavioral insularity and remoteness expresses not merely a fear of rejection but also a primitive unconscious urge to return to the primordial ooze, a lure of ashes to ashes that in all of us interferes too soon with our finest work, corrupts, soils and stains our best interpersonal intentions, and causes us to abandon, often in spite of ourselves, those whom we might love, and those who might love us.

DEVELOPMENTAL CAUSES

Most avoidants react to new relationships as if they were old relationships, avoiding new people and situations now as if they were difficult people or traumatic situations from the past. For example, a patient who at age 3 was severely whipped for "playing doctor" as an adult became a celibate avoidant, his way to stay away from sex in order to keep himself from being whipped again.

Early physical traumata, ranging from sexual seductions to operative procedures such as a tonsillectomy and adenoidectomy, where a patient feels tied down physically and smothered, can contribute to later avoidance. So can early emotional traumata. As examples, excessive parental control can cause a child to grow up feeling as if every new adult relationship is a trap, as one patient put it, "an involuntary commitment." As an adult such an individual can either become a dependent avoidant who gives up and submits and does exactly what he or she is told to do, or an independent avoidant who rebels and does only the opposite of what is expected. Severe criticism of both the child's positive and negative feelings can cause the child to grow up remote and unfeeling to spare him or herself further assault. The child who is told, "It's bad to feel and worse to get angry" might as an adult discourage a relationship in order to spare his or her partner the effect of his or her anger. The child negatively compared to his or her siblings can grow up feeling devalued compared to others and either retreat due to feeling unworthy or, in order to feel more worthy, turn every new potentially loving relationship into one marked by jealous competitive rivalry.

The connection between early sibling rivalry and latter-day avoidance is illustrated by the man who envied a brother who later became a psychoanalyst. The man went on to develop a similar rivalry with a psychiatrist who wanted to be not his rival but his friend. When this psychiatrist friend built a house bigger, and presumably on that account better, than his, he replied by starting an addition to his own house. When the psychiatrist friend came to visit, the man spoke only of his progress—the floors were put in today, the plumber came to hook up the dishwasher, and so on. This single-minded drive to complete the house both expressed and attempted to defend against the terror he felt at being found wanting in comparison to his brother. The guilt over this rivalry took the form of countervailing self-destructive tendencies, so that one evening, in a hurry to complete an installation of a greenhouse, he worked on it while simultaneously cooking for a barbecue he was giving that night. Preoccupied and rushed, he accidentally drilled holes in the glass, smashing several of the panes. When the house was complete he felt, "I didn't do it; his house is still better than mine; his is all new and mine is partly old." Now the only thing left for him to do was to avoid the friend whom he viewed as the source of his bad feelings about himself—effectively declaring his rival dead. In the absence of real reasons to avoid him, trumped-up ones sufficed, created from natural enough occurrences. For example, he complained: "You walked past me at the beach without even seeing me," an insignificant occurrence likely to happen for impersonal reasons on a crowded day.

Parents often create an avoidant-to-be by infantilizing a child. They might keep the child at home away from friends in order to be able to have him or her all to themselves. In the case of the man and woman who were separated and lived apart in the same house divided into two, the mother would not let her daughter visit her father unaccompanied even though they lived in a safe neighborhood and the father lived just down the porch. Instead, she insisted upon escorting the child from her house directly to the father's door and watching until she was certain that the child got safely inside. Infantilized children like this often pay the price, when they are still children, in the currency of defective relationships with siblings and compromised relationships with other children and adults outside of the family. When they become adults, such children often pay another price. They may become Type IV avoidants who have regressive relationships marked by an isolating dependency (codependency) on one associated with an uninterest in, fear of, antagonism to, or jealousy of, all others.

Parents who are themselves avoidant can create an avoidant child in their own image. They can do this directly, by vocally warning the child about the dangers of getting close, or indirectly, by criticizing family and friends for doing normal nonavoidant things. In one case parents who criticized their friends' small interpersonal indulgences like having cocktails each evening before dinner created a child who avoided others because she believed that there was something "evil" about getting together with people and having fun. (Paradoxically, healthy nonavoidant parents can create avoidant children unwittingly should the child counteridentify with them to become a countercultural isolate.)

PSYCHODYNAMIC CAUSES

Interpersonal distancing has unconscious as well as conscious roots, as follows:

Conflicts about Sex

Patients often become avoidant because they experience second thoughts about their romantic (sexual) impulses. Fenichel (1945) comments:

Some adolescents fight their consciences by proving to themselves that they are not worse than others; they congregate on a narcissistic basis for the purpose of swapping stories about sexuality, or even for common instinctual activity; others withdraw, hide their masturbation and their longings entirely and feel ostracized and lonesome, unable to participate in the "sexual" or "knowing" gatherings of the others. Fixations on the first type of reaction are represented subsequently by "impulsive characters, and fixations on the second subsequently by erythrophobics [patients who have an inordinate fear of blushing]. [I might add that the second type of reaction is also represented by erotophobics—individuals who fear their own sexuality much as others fear Friday the 13th.]

It is probably because of social factors that adolescents frequently prefer to meet in homosexual gatherings. In this way they avoid the exciting presence of the other sex and at the same time avoid being alone; thus they may find the reassurance they are looking for. . . . The frequent preference for homosexual objects at this age may be due . . . to shyness in regard to the other sex . . . (p. 112).

Conflicts about Anger

Patients also become avoidants because they experience second thoughts about their anger. Avoidants typically get angry when they cannot be as dependent as they might like to be ("you are rejecting me") or fear becoming more dependent than they want to be ("By attempting to get close to me you are putting me in danger of losing my identity"); when they feel they are not in full control of other people or situations; and when they want to win, but lose, or when, as masochists, they want to lose, but win.

Some do not accept that their anger is a human emotion. Rather they view their anger as an emotion that makes them bad people who should be disqualified from having any relationships at all. So they withdraw to control their anger at other people out of their concern for others' comfort and safety.

However, other avoidants are not so conflicted about their anger. Some avoidants actually welcome and encourage their anger. Getting angry is their way to deal with their fear of being criticized and rejected by becoming the ones doing the criticizing and rejecting. Simultaneously they get revenge on others by humiliating and rejecting them in order to give them a taste of what being rejected feels like.

A patient who lived in Connecticut had a date with a new lover from out of town. The new lover took a bus from New York City to Connecticut to be with the patient. As the bus pulled in, the new lover, from inside the bus, spied the patient waiting for him at the bus station, and waved him a gusty hello, only to have the patient think, "That big wave turned me off—I cannot stand people who are just too eager to see me." Later the patient, to drive the new lover off permanently, openly insulted him by telling him that sex with him was so bad that he never wanted to try it again.

A patient, angry with a woman for liking him too much, told her that he needed a break from their relationship, giving as his reason that she annoyed him because instead of mixing her foods as she ate she finished one food on her plate before going on to the next. The woman's reaction, of being hurt and of never wanting to see him again, was exactly what he intended.

Anxiety

Anxiety (in avoidants, social anxiety or relationship anxiety) is a signal that in interpersonal relationships, forbidden romantic and hostile impulses are about to erupt and cause problems by:

- Creating guilt by running up against one's conscience;
- Creating a loss of self-pride by running up against one's ideals;
- Creating a threat to one's structural integrity by causing emotional flooding;
- Creating a threat to one's structural integrity (particularly in the case of romantic impulses) by causing emotional depletion;
- Creating a threat to one's personal identity (in the case of romantic impulses) by being the first step on the way to a stifling merger.

In the realm of causing emotional flooding, Millon and Davis (1996) suggest that avoidants must "avoid everything which might arouse their emotions" (p. 254) and "seek as far as possible to avoid and deaden all stimulation from the outside" (p. 255). In the realm of depletion, according to legend the artist Joseph Cornell died a virgin because he feared that if he had sex it would destroy his artistic ability. In the realm of fear of loss of identity through merger, one patient was at odds with her sexuality because she feared men would take over her life and keep her barefoot and pregnant, while another patient was at odds with his sexuality because he feared that any woman he got involved with would swallow him up whole and keep him from doing the things he really enjoyed doing, like going out with the boys to the sports and go-go bars.

Patients who feel guilty about their sexual impulses tend to suffer from what I call *sexophobia* (a "love revulsion" technically called an "erotophobia"). They fear relationships (and view isolation as splendid) because they view being in love as they view making love—as something dangerous, dirty, and disgusting. Sullivan's (1953) "primitive genital phobia" (p. 376) (my "sexophobia") is a "more or less contentless aversion to action or thought about 'touching' [oneself] in the perineum; often with a lively, if unwelcome, hope that . . . [one] may be 'touched' by others, and perhaps 'touch' them in turn; after which actual experience [one] would come to 'dislike' and avoid . . . [the other] or, more unhappily, suffer recurrent deeply disturbing revulsion after each of a series of 'conflictful' repetitions" (p. 376).

In some avoidants love revulsion is expressed directly, as disgust with sex. In others it is expressed indirectly, subtly, in such symptoms as a fear of touching, for example, a fear of shaking hands because of the possibility of contamination; avoidant philosophies of life such as the belief that sex is "more trouble than it is worth," which is often associated with the hope that sexual feelings will diminish with increasing age so that one will no longer have to be bothered with them; and the above-mentioned love for splendid isolation when not a real preference but a defense against a forbidden wish to have intercourse with others.

A poignant expression of what might be a form of love revulsion (as usual, rationalized by blaming the lover) appears in Thomas Hardy's *The Mayor of Casterbridge* (1981) when, in a pivotal episode, the hero, Michael Henchard, gets drunk and, generally disgusted with marriage, sells his rather loving and "by no means ill-favored" wife to a passing sailor.

The conversation took a high turn, as it often does on such occasions. The ruin of good men by bad wives, and, more particularly, the frustration of many a promising youth's high aims and hopes and the extinction of his energies by an early imprudent marriage, was the theme.

"I did for myself that way thoroughly," said the trusser, with a contemplative bitterness that was well-nigh resentful. "I married at eighteen, like the fool that I was; and this is the consequence o't. . . . "

"For my part I don't see why men who have got wives and don't want 'em, shouldn't get rid of 'em as these gypsy fellows do their old horses," said the man in the tent. "Why shouldn't they put 'em up and sell 'em by auction to men who are in need of such articles? Hey? Why, begad, I'd sell mine this minute if anybody would buy her!"

"There's them that would do that," some of the guests replied, looking at the woman, who was by no means ill-favored (p. 6–7).

The following are two case histories of patients suffering from love revulsion as a result of anxiety about their romantic feelings:

In his professional life a man's love revulsion was manifest as a dreamy restlessness and desire for change whenever things were going well. He quit one perfectly good job after another and moved on, rationalizing his behavior as "for more money" or "for better working conditions"—ultimately illusory. A doctor, he kept many licenses in different states in case he wanted to relocate, and for a long time wouldn't buy a house or apartment, renting one instead so that he wasn't tied down to one spot. Whenever he did move, he found that he had left behind a job as or more worthy than the new one. Though he recognized this after the fact, the recognition had no effect on his future behavior, so that he continued to look at the ads and apply for new positions. Of course, with each new job, difficulties arose again as his avoidant tendencies reasserted themselves and he felt a new urge to move on.

In his personal life his love revulsion took a parallel form—intense object love alternating with a consuming desire to get away from them all. One night he had the following dream. After waiting in a restaurant for his take-out order, and noting with mixed pleasure and envy the many generations all working under the same roof in splendid cooperation, he heard himself begging his wife to "throw him out" so that he could be alone. In his waking life his ambivalence about his marriage (he was later actually to get a divorce) took the form of an obsessive fear that his wife would get into a fatal car crash. Associated were a series of escapist distancing fantasies and behaviors: shopping alone; going alone on vacations to exotic places or to a remote shack in the woods with a warm fire and steamy kettle; reading escapist books on exploring the Antarctic; traveling "Through the Looking Glass," and going "Over the Rainbow"; wandering alone through the seaside mists listening to the fog horn; taking trains by himself north, to isolated places or to distant remote stations at the end of the line, not because of the pretty, interesting or welcoming things he might find there but because there he would be as far away from home base as possible; and, turning inward in contemplation, taking trips in time to a fantasized past or future, or trips in person—assuming another identity, such as that of a troubadour in the Middle Ages playing ancient music, or that of an archaeologist who uncovered the past, not so that he could study, but so that he could live in, it.

After he got his divorce he decided to actually buy a house in the woods. He couldn't wait to go there every weekend, and even went in winter, using as his excuse, "I have to water my plants." However, when he got there he promptly panicked because he had gone too far and was now all alone with nothing to do. So he called all his friends in the city just to make contact with other human beings, and drank in local bars just to be where other people were, though he hated the people in the bars and the contacts he had with them were invariably superficial and limited. Finally, he sold the lonely country house and bought a house in the city only to find that he constantly dreamed of the splendid times he had alone in his house in the country—of the pleasures of getting into his car in the middle of winter, the cold snow everywhere, driving to the bars with their warm, welcoming lights, sounds, and people, and wonderful, body-strengthening food and soul-softening drink, and of the times when he was isolated, in his beautiful digs, with its beautiful furnishings, living in sin (as an acquaintance once put it) "with the wall board."

In his sexual fantasies one man imagined himself raping his dates. These rape fantasies were his way to deal with his guilt over sexuality by fantasizing women as guiltless when it came to wanting and having sex. By forcing the woman to do it he could maintain the fantasy that "women are good; they don't want it, they don't volunteer for it, they are made to do it, against their will."

Defense and Symptom

Avoidant symptoms such as shyness, withdrawal, and ambivalence are clinical manifestations of the avoidant's internal attempt to defend himself or herself from social/relationship anxiety. More exactly, they are the clinical manifestations of defense mechanisms brought into play to manage this social/relationship anxiety. For example, an avoidant guilty about her sexual wishes *projected* them, and the self-blame for having them, onto others, to develop a symptomatic preoccupation with being sexually harassed, which in her case meant, "See, I don't want to do it with you, and to prove it I chastise you severely for wanting, and trying to force me into, it."

The defenses and the symptoms that represent them are, structurally speaking, compromises, coping mechanisms for dealing with anxiety-laden conflicts by neutralizing them—by creating an inert wish-fear amalgam. For example, the symptom of shyness favored by shy Type I avoidants is a compromise that neutralizes the anxiety-laden wish to connect with a fear of actually connecting. (As we have seen, in social phobics, the compromise involves not generalized, long-term, ingrained, relationship difficulties, expressed as such, without being displaced onto a symbol of what actually threatens, but a transient, reactive withdrawal confined to specific trivial prompts, which are displacements from what is actually feared.)

Type II and III avoidants deal defensively with their anxiety about relating not by shy withdrawal but by symptomatic doing and undoing. They alternate between approach and avoidance so that they first form close intimate relationships (the wish), then break up when commitment (the fear) looms or threatens, only to feel lonely and start the process all over again. Type IV avoidants favor another compromise: defensive regression, a severe form of withdrawal where avoidants form an exclusive relationship with one person for the purpose of walling themselves off from almost everybody else. Their wish to be close is gratified, but selectively, and in such a way that they ruin the rest of their relationships.

COGNITIVE CAUSES

Cognitive errors are "stable underlying [incorrect or partially correct] assumption[s]" (p. 75) that David D. Burns and Norman Epstein (1983) cite as the basis of "negative cognitions or automatic thoughts" (p. 75). In avoidants these negative cognitions, or negative automatic thoughts, distort and disrupt interpersonal relationships by creating irrational disjunctive beliefs about oneself, others, and the world, developed and maintained in the face of evidence to the contrary.

Here are some examples of disjunctive thinking commonly found in avoidants. Ignoring the considerable overlap, I divide cognitive errors into errors of thought *process*, such as some = all errors and errors of thought *content*, such as unduly pessimistic thinking. (Cognitive errors are also discussed in Chapter 15.)

Errors of Thought Process

Part Equals Whole, Some Equals All, Similar Equals the Same Thing Thinking

In this mode avoidant negative thinking results from emphasizing the similarities, while overlooking the significant mitigating differences, between A and B. As a result, avoidants perceive a little criticism (A) to be

a shattering assault (B); see intermittent as constant and complete negativity; view anything short of full love as abject hatred, so that "if he or
she doesn't like me completely then he or she rejects me totally"; believe
that assertiveness is the exact equivalent of aggressiveness, so that for-
wardness = pushiness; and view the vulnerability associated with being
in love as the exact equivalent of being dangerously needy, weak, and
helpless. Advice from others becomes control; kidding, humiliation; constructive criticism, a put-down or personal attack; friendliness, sexual
harassment; and commitment, entrapment. Ordinary desire equals desperation, cooperation equals submissiveness, and submissiveness equals
complete loss of control. The uncertainty associated with all relationships
becomes unpredictability, unpredictability danger, and danger a reason to
stay away or withdraw even from a relationship that has potential "because you can never tell what you might be getting into." Avoidant misanthropy results when others' minor flaws become disqualifying lesions,
so that people who are not all good (which is almost everybody) become
no good at all.

Overgeneralizing

Avoidants who overgeneralize slide too easily from one instance to all
others. For example, a patient views any new relationship as a repeat of
an old traumatic one. A patient traumatized as a child believes that all
future encounters will be equally traumatic, or a patient who has once
fallen in love with someone unreliable becomes certain that no one he or
she loves can ever be trusted.

Thinking According to Exclusive Causes

Avoidants who think this way are effectively blind to alternative explanations for their beliefs. This blindness is selective. Though they see the
possibility of negativity in all positivity, they rarely if ever open their
minds to the possibility of positivity in those situations they perceive as
being completely negative.

Errors of Thought Content

Catastrophic (Alarmist, or Worst Possible Scenario, Thinking)

Avoidants who think catastrophically overestimate the probability of a
disaster befalling a relationship or the impact that an actual disaster,
should it occur, will have on a given relationship, and on their lives. A
patient was afraid to say hello to strangers because he feared that saying
hello would open him up to their not replying, which for him would be
a shattering rejection. The related process of *overexaggeration* also contrib-

utes to the avoidant catastrophic belief, discussed throughout, that commitment necessarily leads to a complete loss of identity, thence to being
trapped in a life of abject submission to a dominant partner whose love
is little more than an attempt to control and dominate. Catastrophic thinking and overexaggeration lead to overreaction, characterized by the taking
of desperate measures. An example of such desperate measures is dissociating into a minifugue to cope with a minor incursion now viewed as a
terrorist attack. Dissociation was discussed at length in Chapter 8 and in
Chapter 10. An example of a minifugue was given in Chapter 10.

Paranoid Thinking

Avoidants who think in the paranoid mode create outer stress from
inner turmoil by projecting their sexual desires, negative biases, and personal guilt onto others. Those who project their own sexual desires onto
others fear sexual harassment along the lines of, "It is not me who is trying
to seduce you, and that is what I hate about myself, it is you who is trying
to seduce me, and that is what I hate about you." Those who project their
negative bias to themselves and others onto the world come to believe
that others have the same negative bias toward them that they have toward themselves and others. That particular projection alone accounts in
great measure for an avoidant's classic fear of criticism, humiliation, and
rejection.

Depressive Thinking

Depressive thinking is self-punitive thinking that leads avoidants to
convince themselves that they are unworthy of being loved. They are hard
on themselves because they believe that they have committed unforgiv-
able sins in the past. For such avoidants to err is inhuman, and to forgive
themselves completely out of the question. If they are shy it is because
they feel that they don't deserve to meet anyone, and if they are commitment phobic or otherwise reject others it is because they wish to spare
others the pain and perils of having to relate to someone as unworthy as
they believe themselves to be.

Obsessional Thinking (Constant Worry)

Some obsessional avoidants are overly worried about the possible negative outcome of what they say and do. As a result they become overcau-
tious to the point that they appear remote, uninterested, and withdrawn.
Other obsessional avoidants are so perfectionistic that they discard any
relationship because of minor flaws, pulling back from social interactions
just because the other person merely makes a single, insignificant, social
blunder.

INTERPERSONAL CAUSES

Interpersonal Dynamics in Children

The *DSM-III-R* (1989) described a syndrome "Avoidant Disorder of Childhood and Adolescence" characterized by interpersonal anxiety manifest in a "desire for social involvement with familiar people, such as peers the person knows well and family members" (p. 61) associated with "an excessive shrinking from contact with unfamiliar people" (p. 61). The child "is likely to appear socially withdrawn, embarrassed, and timid when in the company of unfamiliar people and will become anxious when even a trivial demand is made to interact with strangers" (p. 61) and may even become "inarticulate or mute" (p. 61). For example, a 10 year old has no friends of the same age. Her only contacts are with her parents and their adult friends. She never leaves her parent's side partly because the mother never lets her out of her sight; partly because she is unable to go more than a few feet from home because she fears loud street noises, being stung by bees, riding on public transportation (she fears she will drown when the train she is on crosses a bridge and falls off the tracks into the water), and strangers. (Her preoccupation with details—she is able to list 256 species of dogs as well as all the birds ever found in Colorado—suggests that she might be suffering from avoidance associated with Asperger's Syndrome.)

Along similar lines Kagan, as Ruth Galvin (1992) notes, believes avoidance in children is due to high levels of agitation and irritability in response to the unfamiliar (p. 43), a problem that I call "neophobia." Such children remain quiet in unfamiliar situations and, though externally calm, have a "higher secretion of cortisol (a stress-related hormone)" (p. 43) and a higher heart rate. They "begin to date [only] in late adolescence; [are] likely to marry later than most; [are] likely to take a job involving minimal uncertainty (e.g., bureaucratic); [and are] at risk for panic disorder and agoraphobia in adulthood [because they are ever] concerned with doing the 'right thing,' and not violating standards [having developed a sensitivity] to reprimand" (p. 43).

Interpersonal Dynamics in Adults

The Dynamics of Shyness

Shyness, and the withdrawal associated with shyness, is an active, dynamic, not a passive, static, condition. That is, so often shyness is what Millon and Davis (1996) call an active detachment (p. 253). It is an active defense deliberately and purposively (if unconsciously) installed to deal with anxiety. Four causes of shyness are the following:

1. *Social Anxiety.* Shyness is the chief manifestation of social anxiety.

Sullivan (1953) describes the dynamics of social anxiety, and therefore of shyness, as follows:

Fleeting movements of anxiety . . . are the telltales which . . . mark the point in the course of events at which something disjunctive, something that tends to pull away from the other fellow, has first appeared or has suddenly increased. They signal a change from relatively uncomplicated movement toward a presumptively common goal to a protecting of one's self-esteem, with a definite *complicating* of the interpersonal action. . . . Anxiety appears . . . in the experience of some *complex* "emotions" into which it has been elaborated by specific early training. . . . embarrassment, shame, humiliation, guilt, and chagrin. The circumstances under which these unpleasant "emotions" occur [need to be] observe[d] accurately and . . . subject to the retrospective analysis which is apt to be most rewarding (pp. 378–379).

2. Neophobia.   Shy Type I avoidants are mainly neophobes who have difficulty initiating personal/romantic relationships. In this they differ from Type II mingles avoidants who are neophiles who desire new relationships and initiate them easily, only to have difficulty keeping them afloat. Shy avoidants who fear new contacts have difficulty saying hello to neighbors they pass on the street or meet in the elevator as well as difficulty participating in such group activities as the high-school prom or a friend's birthday party. While some shy avoidants keep on trying to relate, other shy avoidants are either close to giving up on, or have actually given up on, looking for new relationships. Of the latter group some have retreated to living alone, while others have retreated to living with their parents and possibly with other equally avoidant family members. At most they maintain a few distant relationships with casual friends, gay "sisters," or the like, but nothing truly intimate transpires. If they accept new people at all they often choose introverts over extroverts, just as when selecting a pet they tend to prefer cats over dogs.

3. Hostility.   Hostility is often an element in the picture of shyness. Shy people can be very cruel to those who would love them. It is both in their nature and a calculated way to avoid closeness. For example, cruelty came naturally to one avoidant, as she had a secret cache of drawings of pictures of cats being imprisoned and crucified.

4. Low self-esteem.   Shy avoidants tend to suffer from low self-esteem. They avoid relationships because they feel too unworthy to enjoy them, and because before they feel confident enough to relate at all the relationship must meet a number of impossible conditions in advance: constant and unconditional approval and the promise that the relationship will not sour.

An individual with low self-esteem put people off by making jokes on himself. He put himself down by giving himself "back-handed compliments" that were part of his plan to get others to agree that his self-esteem should be as low as it was. For example, he told the following story, consciously meant to amuse, but secretly meant to horrify. When asked on his thirtieth birthday, "How does it feel to be thirty?" he laughingly replied, "At the orgy last night I had anonymous sex with five people, and not one of them complained about my age."

Another time he bragged to his friends what a failure he was in his profession, simultaneously hoping for admiration as the teller of a good story, sympathy for his all too human foibles, and points for being modest. He told of how he started his career inauspiciously by giving "the worst advice he could possibly have given under the circumstances." He had met a stranger in a bar, and asked him, "What do you do?" The stranger proudly replied, "I write poems, and my first poem was just published." "Yeah," this budding mental health worker replied, "do that, but be sure to get a steady job, considering how often people in your field succeed." The punch line that made this a self-demeaning story was that he later discovered the man had become a successful and famous poet. Instead of bragging to friends of his first counseling triumph he was in effect putting himself down, or, as he put it, "goofing on himself," for his first counseling failure. The biggest casualty of all was his career—for instead of building a practice advising real upcoming poets how to succeed in their profession, he had to settle for a mundane, civil service counseling job. Now he had a real reason to be dissatisfied with himself, and a real reason to put himself down.

The Origin of Avoidance in Transference/Parentification

Almost all avoidant behaviors, not only shyness, but also vacillation, unpredictability, hypomanic franticness, fear of commitment, and co-dependency, are partly the result of viewing present relationships in the blinding light of troublesome relationships from the past, then living out relationships with new people as if these new people are old problematic parents, siblings, or friends. For example, as a child an avoidant was raised in the same bedroom as a senile delusional grandmother who regularly and, because of her age and status, with some authority, announced that through the window she could see "kidnappers, and I worry that they will whisk you away." Later in life he stayed away from all involvements with people who were intense, instead preferring bland, unemotional, uninvolved individuals "who instead of worrying throw confetti when disaster looms."

In the realm of the transferential basis of shyness:

One shy avoidant was shy because he was frightened by anyone reserved because he saw reserved people as his rejecting father who paid little attention to him, hardly played with him, and never took him to the movies or museums. Another shy avoidant, in some ways his opposite, was shy because she was frightened by anyone who wanted to get close to her because they reminded her of a father who demanded absolute "apron string" fidelity in return for giving her any love at all.

In the realm of the transferential basis of vacillation and other forms of ambivalence:

A son who loved his father, but was ashamed of the way his father dressed, begged the father to improve his appearance. The father was not only deaf to the son's pleas but also became even sloppier the more the son begged him to change. Later the son, still trying to make the relationship with his father come out differently, developed a series of transference relationships with sloppy men. He would at first fall in love with sloppy men in spite of (really because of) their sloppiness. Then he would fight with them over their appearance and reject them in favor of men who were neat and impeccably dressed. The latter attraction often assumed the proportion of a foot fetish, based as it was on the allure of the well-turned ankle, ending in the perfect shoe, covering the fantasied perfect foot. Sooner or later he would see these men as phonies and would return to loving the sloppy man as someone who was more earthy, sincere, and approachable.

In the realm of the transferential basis of hypomanic franticness:

A hypochondriacal father effectively castrated his son by dressing him in high-shoes to resemble those worn by polio victims, and by keeping him at home for months in quarantine so that he would not come into contact with the poliovirus. "To ice the cake," as the patient said, "to make me even more unattractive," his father forced him to wear knickers after they had gone out of style, and wool pants that itched him so intensely that he could hardly function in social situations. He recalled wearing pajamas under his pants to keep them from itching, only to be humiliated on several occasions when the pajamas spontaneously unrolled and stuck out from below his cuffs. As an adult he became an avoidant who rebelled against this early treatment by going out whenever and wherever he wanted to and doing dirty sexual things to deliberately contaminate himself, and by dressing any way he wanted to even if, or actually because, that meant appearing at professional and social occasions dressed inappropriately or offensively. (One would think he only wanted revenge against his father. Yet another motive existed, his need to please his father and to be loved by him, leading to a positive outcome in the form of a personally and socially rewarding career made out of his eccentric dress—a career as a famous, beloved, much-admired trend-setting fashion designer.)

An avoidant whose mother was distant because she was significantly and chronically depressed postpartum became a hypomanic romantic who, to act as differently from his mother as he possibly could, and to grab her attention, regularly, and with disastrous outcome, gave his love "at first sight, falling in love head over heels, in love with love."

In the realm of the transferential basis of fear of commitment:

When he was a child one avoidant's mother whipped him whenever she sensed he "felt sexual." She meted out a particularly intense whipping when she caught him "playing doctor" with a neighbor's little girl. After the beating he "ran away from home" to a neighbor's apartment only to be beaten again, this time for disappearing. Later in life he avoided getting close to people who stirred up strong sexual feelings, so that he was able to form either close platonic or distant sexual relationships, but unable to combine the two. As a result he became a "big city person," a Type II avoidant with multiple but partial and transient romantic relationships who obtained a large portion of his interpersonal gratification symbolically—from being a sophisticate who "lived in the big city where I feel I belong because it is where it's at, that cosmopolitan place that anyone would give his right arm to live in—look at the crowds and all the activity that surrounds me." He associated with equally avoidant companions who exchanged not affection or love but clever repartee rife with the latest gossip, sophisticated badinage, clever puns, and withering humor. His lifestyle was deliberately created to allow him to get somewhat close while simultaneously reassuring himself that he wasn't going so far that he would be beaten again. As he put it, "I love being surrounded by crowds of clever strangers. I feel as if I'm on the inside, but not so inside that I feel overwhelmed, crushed, or punished."

There are two caveats in studying transference. First, transference must be distinguished from coincidence. Therapists should recognize that because humans can behave in only a few really different ways, everyone in the present is in some respects likely to remind of someone from the past. Second, even when transference is a significant factor in a given relationship, therapists should be practical when intervening and weigh the concern that a patient might marry a parent figure against the concern that the patient might, to avoid any semblance of being married to a parent figure, never marry at all, staying single and lonely merely for theoretical reasons.

Therapists must also remember that early positive as well as negative experiences can create avoidant transferences later in life. For one patient home was so pleasant that she never wanted to leave it. She became an avoidant not because she feared strangers but because she loved being at home with her family and hoped to stay there for the rest of her life.

SOCIAL CAUSES

Peers, teachers, entertainers, religious leaders, and the media often encourage avoidance by word and/or deed. Examples include the Beatles' exhortation to not trust anyone over 30; religious damnation for positive/sexual feelings; and avoidant philosophies including philosophies of Zen withdrawal aimed at reducing personal anxiety by removing oneself from others, philosophies that advocate maintaining a gay identity though this identity is one composed primarily of outrageousness and promiscuity, and psychotherapeutic do-your-own-thing philosophies that overstress the importance of freedom, independence, and individuality while con-

demning any degree of submission and deindividuation, even that necessary to form close loving relationships.

BIOLOGICAL CAUSES

Humans can be rather like animals in their avoidances. Even in such of
our everyday expressions as "badgering," "weaseling," "outfoxing," and
"hogging," we are reminded of the animal origins of some of the most
off-putting of human behaviors. We all have primitive "animal" avoidances such as our reflexive fear of mice and harmless snakes, our super-
stitions of black cats crossing our path, our tendency to curl up in the fetal
position when we feel overwhelmed or depressed, and, what is perhaps
the ultimate biological avoidance of all, our fainting "dead away" in fright
or disgust. Some avoidants in their behavior remind us of a stray cat who,
however hungry it may be, thinks twice before accepting a handout; and
some of a raccoon who strikes a compromise with humans—not bothering
them as long as they don't bother it. Others remind us of dogs—pups
who, thinking only of themselves, push others aside to get to an available
teat; adult dogs who protectively roll over to beg for mercy, playing dead
to retain life, or who retreat to a lair for safety, protection, and territorial
advantage in anticipation of a fight they prefer to avoid; and older dogs
who when ill or about to die remain transfixed within and become remote,
perhaps to anticipate death so that they can deny they love life.

A patient with PTSD saw himself and his prolonged, insatiable grief for his lost
buddies in his cat who after having lost her lifetime companion, another cat, became inconsolable, howling all night, uncomprehending.

An ambivalent avoidant who compulsively left green grass for greener compared
himself to each of his two cats who predictably and perversely wanted the other
cat's food, even when the foods were switched. When living in a small town he
wanted to move to a big city, but when living in a big city he wanted to move to
a small town—never satisfied, constantly changing places and partners, finally
keeping a country and a town house just to be able whenever closeness threatens
to shift from one to the other.

A patient whose social phobia took the form of shame over having to ask for the
location of the men's room and being seen going there compared his behavior to
that of his cat who buried her excreta in her litter "to throw predators off the
scent."

An avoidant with multiple social phobias compared himself to his former cocker spaniel who many years ago (when blimps were plentiful in the skies) developed a fear of blimps and had to scan the heavens for one before venturing out of doors—he speculated as a displacement from a fear of airborne predators. In her inability to walk near large objects like trash bins, he saw his own agoraphobia, and in her fear of walking over grates he saw his own fear of being at the edge of a dangerously high cliff, in danger of falling, about to become nothing.

PART II

Therapy

CHAPTER 13

An Overview of Avoidance Reduction

In the following chapters (Chapters 13–20), I describe a treatment approach to AvPD I call avoidance reduction, a technique dedicated to and focused on handling the causes and consequences of distancing. Avoidance reduction is primarily applicable to, and potentially helpful for, all types of avoidants, I–IV. Almost any avoidant who is motivated can benefit, even those avoidants with such seemingly immutable problems as looks that are less than ideal (in many couples one member of a dyad is better looking than the other); little money (as many poor as rich people have relationships and get married); and severe personality problems (some potential partners prefer people with emotional difficulties because they view them as less bland and ordinary than people without them). It is also applicable to and potentially helpful for patients whose avoidant symptoms are the product of another primary disorder, for example, patients who are withdrawn because they are *depressed*; patients who are overrelated in a way that assures that no real intimacy will occur because they are *hypomanic*; patients who are living in the past as a way to renounce the present because they are suffering from *pathological grief*; patients who are worrisome and have off-putting social rituals because they are *obsessive-compulsive*; patients whose relationships in the here-and-now suffer because due to their *Posttraumatic Stress Disorder* every new relationship reminds them of an old, traumatic, prior interpersonal contact; patients who think only of themselves because they suffer from a *Narcissistic Personality Disorder*; patients who as *bisexuals* reject one sex for another; and patients who as *paraphiliacs* shock and appall onlookers by exhibiting themselves or rubbing in public places.

A *hypomanic*, frantically gregarious single woman had difficulty both in meeting people and in making what relationships she developed last. She ran around in ever-widening but less meaningful circles, like those that come from a rock dropped into a pool, progressively covering more and more territory while each time making a less and less effective statement. Her life deteriorated into swinging like a pendulum from the two-bedroom apartment with the unloving roommates to the lonely studio apartment with the loving cat, then back again; placing personals ads that were geared to fail because they were too hostile to be consonant with their stated purpose; and frantically cruising singles bars, functions, and resorts, drinking heavily to the point that she got too drunk to function effectively.

An *obsessive-compulsive* avoidant deliberately gummed himself up by his rituals so that he couldn't make it out the door to social events. That his rituals were at least partly avoidant in intent became clear from a piece of notepaper he showed his therapist. On one side, under the heading "Things to do today" was a line drawing of people participating in an orgy; while on the other side, under the same heading, was a list of paralyzing rituals, also to be performed today, that would clearly keep him from ever leaving the house to attend an orgy, or anything else of a social nature.

A patient suffering from excessively prolonged *grief* following the death of her lover was grieving less because she was unable to let go of the lost relationship and more to deliberately fill herself with resentful disappointment in a world she needed to view as completely undesirable because it was missing one of its parts. Her goal was to retreat into ghost-like hallucinatory fantasy about her lost lover in order to make all new relationships a casualty of resurrecting the old. Instead of accepting things as they were today, and the world for what it could still offer her, and instead of becoming more of a sport, and making the best of what she had left, she chose to blame the world for its imperfections and horrors, to cry about what she could not change, and to attack God for her fate. In effect she was having spoiled-child temper tantrums, demanding sympathy and coddling so that she could test the patience of others, doing so to deliberately (if unconsciously) isolate herself so that the world would soon in fact exclude her, to the point that she would have a real reason to be resentful, and now a perfectly rational reason to continue to grieve.

Examples of avoidant behaviors that are a product of other *DSM-IV* disorders were given in Chapter 9. A full discussion of primarily non-AvPD patients who present with avoidant symptoms was offered in Chapters 9–11.

CHARACTERISTICS

In the following section I cite four main characteristics of avoidance reduction. Avoidance reduction is as follows.

An Action-Oriented Approach

Avoidance-reduction recognizes that action is the opposite of avoidance. Therefore, avoidance-reduction emphasizes doing as much as thinking. It asks patients to muster enough faith in therapy and the therapist to try living around their withdrawal, and to do so sooner rather than later, and even before they have fully mastered their need to distance.

An Eclectic Approach

Avoidance reduction borrows its methods from the various time-tested schools of psychotherapy in prominence today including psychoanalytic/psychodynamic, cognitive-behavioral, interpersonal, and supportive approaches. By way of an overview that anticipates the fuller material in Chapters 14–20, using an eclectic approach the therapist might, depending on the patient's specific problems and life circumstances, the amount of time and money available for therapy, and the therapist's training, theoretical orientation, and personality, use an admixture of the following approaches.

Psychoanalytic/Psychodynamic Approach

Therapists using this approach focus on understanding avoidance through and through. Therapists attempt to understand here-and-now avoidance by observing it from a historical perspective. They go back over the patient's life to assess how the patient became avoidant, in order to help him or her spot the early sources of damage and make corrections post hoc. A focus might be the contribution of early family interactions to latter-day avoidance. For example, a source of one avoidant's present-day shyness due to guilt about relating was found in her history of excessive closeness to a mother who discouraged her from getting involved with men by telling her that it was unthinkable for her to marry a stranger. A source of another avoidant's present-day shyness due to fear of humiliation was found in her early relationship with her father, a man who never paid her a compliment, no matter how well she did and how much she accomplished. Therapists also attempt to understand avoidance by exploring in depth the patient's here-and-now associations and fantasies, and by identifying and understanding avoidant transference to the therapist, especially the transference resistances patients bring to and develop in the course of treatment. (Transference resistances are discussed further below.)

Therapists also attempt to reveal how a patient's avoidant behaviors are a defense against the anxiety elicited by forbidden sexual and hostile impulses stirred up by relationships. They then help the patient integrate his or her impulses in a healthier way—by becoming less defensive, or, if still defensive, by using healthier defenses, for example, sublimation instead of projection. Finally, therapists using this approach also treat behaviorally. They invoke the phobic parameter, telling patients that to get over their phobia they have to do more than just understand it. They also have to do things that make them more anxious, then bring the aroused thoughts and fears back into therapy for further analysis and integration.

Cognitive-Behavioral Approach

Therapists using this approach correct avoidant thought *process* disorder such as the need to think in terms of some equals all, thereby making minor relationship problems major ("we can't get along *at all* because she eats dinner at 6, and I eat dinner at 10"; "I *can't stand any* man with a mustache—it makes my face all itchy") and avoidant thought *content* disorder such as the belief that "all birds in the bush are better than all birds in the hand" making the patient into a neophiliac who, constantly dissatisfied with old comfortable relationships, compulsively seeks new ones. They particularly focus on exposing and correcting the illogical thoughts that lead patients to distance themselves from relationships due to excessive fears of being criticized, humiliated, and rejected. They reframe negative cognitions such as "Because he criticizes me for this one thing means he hates me completely" into more positive cognitions such as "Her basic feelings about me can still be loving even though she doesn't like how I dress, and says so," or "The person I called at work put me on hold not because she was rejecting me but because she was just momentarily busy." After asking patients to reality-test their fearful interpersonal thoughts by following the rules of evidence, cognitive-behavioral therapists use total-push (exposure) behavioral techniques, asking patients to do what makes them afraid in small, incremental steps as a way to slowly but surely reduce anxiety and enhance motivation. They also directly encourage/cajole the patient to act less avoidant, even to go to nonavoidant extremes, becoming counterphobic as a way to deal with their fear of interpersonal relationships the same way some people become parachute jumpers to deal with their fear of heights.

Interpersonal Approach

Therapists using this approach study the dyadic manifestations of avoidance with a view to resolving distorted interpersonal perceptions that contribute to the here-and-now interpersonal problems that keep the avoidant from getting close and developing anxiety-free intimate relationships. In particular, they focus on a patient's fears of humiliation, criticism and rejection at the hands of others, on the low self-esteem that makes it difficult for the patient to confidently relate to other people, and on the quintessentially borderline belief that serious closeness means complete loss of identity.

Supportive Approach

Therapists using this approach employ exhortation ("I know you can do it"); positive feedback ("you are too good to fail," "that's great that you have succeeded," "your low self-esteem is lower than by rights it should be"); and reassurance ("you can handle and overcome your anxiety"). Simultaneously they give fatherly/motherly advice ("there are other places where you will be happier/more welcome/more popular than in the suburbs.") They do these things under the aegis of a comfortable therapeutic holding environment that serves as a protective bubble for the patient attempting to venture forth into new, anxiety-provoking, interpersonal adventures. As the therapist supports the patient in his or her difficult internal struggles with avoidance, he or she advises the patient to seek additional support from others who are in a position to help the patient become less avoidant—such as secret sharers, counselors, friends, family members, and lovers who can hopefully act as enablers to help the patient deal more effectively with his or her disenablers and even egg the patient on to nonavoidance. Finally, supportive therapists also use relaxation techniques like teaching the patient to breathe more slowly; meditation; and, when indicated, pharmacotherapy.

Existential Therapy Approach

Therapists using this approach reshape the patient's existential philosophy of life by helping him or her rethink favored avoidant positions and goals. Patients can learn a new more nonavoidant philosophy of life directly by identifying with others, including a therapist whose beliefs and ways are less avoidant. For example, patients can make a list of and emulate people they admire for their social prowess. Or they can read self-help books whose authors take valid nonavoidant positions, such as "be flexible about type" and "don't compare yourself to others."

Family Therapy Approach

Therapists using this approach see most or all of the family in therapy. Their goal is to resolve interfamily conflicts that interfere with outside relationships. For example, they might try to convince a smothering family to let go and stop infantilizing the avoidant.

Pharmacotherapeutic Approach

Psychiatrists often recommend the use of anxiolytic/antidepressant drug therapy to reduce anxiety and depression.

My inspiration for the eclectic approach derives from at least four sources: (1) Millon and Davis's (1996) multitasking therapy described in detail in Chapter 2; (2) Benjamin's (1996) practical reconstructive learning therapy that draws from a wide range of available therapies, "from . . . techniques of psychoanalysis, experiential therapy, family therapy, group therapy, drama therapy, educational therapy, behavior therapy, gestalt therapy, and others [that] are appropriate [with] *anything* that leads to one of the five correct categories (enhances collaboration, facilitates learning about patterns, mobilizes the will, blocks maladaptive patterns, and/or teaches new patterns) . . . legitimate" (p. 110); (3) Pinsker's (1997) "supportive-expressive psychotherapy" (p. 2), where the therapist combines supportive and psychodynamic approaches in order to provide the patient with a comforting holding environment while helping him or her resolve specific intrapsychic conflicts (p. 2); and (4) Oldham and Morris's (1995) psychodynamic psychotherapy, which they define as a method that "is based on many of the . . . principles of psychoanalysis, but . . . offer[s] a variety of techniques from support to medication" (p. 405).

The following cases illustrate the use of combined approaches whose therapeutic synergy had an enhanced healing impact.

A patient with social anxiety obtained the most benefit not from cognitive-behavioral therapy alone but from cognitive-behavioral therapy combined with an opportunity to learn about the past, internal, interpersonal, and existential dimensions of her avoidance. She refused to see her lover again because she thought he hated her just because he said that before making the next date with her he had to check his schedule book. However, just correcting the cognitive error that "I will get back to you" equals "I have rejected you" did not free her up enough to feel comfortable making another date with him. Making that correction sink in and stick required taking the next step: tracing the origin of her feeling rejected back to her relationship with her father, a man who, unable to commit himself in advance to a specific day for doing things together, regularly told her when she asked him, "When can I see you again?" that "I will get back to you on that," then did not firm anything up for days, weeks, or sometimes even months.

A shy avoidant learned that she was a remote, formal, rigid, and inhibited adult because she feared acting on her positive impulses without first getting parental approval and because she feared losing control of her instincts in the heat of passion, then saying and doing things that she would be ashamed of—painfully so, because what other people thought of her, that is, her reputation, had become more important to her than what she thought of herself, and ultimately even more important to her than her personal growth and happiness. After challenging the incorrect notions that people frowned upon the friendly woman, that closeness meant losing control, and that what others thought of you was more important that what you thought of yourself, we traced her excessive need for approval back to her parents' warning that people looked down on a woman who was outgoing as being loose—a warning her parents issued to keep her at home so that she would take care of them.

She responded to this new understanding by entering a session wearing a T-shirt whose logo was, "99% devil, 1% angel," her way to tell me and the world that she had finally begun to break free from her inhibitions, particularly her need to obtain parental approval before allowing herself to acknowledge her own feelings and to do things on her own. Her next thoughts (really associations) were about the supposed lack of great women composers these days. In an outpouring that was as much about herself as it was about the topic of which she spoke, she speculated that because Fannie Mendelssohn was a woman she, unlike her brother, Felix, rarely had her works performed. Without performance she had no opportunity for the creative inspiration that comes from the positive feedback of applause. As a result, her music became progressively less and less inspired, more and more tentative and withdrawn, and eventually even deserving of the rejection it at first got only undeservedly. Next she told me that she finally decided that in her own life she would become less dependent on what others thought of her and brave the inevitable criticisms and rejections that everyone gets in life. As she put it, "I am going to become a new Fannie Mendelssohn, a person who, if she couldn't change the world, would at least not let it get to and defeat her." Now, convinced of her value no matter what others thought about, said, or did to her, she was able, with my continuing support and encouragement, to try connecting with men without giving up easily and fleeing if she did not succeed immediately and the first time around.

An Approach with Distinct Social Benefits

Because social avoidances are the product of individual avoidances, treatment of the individual avoidant is apt to bring about positive social change, especially when the individual avoidant holds an influential position as teacher, writer, psychotherapist, or parent. A society made up of fewer avoidants might reward being lovable and related as much as it rewards being moneyed, powerful and smart; give as many accolades to the homemaker and lifetime companion as to the company president, full professor, senator, and bishop; and be more supportive of its well-meaning citizens, however imperfect, ranging from single mothers who need not condescension and hatred for having brought their troubles down on themselves but tolerance and support in the difficult job that lies ahead, to the President of the United States who is doing the best job he can running the country under difficult circumstances and with over 250 million people in ambivalent transference to him.

An Approach That Can Be Adapted for Self-help

Because avoidance reduction can to an extent be self-administered and practiced daily using the intersession homework strategies of cognitive-behavioral therapy, a little therapeutic time can go a long way.

There are some caveats to guide therapists using avoidance reduction. The focus of therapy must remain almost entirely on avoidance. Patients should not be allowed to change the subject, and, on their part, their therapists should hear everything, or almost everything, the patient says as a comment on the present state, or state of disarray, of the patient's relationships. Avoidance reduction should not be used by itself for patients who are suffering primarily from such serious comorbid disorders as schizophrenia or depression and who require specific interventions such as high-dose pharmacotherapy in a hospital. Avoidance reduction is a long-term, not a short-term, therapeutic approach, for nonavoidance and cannot be easily achieved without practice until the nonavoidance becomes automatic and ingrained enough to prevent the patient from slipping back into his or her usual avoidant ways. When therapy is terminated it should be terminated gradually, not precipitously. To avoid seeming to reject the patient, whenever possible avoidant patients who are in long-term therapy should have their sessions tapered over a period of a least a few months, told that they are welcome to return for further therapy should problems arise again, and asked to do so before their problems become serious or irreversible.

TECHNICAL CONSIDERATIONS

Selecting/Combining the Different Approaches

In this section I suggest ways therapists can combine different, even seemingly antithetical, therapeutic approaches into an integrated whole, one in which the disparate techniques of avoidance reduction are united in a holistic approach whose overall therapeutic impact is greater than the sum of the therapeutic impact of its individual parts.

Not all patients should be treated with exactly the same admixture of therapeutic approaches. Different patients will need, desire, welcome, and respond to different therapeutic plans composed of different selections from the menu of available therapeutic modalities. The specific plan chosen will be determined by an individual's diagnosis, specific personality type, preference for intellectual versus practical approaches, current circumstances and needs, personal aspirations, and personal ambition. In the realm of the patient's diagnosis, social phobic avoidants with a fear of public speaking may benefit the most from exposure techniques combined with emotional support as they venture forth trying to overcome their all-the-world's-a-stage fright. However, since social phobics tend to retain relationships with significant others they will likely need less hand holding than AvPD avoidants, who are more likely to be isolated, alone, and lonely. Commitment-phobic avoidants with long-standing deeply ingrained interpersonal anxiety about becoming intimate often need a combination of psychodynamic, cognitive-behavioral and interpersonal therapy with a therapist who additionally acts as a transitional object patients can cling to as they roll over from the isolative to the interactive position.

In the realm of the patient's personality type, some patients are too organized, concrete, or inflexible to feel comfortable attempting more than one approach at a time. Others are more flexible. They are more willing to accept that there are real intellectual and practical difficulties associated with integrating diverse therapeutic approaches, such as the difficulty involved in being supportively noncritical and definitively corrective at the same time. In the realm of the patient's preference for intellectual versus practical approaches, more intellectually oriented and insightful patients tend to want, and benefit from, therapy that emphasizes understanding through insight. They want to learn all they can about themselves before venturing forth. They willingly, even eagerly, analyze their transference to their therapists and use the results of this analysis to highlight and resolve their conflicts. In contrast, more practically minded patients, who are often simultaneously less introspective and more outgoing, tend to want, and benefit the most from, the more manipulative behavioral approaches. While the first group does well being told, "Face your fears of cocktail parties so that we can analyze those fears as they arise," the second group does well being told, "Go to parties for progressively longer periods of time in graduated 'doses' so that you will be able to get used to mingling, slowly but surely." The first group of patients likes to contemplate a journey before during and after embarking on it. The second group of patients is satisfied just to be handed a road map.

With regard to current circumstances and needs, patients who have moved from a small town to the Big City and live alone without family close by, or patients who have many distant but few close friends, may benefit from having the therapist act as a substitute for absent relationships, tiding the patient over until he or she can develop his or her own contacts. In contrast, patients who still live in their hometown, near old friends and family, may not need such replacement therapy. This frees the therapist up from handholding and allows him or her to go to the heart of matters correctively. Of course, practical issues count in the selection of therapeutic approaches, too, such as the amount of time and money available for treatment.

In the realm of the patient's aspirations, avoidant patients who wish to resolve their characterological problems definitively may require long-term insight therapy, while avoidant patients who only want to settle an acute crisis—as might be the case when a patient is currently grieving over a relationship he or she has lost—may only need limited or short-term treatment. Individual treatment might be the preferred modality when the patient is looking for a new committed relationship or attempting to extricate him or herself from codependency, while marital therapy might be indicated when the patient is in, and desires to save, a marriage that is not going well.

In the realm of personal ambition, patients have a choice between accepting essentially complete avoidance, and achieving either partial avoidance or nonavoidance. Patients who select *accepting essentially complete avoidance* are assisted in their pursuit of a lifetime of comfortable avoidance. The patient is allowed, or even encouraged, to keep an isolated job, and permitted his or her solitary obsessions and compulsions, hobbies used to escape, and/or relationships with pets instead of with people.

Patients who select *partial avoidance* are helped to work around rather than attempt to fully overcome their anxiety. Just as patients afraid of being trapped in the theatre can simply sit on the aisle in the back; patients afraid of heights who cannot sit in the theatre balcony can simply buy a comfortable seat in the orchestra; and pornophobic patients who dislike watching sex in the movies can just stay home and watch movies edited for television; patients with a social phobia can take a job where public speaking is unnecessary, and patients with AvPD can seek partial rather than full relationships, such as:

- Relationships with good gang members such as homosexual "sisters." Good gangs offer mutual support without requiring that the individual members of the group sacrifice their autonomy in exchange. They do not infantilize their individual members by encouraging them to avoid people outside of the gang, as do minigangs of summer-share singles who cruise en masse purportedly to meet new people but actually to ridicule and humiliate them so that the group stays intact, or as do capture cults that kidnap their members emotionally, and sometimes physically as well.

- Relationships with paid strangers. Here hairdressers or therapists substitute for lovers, or therapeutic support groups substitute for social gatherings. The best I could do with an extremely avoidant patient was to help him smooth over his fears that he had completely ruined himself with his realtor, accountant, stockbroker, and the waiters at the restaurant where he took his nightly meals. Eventually he told me that he felt happy and fulfilled, was having the best years of his life, and wanted to stop therapy since "with so many friends, who needs a psychiatrist?"

- Relationships with people organized mainly around and subsidiary to impersonal gratifications. Here things become as, or more, important than people, with the relationship partially sacrificed to the accoutrements of that relationship. People do remain in the picture, but play a subsidiary role, one that supports the interest. An example is decorating one's home and improving one's stereo equipment when people are invited into the home to admire the furnishings and the equipment—allowed to enter but not allowed to sit on the sofa, or touch the dials.

- Codependent relationships. Codependent avoidants are Type IV partial avoidants who distance themselves from one large slice of life by becoming resolutely
nonavoidant in another. Type IV partial avoidance is to be distinguished from
healthy avoidance where the patient relinquishes secondary relationships so
that an important primary relationship can survive and prosper—distancing
themselves from a less meaningful slice of life in order to achieve a greater
involvement in another, more important, one, as in the following examples:

For one homosexual couple the advice to get out and actively socialize with as
many peers as possible was less helpful than the advice to avoid social situations
where there was undesirable pressure, as they themselves complained, "to keep
up with others who buy the latest and most expensive trinkets, have extramarital
affairs to expand their horizons (ultimately not their horizons but their avoidance
of each other), and to go to gay movie festivals that in our opinion are merely
pornofests by another lofty name."

A physician took every opportunity to advise a colleague that a patient they
shared hated him. He would sidle up and whisper in his ear, "You know what
Mr. X said yesterday about you—he said he hates you because . . ." The colleague
found that he was beginning to take this personally. Requests to the physician to
stop went unheeded. The colleague came home upset each night because he felt
constantly put down, and with reason. The therapist did not advise his patient,
the physician's colleague, to try to find ways to get along with this disagreeable
person. Instead he told him to just stay away from him. The patient protested,
"But we have to work together." Keeping in mind the considerable pressure this
particular patient was under, the therapist decided that the most therapeutic response was, "Yes, but you also have to restore your self-esteem, and the only way
to do that is to avoid him. Stay out of his way, and even, when you see him coming,
duck into a convenient corridor, to hide, to escape." And the therapist added
reassuringly, "You don't have to get along with everybody you work with."

Finally, if *nonavoidance* is selected, the goal becomes finding and keeping
good friends and one significant other in a close, committed, ongoing
relationship without game-playing or sadomasochistic posturing.

Diverse approaches that at first appear to be mutually inconsistent, or
even mutually exclusive, can still be used together effectively, either alternatively or simultaneously, for several reasons. First, most symptoms
can and possibly should be treated both directly (symptomatically, in effect patching things up) and indirectly (analytically, by getting to the bottom of things). A familiar example involves triumphing over fear by
simultaneously facing it down and understanding it. Second, ordinary
day-to-day changes in anxiety levels or life's circumstances make support
more appropriate one session, insight more appropriate another. Third,

the complex layered personality of the avoidant tends to require, and respond to, different therapeutic approaches. For example, in one avoidant the depressive core responded well to supportive handholding while the worrisome obsessional core, and with it the panicky preoccupation with minor matters, responded better to a combination of insight-oriented psychotherapy and cognitive therapy.

Therapists and patients often ask: "When using more than one approach, which one should be tried first? And what should be the order in which subsequent approaches are applied?" Therapists want and often need a game plan so that they know how to proceed. Patients want and often need an agenda because they tend to get confused when they are offered too many different therapeutic suggestions all at once. They don't know what to do first, how long to keep at it before they move on to something else, and just how selective to be in what approaches they try. Here is how I might proceed:

In the beginning of therapy when many avoidants are very anxious or depressed about their lives, I offer support and sometimes pharmacotherapy. Both together can be especially useful for avoidants who have experienced one or a series of losses. I reserve uncovering approaches for later when the patient's realistic difficulties are fewer, or less urgent, so that what suffering there is is primarily of an existential nature, not "What do I do to survive?" but "How can I look at things differently so that I can feel more alive and joyful?"

Very early in therapy I take a thorough history and do a complete mental status examination. In the mental status examination I make certain to assess the level of the patient's insight to establish consensus about what is wrong so that together we can make it right. Does the patient consider his or her avoidance to be not a problem to be solved but a character flaw to be ashamed of? As a general principle, effective therapy requires that patients accept that they are avoidant, not hide their avoidance from themselves, others, and the therapist.

Next I affirm a basic rule: the focus throughout therapy will be on avoidance as it occurs in both the patient's personal and professional lives. I then explain my eclectic approach and its benefits. I outline its components and then let the patient help me decide which to try first. The one we start out with is the one that in the beginning the patient finds most comfortable. The others we postpone. As a practical matter, if the patient's past is emotionally and physically traumatic, I hold off serious exploration of his or her developmental history until the patient feels up to it. As we go along, I check for possible negative reactions to what we are doing. Does the patient see our going back into the past as a waste of time, or as a diversion from dealing with what bothers him or her now? Does the patient view cognitive correction as criticism, as if challenging his or her thinking is the same thing as being critical of him or her for thinking that way?

Generally I identify and correct cognitive errors first and attempt to understand them developmentally and dynamically next.

An avoidant threatened by closeness worried less about what other people thought of him after asking himself, "What's the worst that can happen if I am rejected?" and after discounting his catastrophic thinking by answering his own question as follows: "I will simply have to go on to the next person." But still his fear of being rejected persisted, making intimacy impossible. We next worked on understanding the origin of his fear of rejection, how in his case it came from a no longer relevant preoccupation with his mother's inattentiveness to him (due to her preoccupation with herself) when he was a child. This understanding helped his "So what if I am rejected" mantra hit home, stick, and translate into real behavioral change.

My sessions fall naturally into the following stepwise pattern. We develop insight one session; use the next session to develop a game plan for putting what has been learned into practice (exposure); have a session or two where we develop further insight into the anxieties aroused by the exposure, accompanied by support and reassurance such as "you can do it" and "you will not faint or die when speaking in public"; have another insight-oriented session; and so on.

I let the patient proceed at his or her own pace. However, I avoid leisurely strolls through the forest in the recognition that time is precious, money is limited, life is short, and therapeutic passivity can send the message that the therapist expects little of the patient and even lacks confidence in his or her ability to improve.

Next comes the working-through process where we cover the same ground repeatedly and in different contexts. Avoidants rarely get better the first, or even the tenth, time they learn, or try, something new. They need to hear the same counterarguments over and over, to revisit and expand on old insights until they stick, and to expose themselves repeatedly to feared situations until they have mastered the threat. This can even take months or years of repetition before results appear and can be transferred from the office to the real world.

Dealing with Resistances

Simultaneously I handle the avoidant's resistances to therapy. Most avoidants start off wanting to be helpful to the therapist and to cooperate with treatment. At first they work with the therapist in a joint endeavor meant to overcome avoidance. They plead with the therapist to tell them what to do to meet people and how to overcome their relationship anxiety. Later in treatment, however, they almost always begin to develop both negative and positive transference resistances.

Avoidants with *negative* transference resistances tend to abuse the repairman, that is, the one who has come to fix the problem. They test the therapist to the extreme. They disregard proffered advice and sometimes even disrupt viable outside relationships in order to make their therapists look defective and impotent. They seek self-understanding only to misuse it. They say, "I will change when I learn," but either they never learn so that they don't have to change, or they learn intellectually but not emotionally so that they can complain, "See, I've got insight, but it doesn't work." They typically develop repression resistances that result from the ego's attempts to ward off threatening impulses by keeping them out of awareness. As Roger A. MacKinnon and Robert Michels (1971) suggest, "the same repression that is basic to all symptom formation continues to operate during the interview. This keeps the patient from developing awareness of the conflict which underlies his illness" (p. 16). Laboring under a poor self-concept, feeling guilty about, or fearful of, criticism for their thoughts and feelings, and worrying about whether or not the therapist approves of what they say or do, they become overly cautious and hesitate to discuss things openly with the therapist. Afraid of closeness, they begin to distance themselves from the therapist by being negative about therapy and to the therapist him or herself. Coming to see the therapist as a parent, they refuse to "get married because mother wants me to," thus turning an opportunity to grow into just another opportunity to rebel. One person speaks for how most avoidant patients treat the therapist as a parent substitute when she says in Ginia Bellafante's (2002) article, "I won't just say yes to any blind date tossed in front of me . . . [my] mother will always say, 'Oh, you never know,' but you know what, I do know, and I don't want to bother with just anybody."

Avoidants with *positive* transference resistances often use the therapist as a substitute for outside relationships, turning the therapeutic encounter into a nontherapeutic Type IV avoidant codependent relationship.

I deal with resistances in two ways. First I deal with them on a conscious level. I advise avoidants to not make their therapy a victim of "Because I have an avoidant problem I can't get help with my avoidant problem," that is, I advise them not to use therapy as just another opportunity to become avoidant. I attempt to undercut resistances directly by pointing out that "I am not a controlling parent, a rival sibling, or an enemy from the past reincarnated on earth to control, defeat, reject, or abandon you." I remind the patient that viewing me in that distortive light undermines the work we need to do. I also remind them that we are both in this together, and suggest that as much as possible they work with me towards our common goal, not against me toward just another avoidant relationship. I note that since avoidance may be the last symptom to go, for now, as I put it, you need to "swim or sink." In effect I ask them to get out on the road before waiting for too thorough an overhaul, beginning their journey to health even though their tires still need a little retreading.

Second, I deal with resistances on an unconscious level. I view them as repetitions of avoidant difficulties now occurring with the therapist, analyze them as I would any other manifestation of avoidance, and subject them to the same avoidance reduction techniques as I would any other parallel manifestation.

The Quality Assurance Project (1991) speaks of a generic curative to patient resistance, noting the importance of mitigating "fear and difficulty with trust" (p. 410) in a therapeutic "atmosphere of sensitive understanding and acceptance in which the patient can learn to modulate his anxiety and express those aspects of his experience which have hitherto been blocked" (p. 410). However, as the authors admit, especially when lack of motivation due to despair becomes resistance, "reassurance, statements about the value of therapy, [and] promises of relief from lifelong isolation, will generally be of no avail" (p. 410).

As a caveat, the therapist must distinguish the patient who is resistant from the therapist whose therapy is deficient. For example, some therapists start therapy without laying down the ground rules and telling the patient how to proceed. Then when the patient doesn't know what to do, and flounders, the therapist unfairly labels the patient as stubborn and uncooperative.

CHAPTER 14

Psychodynamically Oriented Psychotherapy

CLINICAL CONSIDERATIONS

As first mentioned in Chapter 2, according to the The Quality Assurance Project (1991), "Individual psychoanalytically oriented psychotherapy is the treatment of choice for [Avoidant Personality] disorder" (p. 405). In this form of treatment the therapist does the following.

Establishes Patterns

As Pinsker (1997) notes, psychodynamically oriented psychotherapists "understand relationships or patterns of behavior and thinking" (p. 2). As Benjamin (1996) notes, these therapists establish insight into "patterns" (p. 282) without "blaming" (p. 282). As Oldham and Morris (1995) note, the goal of insight therapy is "replac[ing] immature patterns with adaptive, fulfilling, mature styles of functioning that will enable [avoidants] to get more out of their lives" (p. 404). Two patterns therapists might be especially alert to in avoidants are: withdrawal due to a fear of outside criticism and as a way to cope with guilt over one's romantic and hostile feelings; and the tendency to attribute blame to others for one's own interpersonal problems while remaining unaware, as The Quality Assurance Project (1991) suggests, "of the key roles [one plays oneself] in perpetuating [one's] own difficulties" (p. 405).

As I emphasized in Chapter 12, avoidant patterns arise out of conflicts between an avoidant's sexual and hostile feelings and his or her ego ideal, superego, and the society in which he or she lives. These conflicts are resolved by using a number of defense mechanisms, chiefly withdrawal. Hence the psychodynamically oriented psychotherapist's goal is to identify conflicts and pathological defenses and help the avoidant resolve these conflicts in new, healthier, less avoidant ways.

Identifies Conflicts

Conflict with the Ego-Ideal

An avoidant's ego-ideal is a "psychic organ" where his or her self-standards and matters of pride reside. The prideful ideals themselves are to a great extent chosen for, not by, avoidants, making the ideals more like automatic thoughts than like true personal beliefs. Therefore, part of the process of resolving conflicts between instincts and ego-ideal consists of discovering if the ideals themselves, being chosen for, not by, the avoidant, originate in the avoidant's free will or are determined by unconscious inner forces. For example:

A patient insisted repeatedly that she wanted to be free and liberated and that to do that she would have to get rid of her dull and ordinary husband. In fact, that was not what she really wanted at all. Her so-called desires were little more than compulsive needs surfacing in the guise of true longings. Her compulsive need to be free from her husband was the product of catching him up in old persistent problems with her mother. She felt ashamed of her mother because her mother was an ordinary housewife with an ordinary husband. It was this shame that was forcing her to reject her own plebian husband so that she could be different from her mother—as she put it, "I want to be an extraordinary original who stands out from the crowd, not, like my mother, an ordinary woman married to a common drone."

In my experience, few people are alone by choice. Many avoidants who say they are truly happy with their aloneness and isolation, who say that they believe that their isolation is splendid, and who say that they are convinced of the wonders of being able to come and go as they please without that proverbial ball and chain around their ankle, really want closeness and healthy dependency, not the complete freedom they purportedly espouse. For beneath their *desire* for freedom is a compunction to be free. Many of my patients who proclaimed their avoidance to be ideal were in fact angling for sainthood due to a moral compulsion to cloister themselves in a monastery away from normal human intercourse. In effect they were clinging to the cloth to, as they saw it, avoid ending up on the blacklist.

Conflict with the Superego

A harsh rigid superego makes avoidants overly moral people who think too much about good and evil, right and wrong. As a result, they feel guilty and ashamed of their romantic feelings and overly troubled by and at odds with their anger. In response, they condemn themselves both for being loving and for being angry. Then they pull back to distance themselves from people (most people!) they believe are making them feel that way by "leading them into temptation."

Avoidants with a harsh rigid superego also feel guilty and ashamed about being successful (successophobia) and about surviving in situations where others, particularly rivals, go down to defeat (survival guilt). Now messages appear from their conscience to pass on relationships in order to avoid outshining others and gloating about it. For example, an avoidant patient believed that she should not marry until both a favorite maiden aunt and all her sisters found themselves a husband. Like many avoidants, she felt this way because she conceived of the world as a zero-sum place where getting something for herself meant taking it away from someone else.

Conflict with Society

Avoidants are typically highly attuned to and very sensitive about what others think and say to and about them. They worry a great deal about how they look to others and they care a great deal about what others think of them. Next they withdraw in order to avoid any possibility that others will pass negative judgment on them. Their motto might be, "It's better to have never loved at all than to have loved and been criticized for it."

Identifies Defenses

The avoidant conflicts between sexual and hostile feelings and such countervailing forces as pride and shame, guilt, and fear of outside criticism, take place in a theoretical part of the psyche called the ego. The ego attempts to make sense out of, and mediate between, the dissonant feelings that go into making up these conflicts. As first discussed in Chapter 12, the exact method of mediation the ego uses to manage and resolve conflict, and so to reduce anxiety, is called a defense. In turn, AvPD is the clinical manifestation of the defenses avoidants use to deal with their conflicts and to reduce the anxiety these conflicts engender. In the main, avoidants do not deny their pain like manics, project their forbidden sexual and angry feelings like paranoids (who blame others for wanting what they themselves guiltily desire), or internalize their anger like depressives (who typically take their anger at others out on themselves). Instead they use the following defenses, and use them in a pathological—that is, in an easily aroused, fixed, repetitive, and excessive—manner.

Inhibition and Withdrawal

This defense is mainly used by Type I shy avoidants. Characteristically these patients pull back and turn inaccessible, becoming remote, distant, and detached to avoid feeling anxious in social situations.

Displacement

This defense is mainly used by Type I social phobic avoidants who compartmentalize their social anxiety—in effect maintaining their interpersonal relationships by displacing their social anxiety outward, then limiting their avoidance to discrete irritants so that they can have a focused battle instead of an all-out war.

Doing and Undoing

This defense is mainly used by Type II avoidants. These avoidants are *not* social isolates: people who don't relate, or who do relate but rarely, and only when they feel it is safe to do so. These avoidants are mingles avoidants who do relate and relate a great deal—but only when they feel that there is little or no chance of relating successfully, or, if they should be successful in relating, that there is way out at the last minute. Hence, they become unreliable and unpredictable people who start relationships, then panic and pull back before things go too far and, as they see it, get out of hand. Familiar examples of avoidants who vacillate in order to frustrate the full development of their relationships are the perfectionistic avoidant who tries and tries but can never find a partner who is good enough; the eligible bachelor no woman can catch; the individual who assures failure by involving him- or herself in relationships that cannot possibly work out; the man who gets engaged but refuses to make up his mind about getting married or, making up his mind, refuses to set a final date; the archetypal teasing femme fatale who seduces a man, then disappoints him by cutting him off when he tries to get close to her; and the secret relater such as the man who married, then hid his wife from his family, not telling anyone in his family about the marriage so as to not upset them, be criticized by them for making a bad choice of partner, or be criticized for being unfaithful to them.

Ginia Bellafante's (2002) article provides a description of the perfectionistic avoidant who simultaneously relates and defends against relating by setting what can be unrealizable inclusion criteria: "While some therapists have taken note of a greater open-mindedness among single patients who seem more willing to go out with people they might not have considered nine months ago [and are looking forward to a] new mating landscape in which game-playing, manipulation and the ritual of the $175 dinner would become history, [other single patients have been disappointed, noting that their] female friends seem even more focused on their lists, have been willing to compromise less, and are still looking at a guy and asking, 'Did he go to an Ivy League school? Who is his family, and do they have a summer house?'" (p. 2).

Denial

This defense is mainly used by Type II avoidants who become wild cruisers who frantically, and fearlessly, connect with many to handle their fear of getting close to and becoming intimate with one. These are the Type II avoidants who deliberately embrace quantity over quality so that they can appear to be interrelated while nevertheless maintaining relationships that are too fragile and ephemeral to be truly meaningful.

Masochism

All types of avoidants tend to deal with their guilty feelings by yielding to their guilt masochistically. They give in to a harsh conscience that wants them to suffer. Theirs is a lemming-like self-sacrificial, self-abnegating, self-punitive response to forbidden desire, a way to commit social suicide to punish themselves for what they consider to be their unacceptable urges. As examples, some Type I avoidants use isolation to punish themselves. Some Type II avoidants punish themselves either directly by pursuing unavailable or otherwise difficult people or indirectly by giving vent to their temper, driving others away by flaring over minor interpersonal issues that are best overlooked for the good of a relationship.

A woman fell deeply in love and pursued a cyberrelationship with a man from Germany who told her that he was royalty, only to later confess, somewhat ashamedly, that he "picked up waste materials to be moved from here to there on a dispersing truck." Though he promised to visit her, he made one excuse after another for not being able to get to the United States to meet her personally. Eventually, however, he made the trip and, as she put it, "turned out to be a great guy after all." That is when she picked a fight with him, condemning him for his bad grammar, whereupon he packed his bags, stomped out the door, and took the first flight back to Germany.

One avoidant could do no better than to discard a lover for using too many towels, and for always taking a new one instead of using the old ones until they absolutely had to be washed. He justified his action on the correct but trivial grounds that his lover should have known without having to be told that doing the laundry took time and effort and ran up the electricity bill.

Identification with the Aggressor

This defense, used by all types of avoidants, was first described by Anna Freud in 1946. The patient's cry, "I fear you" becomes "I don't fear you— I hate you too much to care about you one way or the other." Avoidants using this defense reject others actively to avoid being rejected by them passively. Some become rejecting by becoming completely, really "brutally," honest. Others become rejecting by becoming the picky perfectionistic people just mentioned—those who look for flaws and slight imperfections and, finding them, express their displeasure about what they found when instead they should be overlooking insignificant transgressions to avoid disrupting significant relationships.

Helps Resolve Conflicts in New, Healthier, Less Avoidant Ways

The ultimate therapeutic task is to help avoidants better manage their interpersonal relationships by finding newer and healthier ways to resolve inner conflict and reduce inner anxiety. The different ways I go on to describe are suitable for different personalities with varying preferences, capacities, and current situations.

Making Defensiveness Less Necessary

Patients can at least theoretically make defensiveness less necessary by subduing their sexual and hostile feelings. Mastery over these feelings can be accomplished pharmacologically via the use of tranquillizers or even alcohol, which, in moderation, can suppress troublesome instincts. (A brief discussion of the pharmacotherapy of avoidance will be found in Chapter 18.) Alternatively, or simultaneously, relaxation techniques, meditation, and deep breathing can control what a patient, or his or her therapist, might consider to be wayward romantic feelings and excessive anger. Patients can also make defensiveness less necessary by reducing their guilt. Through guilt-reduction avoidants can become less rigidly prohibitive of themselves. They can learn, within reason, of course, to be less self-critical and more accepting of their sexual and angry feelings. (When that is not possible, they can learn to deal correctively, after the fact, with any negative consequences of having expressed or acted upon these feelings.) Mastery of guilt can also be accomplished pharmacologically via the use of tranquillizers and even alcohol (again, when used in strict moderation).

Developing New, Healthier Defenses

One healthier defense is sublimation of anger. One way of sublimating anger is to become altruistic, changing anger over into pity and self-sacrifice. Now instead of getting angry at others the avoidant worries about them. He or she asks what is bothering them, and after finding out offers help rather than criticism. Another method of sublimating anger involves dissipating anger overflow with exercise or by the equivalent of "punching a punching bag." Another is counterphobic mastery of anxiety—a forced involvement (without the artificial high associated with hypomania) as a way to master anxiety by meeting it head on. Finally the patient can simply accept his or her anxiety and learn to live with it. This involves, as Anthony and Swinson (2000) suggest, just let[ting] the fear happen" (p. 148), accepting it as the price to be paid for having rewarding interpersonal contacts.

TECHNICAL CONSIDERATIONS

Psychodynamically oriented psychotherapists use transference material—avoidant behavior as it becomes manifest with the therapist—to facilitate the development of insight into avoidant patterns and conflicts. For example, a therapist noted that a patient saw him as her mother, a woman who pushed her to get married though she preferred to stay single. The therapist further noted that the patient's attitude was interfering with her therapy, as it was with her life, because she was spending her therapy sessions not, as she should have, realizing her own potential, but in attempting to defeat her mother (in the person of the therapist).

Psychodynamic psychotherapists also do, or should, use exposure techniques. They ask the patient to actively try new interpersonal situations and make new interpersonal contacts. The therapeutic goals are for the patient to desensitize him or herself to anxiety directly, practice nonavoidance, and release new and deeper anxieties to be brought back into therapy as grist for the mill of the development of further insight. Together the therapist and the patient work the new insight through to integrate it, thus putting the patient in a stronger position to return to the fray for more social exposure, and thus more insight.

Psychodynamic psychotherapists identify and ask avoidants to relinquish the secondary gain they get from being avoidant. While primary gain focuses on relief from anxiety, secondary gain harvests the rewards that accrue from avoidant symptoms once formed, however much these symptoms take their toll on interpersonal relationships. As examples, agoraphobics enjoy having a companion on street outings, social phobics with a fear of public speaking are gratified by not having to do the work that writing and giving a speech entails, and mingles avoidants enjoy the sexual variety that is a side-benefit of their fear of commitment to a single partner. These enjoyments all fall into my category of pleasurable things to give up in order to get something more satisfying in return. As an individual quoted in Ginia Bellafante's (2002) article said, "I was married when I was 19 and divorced four years later . . . I was proposed to three times since then, but I always had a terrible problem with commitment. After four years of being a single woman in New York and really living it up, I realized that love and marriage and family and friends were actually important to me."

AN AVOIDANT PATIENT TREATED PSYCHODYNAMICALLY

A patient entered therapy complaining that he was too shy to meet new people. He was avoidant in both his professional and his personal lives. At work he volunteered for night duty so that he would not have to interact too much with his coworkers and so that he didn't have to spend too much time with his family. In his personal life he had one love affair when he was very young, and never had another. Many years ago when he was a teenager he fell in love with the girl next door, but was too shy to speak to her directly. The best he could do to make contact was to tie a romantic message for her on an arrowhead and shoot the arrow over the fence and into her yard. He thought that that was just the right flourish. Instead he was surprised, and chagrined, to discover that the next phone call wasn't from her, but from the police.

As an adult he had one or two close friends, whom he used to stave off his need for more intimate attachments. They satisfied his minimal need for human relationships to the point that he felt little pressure to meet new people. On those rare occasions when he agreed to go to parties he would mostly stand off in the shadows in a corner of the room looking longingly at all the people having fun. What few people he managed to approach, or who approached him, he antagonized by putting them in no-win situations, rejecting them if they acted friendly because he disliked people who got too close, and rejecting them if they acted unfriendly because he disliked people who were too distant. Then he would go home early, all by himself, to his small apartment where he watched television with the phone pulled and the intercom off, accepting only e-mail because "instead of being the passive victim of anyone who decides to call and bother me I can pick that up when, and only when, I choose to do so."

Once or twice he was able to start a romance only to pull back prematurely after telling himself that it would not work out. First he brooded about all the mistakes he might make that, as he was convinced, would turn the other person off. Then he acted in a way that assured that his gloomy prediction that things would not work out would come true. After thinking, "I already ruined things, so why bother to continue," he became protectively remote and distant, and bolted.

In reality, other people did not much take to him. His appearance did actually handicap him socially, making it difficult for him to connect with the very few people he felt comfortable knowing. As he put it, "They call me 'skull' because of my sunken eyes and cheekbones, 'weird' because my face is asymmetrical, and 'peculiar' because as I walk I keep one shoulder higher than the other." However, he did not do what he could have done to improve his appearance. Rather he confined himself to checking in the mirror from time to time, assessing flaws, overlooking virtues, and not really thinking about making those repairs that were both indicated and possible. Unconsciously, he held himself back because he actually wanted to look strange to others so that others would not become overly familiar with him.

Over the years he developed a number of social phobias relating to specific trivial prompts that symbolized deep interpersonal terrors. In part he installed these phobias so that he could avoid being close to people, his way to live out his motto, "If you don't visit them you don't have to invite them back." He could drive over bridges when he was not going to a date's house, but when he was, he could not drive over bridges due to the fear that he would faint, lose control of his car, hit an abutment, and have a fatal accident. He was equally unable to take the train because he feared a train crash. He also developed a phobia of going to church. During the service he had to sit near the exit door in case he should feel faint, so that he could get out without calling attention to himself. This church phobia expressed both a fear of being controlled and having to be submissive and a fear of being embarrassed publicly should he get too emotional about the service and lose control of his feelings. His fear of losing control had some basis in reality, for on more than one occasion just a little alcohol released his inhibitions to the point that he acted too aggressively and said nasty things underneath his breath to people he hardly knew.

Eventually he began to have some difficulty venturing out of doors at all. During the day he had trouble going out because he feared being stung by flying insects, particularly wasps, and because he feared a repetition of an incident where a policeman had stopped him for no reason at all and asked him, in an accusatory fashion, where he was going. Next, he completely stopped traveling from his hometown to the Big City for all the reasons just mentioned and because he became convinced that the second he got off the train someone would approach him, pick his pocket, and strand him by taking the money he needed for the return trip.

In spite of all the problems, he claimed that being an avoidant had its advantages. As he in essence put it, "I prefer to keep my positive emotions in check to avoid embarrassing myself by expressing feelings that I consider to be so common as to be trite. Besides, I do not really need other people. All I need comes from within. I enjoy my own company best. I like being isolated and get a great deal of pleasure from being able to go home, sit there surrounded by the things I love, and come and go as I please. I enjoy collecting things so much that I feel that the worst day at the flea market is better than the best day at the meat market, and anyway, my cat is my best friend, someone I can always count on, unlike everybody else I have met up to now."

One goal of therapy was to understand how his avoidance began. We learned that his fear of criticism went back to his relationship with a mother who criticized him when he did things wrong without also complimenting him when he did things right, to the point that, as he put it, with a sort of humorous resignation, "she actually died before she could ever say a single nice thing about me."

Another goal of therapy was to uncover the present fantasies behind his current avoidant symptoms. We discovered that his shyness originated in part in his concern that he would take anyone he met away from someone else, just as his father took his mother away from him. He also feared being criticized for his sexual feelings, a fear that was in turn the product of an intense religious scrupulosity. There was also a morbid fear of making any mistakes at all. As he put it, "In my whole life I never made a slip of the tongue because I never spoke before I thought carefully about what I was going to say. For me slips of the tongue are like wrong numbers. If you dial one you didn't get a wrong number, you dialed the number wrong." He also wanted to be a good role model for others he believed should, when it came to interpersonal relationships, follow his lead and be just as spartan and abstemious as he was. As he described it, he was an advocate for the highest level of morality. His means of getting rid of temptation was not, as Oscar Wilde said, to yield to it, but to get rid of the people who tempted him.

We also discovered that for him stinging insects symbolized his mother, as did the preacher and the policeman. We further learned that he could not take the train because the moving train symbolized his impulses, and train crashes the dreadful consequences of expressing them. Driving over the bridge symbolized his fear of forward movement and his fear of success, translated into the symbolism of reaching the pinnacle only to be mauled physically (that is, castrated) as a consequence of soaring.

After several years of therapy he was able to deal with his relationship anxiety enough to form tentative, partially intimate relationships. He kept his old friends and developed a few new ones. He moved in with a woman he felt comfortable with partly because she was an avoidant herself: an unassuming undemanding person who desired little closeness and intimacy from him or from anyone else. They fought a great deal and threatened to leave each other on a regular basis, but that was mainly their way to reassure themselves that neither was engulfing or being engulfed by the other. On follow-up he said that now was the happiest time of his life, though he recognized, "As my therapist you are probably disappointed in me, thinking that the adjustment I made is somewhat less than ideal, at least according to your overly rigorous standards."

CHAPTER 15

Cognitive-Behavioral Therapy

COGNITIVE THERAPY

Clinical Considerations

Therapists who treat avoidance using cognitive therapy identify, illuminate, challenge, and correct logical distortions in order to help patients think and act more rationally and productively, so that they can connect with others and commit to a lasting, loving relationship. As Beck (1999) puts it, cognitive therapists take the role of impartial observers "reframing . . . conclusion[s] about the supposedly noxious behavior of another person" (p. 252). They do this so that patients can "put aside the subjective meanings they attach to a communication and focus on the objective content" (p. 254). Now patients can become less "prone to arrive at biased explanations" (p. 253) and "respond to the manifest problem" (p. 254), instead of, in the words of Burns and Epstein (1983) "responding to . . . activate[d] stable underlying assumption[s]" (p. 75) and so drawing nonobjective conclusions about content.

A shy patient hesitated to leave the house because some of his neighbors did not say hello to him, he thought because they did not like him. I helped him reframe conclusions about the supposedly noxious behavior of his neighbors using Beck's (1999) strategies of "applying rules of evidence" (p. 252) and "considering alternative explanations" (p. 252). I suggested the possibility that while some of his neighbors might dislike him, others were simply caught up in their own little world, or thought *he* didn't see *them* and did not want to call out his name because it was early in the morning and they were afraid of waking up the whole neighborhood.

Therapists can correct cognitive errors both directly and indirectly. They can correct cognitive errors *directly* by *reality testing* a patient's inappropriately negative beliefs, doing so by challenging the logical basis of his or her fear of criticism, humiliation, and rejection. They can correct cognitive errors *indirectly* by exploring and understanding the context in which they occur. Cognitive errors do not exist in a vacuum. Rather they appear, take shape, and develop within a facilitating matrix of disruptive developmental events; internal conflicts inadequately resolved by pathological defensiveness; negative behavioral conditioning; interpersonal distortions formed in childhood that persist into adulthood; misguided existential philosophical beliefs; and comorbid emotional disorder. In the realm of disruptive developmental events, sometimes adults think in an avoidant manner in the here and now because as children they identified with parents who thought the same way, or because as children they jumped to false conclusions that the adults in their lives were rejecting them. In parallel situations today they continue to jump to the same unwarranted conclusions. For example, a patient continues to react in the here and now as he reacted to his mother when he was a child. Then, if she got even a little angry with him it meant that she didn't love him at all, or if she set any limits whatsoever on him it meant that she criticized and rejected him completely. Cognitive errors often have roots in past traumata. For example, in one case a patient's current hypersensitivity to criticism and rejection could be traced back to his family's rejecting him by showing a clear preference for his brothers and sisters almost from the day he was born.

A shy hypersensitive avoidant patient felt uncomfortable meeting new people because he failed to distinguish making a social blunder from ruining himself completely socially. He believed that others' basic feelings about him could change without warning from positive to negative the same way his parents' basic feelings did change toward him when as a child he did something they disapproved of. I attempted to convince him that in reality interpersonal relationships have built-in margins of error, so that most people's basic feelings do not change from positive to negative over something trivial. Thus, fewer people than he thought were parental clones who would turn on him the same way his parents did when he made childish mistakes.

In the realm of comorbid emotional disorder, cognitive errors are often generated by paranoid suspiciousness, depressive pessimism, obsessive perfectionism, histrionic overexaggeration, or a masochistic need to suffer.

It was difficult to effectively challenge the fear of flying in a depressive avoidant whose negative ideas about the outcome of a plane trip originated in, and persisted because of, a generalized pessimistic world view, one based on the conviction that bad things happen to good people because even the best of us come from original sin. It was equally difficult to effectively challenge the fear of flying in a histrionic woman whose fear originated in an unconscious sexualization of the act of taking off, and in an equally unconscious fear of success due to her belief that reaching one's destination in life equals fulfilling one's incestuous wishes.

"Illogical" cognitions are particularly resistant to logical assault when the so-called "illogic" has a basis in reality, making full reality testing and complete reassurance difficult or impossible. For example, because planes do sometimes crash, it is not possible to completely reassure patients that flying is as safe as walking, and safer than driving, any more than it is possible to completely dismiss the appropriateness of opening night jitters when performing before critics, or the possibility of rejection when meeting new people.

Here are some specific cognitive errors leading to avoidant shyness and withdrawal, vacillation, unpredictability, and regressive immersion. Some of these were also listed and discussed in Chapter 12.

Some Equals All, Part Equals Whole, and Similar Equals the Same Thing

Avoidants become sensitive to criticism when they define criticism as anything short of complete acceptance and so come to believe that if you criticize me a little you criticize me a lot. Avoidants develop low self-esteem when they define any slight imperfection of theirs as a fatal flaw and so come to believe that if they are not all good they are no good at all. Avoidants fear losing their identity completely, if they get at all close to someone, when they view closeness as merging, that is, as entirely engulfing, and come to view marriage as the proverbial ball and chain forged to keep them from completely realizing their individuality.

Thinking According to Exclusive (and Exclusively Negative) Causes

Unable to think of positive elements in and alternatives for others' negativity, avoidants explain others' behavior as being strictly antagonistic and rejecting. For example, "He didn't return my phone call yet" becomes "He does not like me enough to want to get back to me ever." Self-critical attitudes originate along similar lines, so that instead of "I am too shy to connect" we hear a much more pejorative, "I don't have what it takes for anyone to love me, so why even bother trying to extend myself?"

Overgeneralizing from One Specific Instance to All Other Instances

Avoidants make no attempt to connect when they come to fear that all new relationships necessarily replicate old problematic traumatic relationships. For example, many avoidants, basing their conclusions on shared characteristics, however inconsequential, parentalize present people so that these people come to remind them of their mother and father. They think, "He does this, my father did the same thing to me, therefore he is my father," or "She is this way, my mother was that way, too, therefore she is my mother."

Thinking Catastrophically

All-is-lost avoidants make mountains out of molehills when they assign absolute rather than relative meaning to problematic events, then overreact to unimportant occurrences as if they were major negative developments. Now they become unable to say, "So what" and "Big deal" and remain calm and unemotional about things that don't really matter, or even about things that do but not that much, or, if that much, are best overlooked for the overall good. Developing a Pandora's box mentality as a result of their catastrophic thinking, they believe that being true to themselves and opening up to others will predictably lead to their flooding the world with their evil sexuality and anger. Or, thinking like Joseph Cornell, they decide that having sex will empty them completely and, thoroughly exhausting and depleting them, make them no good for anything else.

Many avoidants make two or more cognitive errors simultaneously. For example a patient felt too frightened and devastated to relate intimately to anyone due to his taking criticism too seriously. His fear of criticism started with *similar equals the same thing* distortive thinking, so that if someone merely requested that he do something that became an intended criticism that the thing was not done. Next, *thinking catastrophically*, he perceived the imagined criticism as a rejection ("if you really loved me, you would have spared me, even if it meant doing the thing yourself, but since you did not spare me, that means you hate me"); and the rejection became a dire warning that the relationship was in serious trouble, and about to end badly.

Technical Considerations

Some cognitive therapists focus on cognitive errors as they appear in dreams, such as the catastrophic thinking in the following nightmare:

A man dreamt that his lover was spending too much time at the gym. Thinking catastrophically in the dream itself, he viewed his lover's dalliance there as a shattering personal rejection. Next, and also in the dream, he got back at his lover by rejecting him in turn and in kind. He told him that he would be going out before dinner, and would not be returning until after midnight. Then the dream turned to his being punished for what he said and planned to do. In the dream he had fallen over a cliff and was attempting to climb back to his lover, but, without an adequate foothold, was about to slide down the cliff into the water below.

Therapists can effectively use cognitive distortions about the therapist to challenge and repair negative interpersonal beliefs about therapy and the therapist, and then apply what is learned in situations outside of therapy. For example, an avoidant learned that her therapist was not being critical of her simply because she was correcting her cognitive errors, as she also learned that her husband still loved her even though he sometimes did not agree with everything she said.

Some cognitive therapists use role-playing to help their patients correct false assumptions about what others have in mind. Patients are asked to put themselves in another's place. In one case, a patient—who felt he was being rejected because he didn't get an immediate reply to an e-mail he sent—was able, after putting himself in the (overworked) recipient's place, to understand that the response was delayed simply because the person who received the e-mail was currently busy.

Some therapists take the next step and suggest positive thoughts patients can have to counter their negative thinking. For example, a therapist helped a patient, who feared public speaking because he feared he would faint, to think less catastrophically. He next suggested that the patient hold a countervailing reassuring thought while giving his speech: "My anxiety always dissipates a few minutes into my talk."

Millon (1981) speaks of a downside of cognitive therapy rarely mentioned: the patient becoming "unduly guilt ridden, depressed, and suicidal" (p. 272). Cognitive therapy is by nature somewhat unsupportive and invalidating, offering the patient a blaming, "The problem is not your difficult situation but the way you misinterpret it." For example, Rapee (1998), assigning full responsibility to the patient for thinking negatively, states, a bit too categorically in my opinion, that "feelings and emotions are directly caused by our thoughts, attitudes, and beliefs—in other words, by what goes on inside our heads" (p. 24). This line of thought, that how we react is strictly attitudinal and never situational, can, among other things, undercut a patient's anxiety-reducing not-me projective defenses—that is, the defensive "it's your behavior, not my distortions, that makes me feel the way I do about you." Next the patient responds by feeling guilty and getting depressed, developing somatic symptoms like headaches, or becoming resistant to, or even leaving, therapy.

Therefore, therapists should take care to do cognitive therapy in the context of a supportive holding environment. They should make an effort to offer patients comfort, reassurance and understanding throughout. They might say something supportive such as, "Most people share your anxiety and fears, at least to some extent" and that "While it might be necessary for therapeutic purposes to act as if you are entirely responsible for your cognitive errors, we both understand that even the most unrealistic negative cognitions are to some extent provoked by the negative behaviors of others."

BEHAVIORAL THERAPY

Clinical Considerations

Behavior therapy can be used by itself to help patients overcome their avoidance. Alternatively, behavior therapy can be an ancillary method for catalyzing psychodynamic, cognitive, and interpersonal interventions—chiefly a means to the end of bringing negative cognitions and bodily sensations to life—highlighting thoughts and feelings so that they may now be brought back into, and become the focus of, uncovering psychotherapy.

Here are some behavior approaches I frequently use for treating avoidants.

Maintaining the Focus on the Goal of Nonavoidance

I condition patients to focus on their avoidance, making forming and maintaining relationships their first priority.

An avoidant patient said of a friend, "I basically like her, although she puts me off by constantly talking about material things. Still, I don't want to visit her if she is only going to talk about her house. But she's my best friend and I don't want to give her up. What should I do?" A previous therapist suggested that the patient give up the relationship because "it's stressful, and giving up stress is your first priority." Following this advice destroyed a valuable friendship, with negative consequences for all concerned. The therapist's advice, the product of an unbalanced do your own thing philosophy, overlooked both the well-being of the patient (the relationship was important to her) and the well-being of her friend (giving up the relationship badly hurt the friend's feelings).

An avoidant woman whose chief complaint was "I never meet anyone nice" at the gym placed her scorecard on the seat of a machine to reserve the machine while she rested, whereupon an equally avoidant man said to her, "I'm in a hurry to use the machine; is this yours?" This was really a hint to remove the scorecard, probably given less because he wanted to exercise than because he wanted to make the point that he did not like her hogging the machine. She replied in a counter-hostile fashion, "I'll remove it," but because she resented being told what to do, she first removed it, then made a great show of going back to exercising, and made it a point to do more than one set. He next asked her, in an even more hostile fashion, "When do you plan to move on?" She replied, further escalating the hostility, "Soon enough," yet still continued to exercise. In the end, both walked away angry. The man's therapist commented, "You did the right thing by standing firm—it showed her that you are castration-proof." I would have said, "Instead of escalating, as lonely as you are, you might have made a friend by giving in and apologizing, perhaps adding, "I've had a rough day, let's not fight, it's only a machine."

I do not emphasize removing nonavoidant comorbid symptoms when these are mild and soak up energy that might otherwise go into the creation or maintenance of avoidance—that is, I bypass those symptoms that, however pathological in themselves, at least enhance interpersonal relationships by binding interpersonal anxiety.

I did not actively intervene in an angry depressive avoidant's need to take his anger out on himself instead of on others. Instead I even encouraged it in a roundabout way—by discouraging him from expressing his anger with the world, leaving him no target for his anger other than himself. In the beginning, taking his anger out on himself intensified his (mild) depression somewhat. Soon, however, his depression improved because his self-esteem increased as others reacted to him positively for being "such a nice, all-suffering guy."

Because he was alone when leaving the house I did not discourage an obsessional patient from going back to check and recheck the door to his house to see if it was locked. I did, however, discourage him from going back to recheck his work desk in the center of a busy office to see if he had locked it, from going back to look under the table after a pleasant restaurant meal in the company of others to see if he had dropped anything, and from asking his lover if he had somehow contaminated him during sex.

I worked with another obsessional's fear of the germs on his coworkers' hands because this fear kept him from shaking hands with them. I left untouched his fear that he had demagnetized his backup computer discs by putting them too close to the telephone, a fear that allowed him to keep old friends, because it only required that he make new backups.

A phobic who worked on a high floor in a high-rise building suffered from both an elevator phobia (actually a claustrophobia and a fear of heights combined) and a fear of open-air heights that appeared when he hiked in the mountains. We worked on his elevator phobia so that he could keep his job in the city. We left untouched his fear of heights so that he could appease his guilty conscience by sacrificing the pleasures of his country hikes.

A hysteric in the public eye suffered both from symptomatic frigidity associated with a persistent vaginal itch and from an interpersonal frigidity characterized by remoteness and a need to keep her distance from, and be cold towards, her fans, displayed when her admirers came to her dressing room door only to be turned away for "annoying me by raving about how fabulous I am." I chose to work with the second display of frigidity while virtually ignoring the first, because the first was a symptom she could have in private between her and her doctor, while the second was a symptom that by making her remote from her public threatened her career.

Increasing Motivation

I help motivate patients to become nonavoidant by inspiring them. I do this directly by telling them to "take yourself in hand and act less shy," and "that you can do it, and you can do it now," and I do it indirectly by enumerating the benefits and rewards of relating. I note that the rewards of relating are sufficiently great to make it worthwhile to experience the discomfort everyone experiences when attempting to get close to, become intimate with, and to commit to a significant other. I might mention such long-term benefits of nonavoidance as: more satisfying social contacts; experiencing greater admiration from others; having more satisfying sexual relationships; replacing compulsive decision-making with true freedom of choice; developing self-pride over personal and professional achievement; and leaving a worthwhile interpersonal and professional legacy behind.

Suggesting Graded Exposure

Most cognitive-behavioral (and interpersonal) therapists sooner or later ask avoidants to expose themselves to the relationships that they fear undertaking, citing as advantages the following: First, exposure helps many avoidants get started relating because they find that they like relating once they try it—with motivation coming as much from doing as the other way around. Second, minor successes help protect against the despair related to future fears of, or actual, social failure. Success breeds success, because real accomplishment enhances self-esteem by promoting self-pride. That in turn enhances self-confidence, which leads to improved functionality. Patients relate successfully, relationships make patients feel good about themselves, patients who feel good about themselves feel more worthy of relating, and patients who feel more worthy of relating relate even better. Third, actually being in a positive relationship helps reduce phobic symptoms. For example, a patient was unable to ride on a train until she had to meet a potential lover she met on the Internet at the airport. Now, feeling enveloped in his protective warmth, she became able to make the trip, virtually anxiety-free. Fourth, attempts at nonavoidance interrupt the self-sustaining vicious cycle that creates avoidant gridlock when a patient's anxiety leads to defensive avoidance which antagonizes and provokes others, who then become rejecting, making the avoidant even more anxious about rejection and so even more avoidant, until disuse atrophy sets in, further diminishing the ability to form relationships.

However, exposure techniques are not suitable for all avoidants. In my experience, the patients who do best with exposure are those whose avoidance is relatively mild (here exposure techniques can even be curative by themselves) and Type I avoidants who are shy or suffer from discrete social phobic symptoms. Other avoidants do better with more subtle persuasion via subliminal therapeutic message transfer through innuendo, clarification, and interpretation. These include patients whose ambivalence is severe and patients who have ongoing problems with commitment and intimacy. The shy patient who fears meeting someone new at a party can attempt trial connecting, but the outgoing patient who can start but not see a relationship through to its conclusion cannot be reasonably expected to attempt trial committing.

In the realm of specific techniques for creating exposure, I often ask my avoidant patients to start relating somewhere, anywhere. Some patients have the motivation, the personality, and the right circumstances to be able to start at the top, in effect taking the nonavoidant plunge by performing the most difficult tasks first. Other patients both need and prefer a more gradual, more incremental approach where they start at the bottom and go on to the top through graded tasks of progressive difficulty. Here are some ways a representative sampling of my avoidant patients started small:

- They got out of the house and talked to strangers, saying hello to just one person a day. They responded to a stranger who said hello, instead of questioning the stranger's intentions, then averting their eyes.

- They treated people better. They said hello to the gay couple who lived on their block, instead of snubbing them for moral reasons. They discussed a problem they were having with the person they were having it with, instead of retreating from or punishing that person for being difficult. They tipped the waiter even though the coffee was cold, instead of complaining to and about him, thus killing the messenger. They forced themselves to wait patiently for a driver in front of them who reacted slowly when the light turned green, instead of honking their horn. They waited patiently as the person in front of them in the checkout line at the supermarket wrote a check, instead of glowering or muttering under their breath that the sign says "cash only." They fell back when an infirm person or a woman with a baby carriage walking in front of them was going too slowly for their schedule or taste, instead of muttering or complaining about old people or mothers with children. They averted their eyes from someone who was dressed differently or behaving strangely, instead of staring them down incredulously. They smiled knowingly at an unruly teenager, instead of frowning after forgetting that they were once unruly teenagers themselves.

- They broadened their interpersonal horizons. They answered the phone instead of letting the answering machine pick up the call. They went into work when they did not feel like it, instead of calling in sick in order to have a mental health day. Though they did not have a partner, instead of staying home and eating by themselves, feeling sorry for themselves, they went out to dinner alone. They bought a computer so that they could get e-mail from their friends, modified favored hobbies to put them in contact with other people—collecting stamps in a group instead of by themselves, or buying a book in a real bookstore instead of in the remoteness of cyberspace. At work they joined in a water-cooler conversation, or sat with a group in the cafeteria, instead of sipping coffee alone or taking their lunch to a park bench and eating it there in isolation.

Technical Considerations

Some therapists use the following ancillary behavioral techniques to help patients better tolerate or actually reduce interpersonal anxiety.

- Advocating relaxation techniques like deep breathing and muscle relaxation to help induce a state of calm and control the hyperventilation that often accompanies anxiety.

- Creating right-brain activity (that is the product of emotions) to blot out left-brain faulty worrisome thinking. For example, a therapist suggested that to blot out stage fright a patient anxious about public speaking could think about a joyous dinner and sex to come after the speech was over.

- Suggesting the patient admit his or her anxiety to others, in effect throwing him or herself on the mercy of the court. Patients who confess to others that they are shy at least get over the fear that their shyness will be inadvertently discovered, and avoid seeming to reject others who mistake their shyness for remoteness.

- Suggesting joint exposure by getting together with an avoidant friend and egging each other on as powerful allies joined together to conquer the temptation to panic and retreat.

- Suggesting consultation with ex-avoidants to find out how they became nonavoidant.

- Offering social skills training where patients are instructed on how to behave with others. Patients can benefit from being told what they should or should not do in order to become more favored among people. For example, I tell patients to look people directly in the eye and to not look off into the distance, ostrich-like, thinking, "If I don't see them, they don't see me." I also suggest actions patients can take to turn a situation of mutual antagonism around, such as the following:

Once when at an art gallery a patient spied a price list of the art, walked over to the counter where it lay unattended, and started to make off with it, only to have a woman standing two feet away from the list complain that she was just about to use it and demand its immediate return. The patient then started to retreat in anger and abject humiliation but, thinking better of it, instead responded to her complaint by saying, pleasantly, "Well, how was I supposed to know you wanted it, I'm not a mind reader." He then asked her out on a date.

- Advocating role-playing with rehearsal to help patients spot their relationship problems, and practice relating in new, less tentative, more effective, less self-destructive, ways.
- Injecting the therapist's personal nonavoidant philosophy into the sessions. Hoping to teach a patient how relationship difficulties can be overcome through yielding, compromise and positivity, a therapist once quoted W. H. Auden's (1960) poem, "The More Loving One": ". . . let the more loving one be me."

Some therapists use Jay Haley's (1976) *paradoxical therapy*, a form of behavioral therapy that is the *opposite* of exposure therapy. Here patients are asked, or told, to *not* do the very thing that they should be doing, the very thing that makes them most anxious. The therapist counts on the patient's native stubbornness and oppositionalism to surface and propel him or her to overcome fears. For example, one therapist suggested a patient take a vacation from relationships, anticipating that as a stubborn resistant avoidant she would do exactly the opposite of what he suggested, just to defy him. Of course, defying him was just what the therapist wanted the patient to do in the first place.

Paradoxical approaches can work especially well with avoidants with sexual inhibitions, which the lure of the forbidden regularly helps overcome. Patients often experience an enhancement of sexual desire plus an urge to have the prohibited sex they were formerly unable to have simply because now they are having it behind the therapist's back.

CHAPTER 16

Interpersonal Therapy

CLINICAL CONSIDERATIONS

In interpersonal therapy, the therapist, as Oldham and Morris (1995) suggest, views people as belonging to "an interdependent system and views their emotional problems as developing within a dyadic or inter-familial context." Oldham and Morris treat these troubled units as a way to manage their individual members (p. 407).

An important cornerstone of interpersonal therapy involves asking patients to identify the contribution they themselves make to the distancing process—how they determine the negative outcome of their relationships by what they say and do. Interpersonal therapists ask patients to determine if they might be:

Rejecting. Rejecting avoidants are right to fear rejection, for it is only human nature to reject people who reject you first.

Angry. Angry avoidants do not so much avoid people as they push them away. Some put other people down directly. They do so by being obviously and openly critical. For example, an avoidant severely castigated her hairstylist for taking a bit too much off her front bangs, loudly, angrily, and nonsensically complaining, "You made me look like a peanut." In a restaurant a gay man responded to his partner's asking the waiter to take back his coffee because it was cold by loudly proclaiming to everyone in the place, "Aren't you all glad you aren't married to him?" Others put people down indirectly. They do so with a hostile shyness that conveys the message, "I don't want to have anything to do with you." Or they put others down to a third party, knowing that what they say will get back. For example, a single woman, a nurse, announced to everyone at work that she would rather spend the rest of her life alone than get married to any of the doctors she worked with because "they are all so stuck on themselves." A husband greeted the late arrival of his wife at a party they were both attending with the following aside to their son, a man who was very close to his mother: "Here she comes, so let's all go—out the window."

Rigid. Rigid avoidants are unable to relax and yield into a healthy merger with others. As excessively inhibited remote individuals they stifle their interpersonal affection, and squelch their warm feelings out of guilt, shame, misplaced pride, and the twin fears of flooding and emotional depletion. Hug them and they become even stiffer.

One avoidant did not respond affectionately to people because he feared being flooded by the feelings that others would arouse, in part because he believed that having strong feelings was a sign of femininity and so of weakness. For this man, avoidance was a way to detach from others in order to be able to proclaim, "Because I don't have feelings I'm not a sissy, or a mama's boy, but a strong person, in control of myself, and intact."

Perfectionistic. Perfectionistic avoidants are much too selective and demanding for the good of their relationships. They look for ideal partners and discard those they believe to be merely adequate.

Suspicious. Suspicious avoidants lack basic trust. They assume that others mistreat them without first determining if there are alternative, more positive, explanations for what they too readily believe to be others' unsupportive words and negative deeds. For example, one patient felt that his sister-in-law was ignoring him for the holidays when the real reason that she was unavailable was that her husband insisted that they spend every holiday with his own family.

Self-centered. Self-centered avoidants determine who is right for them but not whom they might be right for. Their needs come first as they call in sick to work because of how they feel without concern for the disruptive effect their absence might have on their coworkers. They turn others into a captive audience as they talk about themselves without letting others get a word in edgewise, pinning them to the wall with their verbiage, and making them squirm as they recite their latest conquests, grandchildren's antics, stage appearances, rave reviews, or terrible troubles. They use others for what they can get out of them, then drop them. For example, they call upon them only when they need a favor, and at no other time, or treat them as trophies to enhance their own image and improve their own social status.

Unreliable. Unreliable avoidants, often Type II and Type III avoidants, might cancel a date at the last minute instead of forcing themselves to go in spite of their fear and discomfort, or abandon a relationship, even one that works, because they are restless, bored, or thrill-seeking. Many are teases who distance by promising, then failing, to deliver. For example, they might tell people, "We must get together sometime," then not follow up with an invitation. (Either they should not offer the invitation in the first place or they should offer a specific invitation, and then honor it.) They might be manifestly adoring but secretly unfaithful.

For example, the German man from cyberspace referred to in Chapter 14 undid his confession of undying love to his new companion and corrupted his suggestion that they become lifetime partners by dating other women behind her back, then "letting it slip" that he was being unfaithful.

As should be evident from Chapters 9–11, another important cornerstone of interpersonal therapy involves identifying and treating the interpersonal manifestations of comorbid disorders that underlie the interpersonal distancing, as follows.

Paranoid avoidants distance themselves from others by coming across as mean, spiteful, vengeful, punitive individuals eager to retaliate for the negative things they imagine others are thinking about, and doing to, them.

A patient feeling rejected because her next-door neighbors did not invite her over to join them for their family barbecue got back at them by haranguing them to stop letting their ivy grow onto her fence. Shortly afterwards her next-door neighbor's child was sitting quietly in her own yard, watching the birds at the feeder in the patient's yard. Feeling "observed," really intruded and spied upon, the patient yelled at the child: "Stop it, and stop it now. Stop watching *my* birds!"

Depressed avoidants distance themselves from others by being self-critical individuals who put themselves down partly in order to make others feel that "I am not worthy enough to associate with." They wallow in low self-esteem in order to make others feel too guilty and exasperated to comfortably continue relating to them.

An attractive intelligent woman worked in the coffee shop at an upscale gym. A perk for employees was permission to use the gym facilities. One day she found herself on a machine that a club member was waiting to use. As soon as she saw that he was waiting she stopped what she was doing, got up, apologized for taking up a machine that he wanted, and, by way of explanation and apology for her actions, noted that she wasn't supposed to get in his way because while she was only an employee, he was a paying customer.

Hypomanic avoidants distance themselves from others by being frantic, turning relationships into fatuous, meaningless interactions with many that keep them from getting too close to one. An excerpt of a conversation between one such hypomanic avoidant and a close friend about what the avoidant considered to be an ideal Saturday night is illustrative: "Cool. Dinner somewhere would be cool. Then we can head for the party and do something afterwards, like going to the new singles bar down the block, staying up all night, getting smashed, and finding someone for a hot relationship, like, you know, that would be cool too."

Borderline avoidants distance themselves from others because they are, as Beck (1999) suggests, equally threatened by the "affiliative mode [which] promotes bonding and dissolution of boundaries, and the autonomous mode, which maintains boundaries, erects barriers against incursions by others, and facilitates freedom of action" (p. 108). As a result they become Type II avoidants who alternate between a fear of commitment and a fear of being abandoned, first isolating themselves from others, then panicking, becoming too dependent on others, then panicking again, pulling back from and isolating themselves once more, ad infinitum.

Sadistic avoidants distance themselves from others by being either passively or openly aggressive. A passive-aggressive avoidant might reject others for their own good because "You don't want to get involved with someone like me—I'm nothing but trouble." Here are some examples of openly sadistic avoidants:

A housewife saved her money for months to travel to Manhattan to a salon for a complete makeover. Her husband disliked her leaving him for the day, and even suspected that she might be meeting a secret lover in New York. As he put it, "You wouldn't be making yourself over for me, I no longer care how you look." Upon her return, instead of telling her, "You look beautiful," he launched into a tirade about how much her cat missed her and how pissed-off the cat acted because she left her alone for the day.

A patient's husband told her to go to a dangerous New York neighborhood to buy him the Boston newspaper. Secretly he wanted her to get hurt more than he wanted the newspaper. Later when she had a bilateral mastectomy, he made fun of her for not having breasts and said, "Just my luck to have to spend my final years with someone deformed."

A patient contemplated teaching her son a lesson for getting a C in English: leaving him home in summer school with an aunt while the rest of the family took a long trip to San Francisco.

A veteran refused to take his antihypertensive medication to pay the clinic back for its policy of charging $2 for a prescription he believed he should have free. He deliciously contemplated getting his doctors into big trouble by having a stroke, then suing them for malpractice. When I pointed out that he would be hurting mainly himself, he glowingly replied, "If I have to drown, I will at least take every one of you down with me."

Masochistic avoidants distance themselves from others by arranging to suffer by having relationships that fail. An ordinary-looking man sought out one beautiful woman after another to love, in spite of knowing that beautiful women tended to avoid him on account of his ordinary looks. Since these were the only women he would consider, he found himself rejected on a regular basis, and finally gave up dating altogether, his only pleasure the pleasure he obtained from sharing his pain with his gym buddies, commiserating with them about how these days there was something wrong with every woman you meet.

TECHNICAL CONSIDERATIONS

Interpersonal therapy can take the form of individual, group, or marital therapy.

Individual Therapy

Individual interpersonal therapists identify avoidant behaviors, bring them to the patient's attention, and then focus on the specific circumstances under which these avoidant behaviors appear, that is, the exact moment when patients begin to pull back from others. Most avoidants are selective in their avoidances. They are phobic in some situations but not in others, and withdraw from some but not from all situations. For example, some individuals feel comfortable with someone on their own social level, or "of their own kind," but withdraw from people unlike themselves in significant ways (avoidant endogamy). In contrast, others feel more comfortable with people of a different color, race, religion, or social status, and withdraw from people who do not meet these criteria (avoidant exogamy).

Also, individual therapists employ some or all of the following specific interpersonal therapeutic techniques for helping patients overcome their avoidance. Obviously, the therapist will be selective in choosing which techniques to use based on a patient's individual needs, preferences, problems, and possibilities—the latter depending in great measure on the patient's circumstances. The overlap between interpersonal and other forms of therapy will become clear from the following discussion.

Offering the Patient Inspiration

Some therapists inspire selected avoidant patients by stressing the downsides of being alone while affirming the positive aspects of closeness, intimacy, and commitment. Positive aspects of closeness, intimacy, and commitment range from having a stable life and being loved and supported to not contracting a sexually transmissible disease. These issues were also discussed in Chapter 15.

Analyzing the Patient's Distancing

In one case a dream with sexual and oedipal overtones revealed how a patient's distancing originated in his too-close relationship with his mother, and also foretold what he planned to do about it. "As I sit next to my mother on a couch, I note that my mother's dog is escaping. I next see the dog outside, sitting on a fence. The dog, pale-colored, limpid, and drained of blood when with my mother, changes to become pink and blue, then leaps off the fence and runs off to enjoy itself, at play."

Teaching/Instructing/Coaching the Patient

Some therapists teach avoidants how to improve their interpersonal skills. Some avoidants need to wipe a panicky grimace and off-putting frown from their face. Some avoidants need to become more assertive, while others need to become more submissive—to learn the art of interpersonal negotiation and compromise. Almost all avoidants can benefit from confiding in others. Just telling others "I feel anxious because I have problems getting close" puts others at ease by relieving their guilt as they think, "It's not my fault, it's his or her problem." It also makes others more simpatico—to the point that they demand less of, and become more flexible in their approach to, the avoidant. Now instead of making the avoidant's anxiety worse by being challenging and confrontational, they become more supportive, helping the avoidant feel more comfortable and relaxed.

Having the Patient Undergo Exposure

Exposure, as much a technique of interpersonal as it is of behavior therapy, is a direct way for avoidants to master their shyness and anxiety about meeting new people. I often ask avoidants to purposively set out to make new friends and get closer to people. As I mentioned in Chapter 15, I sometimes suggest that they do this gradually, doing a few minor nonavoidant things each day, then progressing step by step through exercises of increasing difficulty and complexity on the way to true closeness and intimacy. Some who started small, for example, by saying hello to strangers, are able to go on to accept a date, go steady, get engaged to be married, set a date to get married, then actually go through with the wedding. At other times I suggest that, instead of step-by-step exposure involving tasks of progressively increasing difficulty, avoidants start at the top and take the plunge, deliberately increasing their anxiety to a painful level all at once, in an attempt to bypass their fears of relationships and to instead at least act resolutely unafraid. In some cases it has been possible for an avoidant to become intimate with a significant other even before deep fears of closeness have been resolved. Of course this method requires picking the right person in the first place to avoid getting seriously hurt or hurting others in the process.

Interrupting Vicious Cycles

I help my avoidant patients interrupt vicious cycles of rejection, distancing, and more rejection, and turn these vicious into virtuous cycles. One good way to do this is by becoming less sensitive to and more accepting of what criticism/rejection they get and cannot ignore. They can tell themselves "rejecting me is your problem, not mine" and that "not everything that happens *to* is meant *for* me." Sometimes they can even bring their critics around, turning them into friends and supporters using the methods for handling critical people I describe throughout and in detail in Chapter 20.

Conquering Bad Reminiscences of Things Past

I urge my avoidant patients to not allow past traumata to create a Posttraumatic Stress Disorder. I help them discriminate between bad past and good present relationships so that they do not generalize from old bad experiences to new, unrelated, potentially satisfying involvements. This generalization is exemplified by the cat that, burned by jumping on a hot stove, fears and avoids not only hot stoves but cold ones as well. I remind avoidants that just because as children they experienced ill treatment from a parent does not mean that everyone else will treat them the same way, so that it is not necessary to avoid all men and women in the here and now as hot stoves when in fact they are cold stoves.

Increasing Self-Esteem by Encouraging Self-Acceptance

Many avoidants withdraw to increase their self-esteem by avoiding a test of that self-esteem. I ask them not to attempt to increase their self-esteem this way. I suggest that instead they increase their self-esteem by accepting themselves as they are, warts and all. I remind them that everybody has imperfections and makes mistakes, that one relationship failure is not a sign of personal deficit, and that, as I might put it, "it is okay to have even kinky sexual feelings, as long as you do not translate them into dangerous or hurtful action, and to have paranoid hostile thoughts as long as you do not actually live by them." I suggest that they stop comparing themselves to others and instead start viewing themselves as individuals, asking themselves, "Do I have what it takes?" not, "Do I have what he or she has?" I further suggest that instead of looking back in regret to the bad things they did when they were young, they look ahead, burying their past mistakes, and just not repeating them as they grow older.

Encouraging the Patient to Give Up Something to Get Something

I reassure avoidants afraid of relinquishing their identity to a significant other that new and often superior identities emerge in close intimate relationships, such as the identity of being a happily married man or woman. I also suggest that they can compensate for any loss of personal identity that may occur by developing new and stronger professional identities.

Encouraging the Patient to Develop a New, Less Avoidant,
Philosophy

Lonely individuals who consciously complain about relationship difficulties but unconsciously remain aloof from close relationships offered, or rupture close relationships that promise, really threaten, to work, often do so because philosophically they believe that isolation is splendid. Individuals like this must make enemies with their avoidant value system before "I like being alone" becomes, "And besides, I have no choice." They must convince themselves once and for all that isolation is not splendid but is an unpleasant lonely condition that ranks right up there with pain and hunger. They must tie themselves to the mast and refuse to allow themselves to be carried away by siren songs about the pleasures of being by oneself. Intellect must become the patina over passion, putting the recognitions that "It's not better to be alone than to be in a relationship" and "It's worth whatever trouble it takes to sustain a relationship" in place like a helpful companion to warn that such beliefs as "The single life is for me," "I can get along better without you from now on," "Life will be better after you've gone," and, "I will be in great shape when you die and I get your furniture" are preludes not to self-fulfillment but to self-destruction.

As discussed in Chapter 14, developing a nonavoidant philosophy requires distinguishing preference from compulsion—one's true ideal, and what one really wants out of life, from one's automatic thoughts and behaviors that in effect tell one what to want, and do. I ask avoidants to answer the following questions truthfully: Do I want to be alone or do I fear commitment and intimacy? Do I really believe that isolation is splendid or does something inside warn me of the terrors of connecting, and tell me to stay out of a relationship because my dreams of intimacy will never come true or turn into nightmares? Do I really want to do my own thing or am I afraid of doing my thing with you? Do I truly like my fantasies of walking alone into the distance through swirling mists or am I conjuring up those mists in order to hide my desire for a close, warm loving relationship? Do I truly identify with songs that speak of being a rock and an island, say I should be glad that I am single, and proclaim that never, never will I marry, so that I really want to be insular, or am I really afraid of singing another tune, leaving my avoidant island, taking the plunge, and swimming to shore?

I help avoidants distinguish preference from compulsion by having them look back over their lives to see if they can spot the historical moment when approach became avoidance as an original desire to relate turned into a fear of closeness and intimacy. I also ask them to look inside themselves for present signs of conflict between approach and avoidance, identifying wish-fear/desire-guilt/rebellion-submission conflicts, and the anxiety associated with these conflicts, to determine if these, not free will, are prompting them to take heroic defensive measures against welcoming others into their lives.

Role-Playing

I sometimes ask my avoidant patients to role-play, putting themselves in the place of others so that they can see exactly how they come across to them, in preparation for making necessary repairs. Family members and friends can often give valuable feedback, and videotaping can help with self-assessment, especially for avoidants who alter their appearance and behavior in an off-putting manner by rejecting the very social values they need to accept so that others will accept them, and in turn take them into their lives.

Calling in Third-Party Reinforcements

I advise my avoidant patients to call for help from people who encourage nonavoidance, are supportive of their progress, or who can actually help them directly by introducing them around. However, avoidants need to be very careful in picking third-party assistants. Impressionable avoidants should not become soul mates of infantilizing people with an avoidant philosophy of life who do not want to let them go and roam free. They should challenge gurus who advise or recommend avoidance in subtle ways—such as those who subscribe to and advocate avoidant Zen-like philosophies of removal. However much Zen may be a good way for nonavoidant patients to handle anxiety, it is not always the best idea for avoidants, who are usually already, to coin an expression, all too Zenned-out for their own good.

Advising Accepting, or Being Resigned to, Being an Avoidant

Avoidants who, right from the start, simply accept their avoidance and decide to live with it can build their avoidance into their daily routine, willingly giving up the pleasures and rewards of nonavoidance in exchange for remaining relatively anxiety-free. This is a technique of last resort, best reserved for those situations where a realistic assessment of the patient's possibilities and progress to date suggests that some pessimism is indeed indicated.

Marital Therapy

Marital therapy is essentially a subtype of interpersonal therapy dedicated to helping two individuals who are basically committed to each other work out their unilateral or mutual avoidances. A review of the literature and an informal sampling of therapists reveal that marital therapists do not always agree on exactly how to help couples work out problems when one or both members of a dyad are avoidant. Different therapists advocate different methods for resolving the interpersonal difficulties found under such circumstances. Methods advocated include psychodynamically oriented couple psychotherapy, the goal of which is developing interpersonal insight to resolution; abreaction of feelings in order to obtain at least temporary relief of tension and pressure; forbearance and compromise in relationships where change is unlikely, that is, accepting a difficult partner as he or she is and learning to live with, and even to like, him or her; and ending a relationship with a partner who is too remote, too uncaring, and unwilling to change.

Group Therapy

In group therapy with an interpersonal focus the therapist, as Oldham and Morris (1995) note, facilitates the group members in observing the patient's problems as manifest in the group, with the group giving the individual members help through "feedback" (p. 408) and "mutual problem solving" (p. 407). An advantage of treating the avoidant in group therapy is that the group can provide an encouraging and motivating nonpunitive setting in which the patient can feel comfortable coming out of his or her shyness and remoteness. A disadvantage is that the group members are often neither inclined nor trained to deal with shyness and remoteness, so that instead of being therapeutic, they have negative retaliatory knee-jerk emotional responses that are not helpful to avoidants whose problem is one in the first place of putting people off—a difficulty that needs to be treated, not a misbehavior that, as can happen in a group setting, needs to be condemned.

Pharmacotherapy

There are medications that can help a great deal with interpersonal anxiety. Patients should consult with a physician. They should think twice about taking Rapee's (1998) blanket advice to "go back to [your] doctor and ask him or her to help you stop taking the medication" (p. 116).

CHAPTER 17

Supportive Therapy

Supportive therapy, as Pinsker (1997) defines it, is a form of treatment that is "encouraging" (p. 1), where the relationship with the therapist "is a real relationship and is not usually analyzed" (p. 1), where "defenses are generally supported unless they are maladaptive" (p. 1), where the therapist attempts to "minimize frustration and anxiety in the therapy" (p. 1), and where the therapist uses "direct measures to ameliorate symptoms and to maintain, restore, or improve self-esteem, ego function, and adaptive skills" (p. 1). The following are three of the main cornerstones of supportive therapy for avoidants: liking and respecting the patient, offering the patient reassurance, and giving the patient good (while not giving the patient bad) advice on how to become nonavoidant.

LIKING AND RESPECTING THE PATIENT

Even badly done psychotherapy can be supportive as long as the patient feels accepted, not rejected, and believes that the therapist likes, respects, and wants to help him or her. The positive effect of liking and respecting is not a placebo effect. Rather it is a real health-giving response to a therapeutically corrective emotional experience. This positive therapeutic response can persist long after psychotherapy is over as the patient carries the "helpful therapist" around in his or her emotional life as a fan-club-of-one, perhaps the first person in the patient's life different from his or her rejecting mother or castrative father.

OFFERING THE PATIENT REASSURANCE

Here are some reassuring messages that have helped selected avoidant patients feel less anxious, often enough to enable them to act in a more conjunctive fashion:

Social anxiety can be overcome. Avoidant patients almost always feel reassured to learn that their prognosis is good—that is, as Oldham and Morris (1995) suggest, "people with Avoidant personality disorder are luckier than they may think" (p. 201). One reason for the good prognosis is that avoidants have the gift of relating already there inside, and all they have to do is unwrap it. Another reason is that so often AvPD improves with the tincture of time. This was the case for a patient who simply grew bored with his fear of success, mastered his fear of interpersonal relationships by understanding it, and lost his success-discouraging parents to death, in time for him to have a career/relationship later in life, to have a best last marriage, and to blossom artistically after an early, unsuccessful, pedestrian career. (As emphasized in Chapter 8, avoidants can also get worse with the passage of time.)

Everyone experiences a degree of social anxiety. Avoidant patients who feel singled-out and uniquely troubled, or even uniquely bad, are often reassured to learn that they are not alone. In fact, most everyone gets anxious in social situations. Often the difference between a healthy and an avoidant response is the willingness to accept and tolerate a degree of social anxiety, and to force oneself to continue to function nevertheless.

People have some control over how others treat them. Avoidants often have the option of staying away from, or getting out of, relationships with difficult avoidogenic individuals, those who would make anyone anxious and drive them away.

Criticism is rarely fatal. Most of us are severely criticized from time to time no matter who we are or what we do—yet we survive. For example, most of us find ourselves in can't-win situations similar to that of the woman who was criticized for being a slut for showing her sexual feelings, then criticized for being cold, unavailable, and unresponsive for hiding them, or like the situation a critic put me in when he complained that my desire to help gay men find a long-term satisfying monogamous relationship in fact revealed a sinister desire on my part to devalue gay men who were single.

There are ways to make even devastating criticism more tolerable. One can find strength and approval from within, and refuse to calculate one's self-worth by one's reputation. It also helps to recognize how often not us but our critics are the ones with the problem. In my experience, many critics are individuals with a personal agenda geared to elevating their own self-esteem by lowering the self-esteem of others. For example, a critic took me severely to task for suggesting that some gay men were too promiscuous for their own good. He did this because he was promiscuous himself, and guilty about it. Shooting me down was his way to justify his behavior to himself. Also, there is often a bright side to being criticized. People identify with, sympathize with, and move in to support the underdog. Ways to cope with and tolerate criticism are discussed in detail in Chapter 20.

Fears are worries, not realities. Avoidants can be reassured that there is no reason to fear that allowing themselves to have feelings means that they will become depleted. While a degree of depletion can be the result of intense emotions, such depletion is almost always mild and temporary, little more than a transient feeling of fatigue. Therefore, it is a stretch to feel with Joseph Cornell that having sex can either literally or figuratively destroy one's artistic capacity. Avoidants can also be reassured that in the absence of severe ego deficit, such as the deficit that can occur in schizophrenia, flooding, as with depletion, is almost always mild and containable. Finally, people who fear that they might faint while speaking in public almost never actually pass out. While there are documented cases of grooms and best men passing out during a wedding ceremony, I know of no documented case of a public speaker actually fainting while giving a speech.

Guilt is often an overresponse. Much that we call guilt is an overwrought reaction to minor psychic events and behavioral peccadilloes that in reality don't amount to much. While sometimes guilt is justified, mostly it is the product of erroneous distortive thinking such as confounding reprehensible thoughts with reprehensible actions, equating being successful with destroying a rival, and deeming it sinful to survive should others close to us falter. In turn, the low self-esteem that often accompanies guilt is mostly less the product of realistic self-assessment than the outcome of vicious cycling, where a little low self-esteem starts with an inability to give oneself a vote of confidence about something minor. That breeds self-criticism, and the self-criticism breeds self-esteem that is even lower.

Anxiety almost always subsides after starting an activity. I remind patients with a Social Phobia that their symptoms almost always diminish once they start and get involved with a feared activity. When they crest over their "phobic hump," their anxiety disappears, to be replaced by positive feelings of mastery, pride in accomplishment, joy in activity, and a general sense of elation—feelings both pleasurable in themselves and a source of courage to try again, as in the following example:

An individual afraid to drive over a bridge at first refused to try because he was generally too anxious to leave home and because of specific fears that something terrible would happen if he got behind the wheel: he would faint, lose control of his car, and, bumping and crashing into other cars, die in a fiery crack-up. One day he forced himself to drive over a bridge. Predictably his anxiety started up as soon as he got near the base of the bridge and increased as he ascended, until he crested and began to drive down the other side of the bridge. Now anxiety turned into a feeling of euphoria due to delight in his accomplishment, happiness about his triumph both over the obstacle bridge and his need to avoid it, and pleasure in actual success that was equal in intensity but opposite in direction to his dismay about his past failure. (However, the entire cycle began again the next time.)

Things were much the same for him when he forced himself to attend a cocktail party. He felt anxious at the beginning of the evening. The anxiety worsened as the evening progressed. However, after an hour or so, the anxiety peaked and began to diminish, to the point that he was able to introduce himself to one or two people. Now he felt quite pleased and delighted with himself. This feeling lasted for the rest of the evening, only to have the anxiety start up again the next time he went to a party.

Things can usually be worse. When all else fails I remind avoidants that things could be worse. The prototype of this interpretation is one that I gave to a man who became seriously depressed because his mother developed Alzheimer's disease when she was 84. I told him that it could have been worse, for some patients develop Alzheimer's disease when they are 54. (A caveat is that paranoid avoidants tend to think that therapists who offer them blanket reassurances are belittling their personal plight.)

GIVING THE PATIENT ADVICE

General Principles

Pinsker (1997) generally discourages giving patients specific advice. He tells his patients that "for $11.98 you can buy books that tell you what to do" (p. 162). He prefers to outline general principles. I feel that outlining general principles (as distinct from giving specific advice) is a particularly good idea for treating most patients, in particular passive-aggressives whose ambivalence and stubbornness leads them to discredit the therapist, making specific advice-giving problematical. However, for avoidants, merely outlining general principles may not be enough. Avoidants tend to misuse hands-off approaches the same way passive-aggressives tend to use hands-on advice—to resist getting better.

The advice I give to avoidants often amounts to the information therapy Laura Landro (2002) describes in her *Wall Street Journal* article, "If Doctors Prescribe Information, Will Patients Pay or Surf Web?" (p. D4). I sometimes advise avoidants on how to relate much as an English teacher advises a student how to parse a sentence. Several considerations apply. Therapists should explain that taking advice does not make one dependent, or a pushover who too easily yields to therapeutic authority. Therapists should caution patients to do what works for them, not what works for someone else, regardless of any myths of the moment, and of what anyone else, including the therapist, thinks they should do. The safest, best, and most effective advice therapists can give is advice geared to overcoming specific avoidant pathology. For example, in all but the most egregious cases, it is presumptuous for a therapist to decide who is wrong and who is right for avoidants, or for that matter for anyone else. In contrast, it generally makes sense to tell Type I avoidants to overcome their shyness by "getting out there and meeting new people," and to helpfully suggest some places they might actually go to try to connect.

As I mentioned in Chapter 13, therapists giving advice should respect the level of nonavoidance a given individual wishes to achieve—how much closeness and intimacy a particular patient wants out of life and is capable of accomplishing. Some so-called avoidants truly want to be loners; still others long for a close but not a fully intimate relationship. For some, marriage is the right and only goal. Each avoidant has to determine for himself or herself what—on a continuum from social isolation to full closeness and intimacy—is desirable, possible, and right for him or her as an individual, and the therapist should take his or her cue from the patient on how to proceed.

Good Advice

Develop a Relationship-First Philosophy

Avoidants must recognize how important relationships are and how they are worth making sacrifices for, including the sacrifices of a degree of self-pride, autonomy, independence, the need to express oneself completely and honestly, and a consuming desire for revenge against those who have been rejecting.

Learn to Think before Avoiding

Avoidants should evaluate every statement before they make it and consider and reconsider every action before they take it. Angry avoidants need to be especially careful to think about what they are about to say or do before they say or do it, deleting any knee-jerk counterproductive angry avoidant responses in ascendancy, that is, catching them early, making sure that they do not actually emerge.

Handle Sexuality in a Healthy, Interpersonally Conjunctive, Way

Premarital sex should not be used to express avoidant desires in the sexual mode. That is, it should not become a substitute for true relatedness, be a way to rebel against a society believed oppressive, serve as a form of masochistic begging (submitting to premarital sex in order to retain a relationship, along the lines of, "I'll do anything you want me to do if only you will love me and not leave me"), or be a way to express aggressiveness to a partner by telling him or her, "I only want you for your body." Expressing aggressiveness via sex is doubly bad because it is both bad sex and bad aggressiveness.

Infrequent Sex/Abstinence Is an Option in Relationships

Avoidants who abandon relationships because the sex isn't great can be advised that it is as possible to have a good relationship with bad or no sex as it is to have a bad relationship with good or a great deal of sex. Even abstinence within a relationship/marriage is neither necessarily abnormal nor unpleasurable. Some people perceive sex as generally not all that wonderful, while others (the more obsessive, but still normal, among us) feel controlled by their sexual feelings, feel that sex is overly primitive and excessively uncivilized, or simply find the pursuit of sex too time-consuming and too much a diversion from other purposes. For such people it may be enough to cuddle.

Strive for 100% Fidelity within Relationships

I believe that infidelity is per se an act of avoidance and that for avoidants who are not abstinent, 100% fidelity cements relationships. In my view, cheating is usually an avoidant problem, not a nonavoidant solution. That is because it usually puts distance between people by creating personal guilt and resentment in one's partner, even when both partners have an arrangement. (As least some of these arrangements are false preferences created out of a willingness to be submissive, with the rebellion of morning-after regrets the predictable result.) Therefore, within my (admittedly rigid) schema, the only entirely comfortable nonavoidant extramarital relationships are incomplete relationships that are selected to supplement, not replace, spousal relationships: a relationship with a pet (where the nonhuman aspect makes the closeness both acceptable and tolerable); a relationship with a non-trouble-making friend (a member of the same sex in a heterosexual marriage/opposite sex in a homosexual marriage works well); a relationship where age differences are reassuring (so that homosexuals/heterosexuals may more comfortably adopt an older man/woman as a close companion than a younger one, or one of the same age); and family relationships, so that a male homosexual's close relationship with his nephew would be nonavoidant vis-à-vis his relationship with his lover, whereas an equally close relationship with a younger stranger might be avoidant. Of course, almost any outside relationships can work as long as the partner is somehow reassured, "I will not allow this person to come between us or take me away from you." Indeed, not giving the necessary reassurances can be a passive-aggressive form of avoidant troublemaking, part of the distancing pattern inherent in pathological "cross cruising."

Go to Singles Bars to Meet People

Most single avoidants sooner or later ask their therapists whether to try to meet people in singles bars. I used to think that singles bars were okay places to have a drink, and socialize with old and meet new friends, but were not productive places to find love since they were nests for untherapeutized avoidants who put others down when they tried to make contact with them. I reassured my avoidant patients that those who don't meet anyone in a singles bar should not think, "That's because I haven't found the right singles bar, stayed there long enough, had enough to drink, worn the right outfit, or developed the right clever opening line." Instead I suggested that they think, "Finding someone in a singles bar is difficult. That is why they are called singles bars."

My attitude about singles bars has changed somewhat. I still suggest that patients go to bed early on a weeknight. I still tell them, "You need the sleep; you will look, feel, and act better the next day; and your work will thrive. Your being professionally successful will next become a source of self-pride, and the admiration you get from others will help you overcome your low self-esteem." I still take pains to advise my patients to not stay up late cruising every night thinking that the longer they stay up, the more they will accomplish, for it is just as fallacious to equate hard work in a bar with success at relationships as it is to equate getting good grades in college with being successful professionally.

But now I advise my patients that singles bars, used appropriately and in moderation, do have their place, and that avoidants can find a lasting relationship there if they work the bar creatively. They should not engage in frantic pub-crawling behaviors or manic cruising. Rather they should use the bar for networking. Networking involves slowly but surely establishing capillaries between the artery of loneliness and the vein of interpersonal contact, making as many acquaintances as one can, deliberately spreading oneself thin in the beginning hoping to make multiple contacts, developing a circle of acquaintances, then narrowing the resultant wide band of relationships down to one significant other, the most important individual in one's new life, the ultimate contact of them all: the one with Mr. or Ms. Right.

Because all contact is by nature nonavoidant, at least in the beginning, avoidants desiring to network need only start somewhere, almost anywhere. Avoidants can and often should start small by being nice to the local "stray cats." Someone may see them doing it and recommend them to other stray cats. They can be nice to the newspaper person, hoping he or she may say something positive about them to another client. Avoidants can even enjoy neurotic experiences for what they have to offer—as long as they are only momentary interludes and not the start of a lifelong self-destructive pattern. Therefore, as long as they stay safe and do nothing irreversibly damaging to themselves or others, it is okay to meet and have a fling with unsuitable people, be temporarily codependent, or experiment sadomasochistically, especially if these activities serve the purpose of loosening up, practicing relating, getting a nonavoidant reputation, conditioning oneself not to fear rejection, advertising one's availability, and showing other people that they want and are willing to accept them.

Accept Blind Dates

I strongly suggest avoidants freely use, not condemn the use of, blind dates. These can be arranged either by amateur or professional matchmakers. The usual criticisms of blind dates are part of the avoidant folklore. There is in fact nothing per se wrong with blind dates. Often the only reason why good things don't come from blind dates is that the participants, because of preconceived notions (that reflect preexisting avoidances) use the dates as new opportunities to avoid. If both partners are motivated and not self-defeating, blind dates should work out as often as any other encounter—which is all anyone can really ask. However, avoidants should take care not to fall for the come-ons of dating services that offer miracles in the form of alluring advertisements virtually guaranteeing the offer/presence of other suitable singles. They should also avoid books and gurus that tell them how to succeed effortlessly and in short order, promising an immediate and easy solution to a complex problem that will almost certainly take time and effort to resolve.

I sometimes back up my advice by making specific suggestions as to how avoidants can act in productive ways that will make it more likely that they can successfully connect to the new people they meet. However, I do not ask my patients to practice meeting new people with me during the therapy hour. I believe that friends and family can do that particular job better than I can.

Pick Good and Avoid Bad Companions

Bad companions validate avoidants' fears of being rejected by actually rejecting them. They also serve as bad examples by what they say and do. For example, putting things before people, they become fussy housekeepers who won't invite people over to the house because they fear that they will ruin the furniture. They excuse and justify inappropriate aggressiveness as assertiveness, a distinction mostly lost on the victims of avoidants. They reserve their highest praise for fictional writings about love affairs that end tragically, such as books where the hero's lover dies in the end, leaving the hero in the lurch and extremely depressed. Their favorite songs contain avoidant lyrics, such as the one about being a rock and an island. They warn that, in any event, when it comes to relationships the future is bleak. For example, they encourage a paranoid attitude about connecting by warning avoidants that you cannot trust anyone except yourself (and them). They have, and pass on, a strict sphincter morality that leads them to condemn romance and suggest that others renounce what they consider to be its sins, a list of which they bring out at the first sign that a friend or family member might be becoming too independent, getting too close, or just having too much fun. For example, they might warn avoidants embarking on a serious relationship that it is a sin to abandon, not stick close to, their parents, and to not honor and obey them, and take care of them, no matter what, even if that means never moving away from home, going out on one's own, and getting married. They undermine any real relationships that form. They might attempt to destroy a budding relationship by viewing anyone new the avoidant meets as an interloper, whom they proceed to backbite. Or they might accomplish much the same thing by acting hurt and announcing that they themselves feel like a failure when the avoidant reports being successful in connecting. For example, a man responded to an avoidant friend's bragging that she met a new lover not with congratulations but with a plaintive "Boy you are lucky; I cannot meet anyone, I guess that there is no hope for me." Simultaneously they offer themselves up as platonic substitutes for romantic relationships, jealously guarding the avoidant so that he or she does not wander off. They keep tabs on avoidants, calling them constantly to check up on them to find out what they are doing, who they are doing it with, and if they plan to continue, and for how long. They also lure the avoidant into groups, ranging from therapeutic support to Web chat groups intended to offer an immediate, ready substitute for individual relationships, while demanding group cohesion at the expense of these individual relationships by putting group loyalty before individual achievement and fulfillment. As an example, a bad companion lured an avoidant into a group house on Fire Island. Whenever the members of this house sensed that an individual member was on to something, about to connect, they suggested that they all go to the local ice-cream parlor and look for men. Significantly, the place was called *Unfriendly's*. Favorite groups they advocate are those that demand an excessive outlay of time from their members, meet only occasionally and then in order to promote solitary activities outside of the group the rest of the time (a problem with some religious groups); espouse a Zen-like philosophy of removal as the best or only way to reduce interpersonal anxiety; advocate antisocial behavior, as do some rumbling motorcycle clubs; or advocate bigotry by word or deed, for example, with their own seriously exclusionary bylaws.

Almost predictably, sooner or later bad companions like to do an about-face, find an intimate relationship for themselves, then reject the avoidant suddenly and without warning. For example, a psychiatrist leaned heavily on and formed a codependent relationship with a psychologist friend who willingly listened to her troubles for 30 years. Then when the psychiatrist got married, and no longer felt so needy, she told the psychologist, "I am out of the shrink realm and into the art realm, so because we no longer have anything in common I won't be seeing you any more."

Paraphrasing Dorothy Parker, I advise avoidants with companions like this to get a whole new set of best friends. I advise them to find supportive noncritical, unselfish, altruistic people to relate to, people who encourage them by giving them the support and good advice they need to get over their social anxiety. I also advise them to only join groups devoted to expanding horizons, not groups dedicated to maintaining the avoidant status quo of its individual members.

Maintain Your Physique/Physical Health

I often recommend a complete cessation of smoking, limiting one's use of alcohol, and using only prescribed medications—and these in as much moderation as one's physician will allow. On the positive side, prescribed benzodiazepines and antidepressants can help avoidants become less anxious and fearful, while antidepressants can help relieve an avoidant's depression. On the negative side, both can interfere with relationships. Both can create a chemical nirvana that removes motivating depression that warns avoidants to do something with their lives before it's too late; take a needed edge off the socially useful (protective) paranoia that allows avoidants to determine if there is anything wrong with, or even dangerous about, others; soften the craggy neurotic profile an avoidant needs to not become uninteresting/bland/pedestrian/ordinary; and lyse the prosocial interpersonal sensitivity and capacity for empathy that so often originates in being anxious, depressed, and paranoid. A more complete discussion of pharmacotherapy is available in Chapter 18.

At times I refer my avoidant patients for an appearance makeover, to an exercise guru, or to a physician.

A physician noted that in his gym there were some men who had untreated but treatable skin lesions. He overheard some of these men complaining that they couldn't keep relationships going and that they did not know why. He speculated how their partners might react to the sudden presentation of these lesions thrust upon them on a first date or during a first sexual encounter. Yet few of these men seemed to view their lesions as significant. They denied their importance, or if they admitted it, said, not necessarily convincingly, "If she really loves me she will overlook such a small thing." These small things, however, might have put early and late love to an impossible test. Moral: while it is common for an old partner to overlook a new lesion, it is uncommon for a new partner to overlook an old one.

Use Tricks to Cope with Social Anxiety

Here are some tricks avoidants can use to master the anxiety associated with giving a speech or meeting people at a social gathering, and to cope with the consequences of that anxiety. Public speakers can deal with the fear of fainting associated with stage fright by reassuring themselves that they are still conscious, doing so by moving about in place, wiggling toes, tightening the thighs and buttocks in an attempt to get the blood to flow back to the brain, sucking on a mentholated cough drop or sugar candy to refresh themselves, or having a sip of ice water to shock themselves back into focus. They can also make their audience seem less frightening by demeaning them, for example, by imagining them in a ridiculous pose so that the audience looks to the speaker as ridiculous as the speaker feels he or she looks to the audience. I don't give talismans, but other therapists, noting that phobic avoidants respond to magic, give their patients a slip of paper signed by the therapist that says, "You will be okay on your date tonight" or "You will be able to get through your speech without passing out, or having your voice crack."

Revamp Your Defensive Structure

The following defenses are potentially viable substitutes for withdrawal:

Healthy avoidance, which is limited, small scale, creative avoidance that is both appropriate to the circumstances and for an ultimately greater nonavoidant good. Healthy avoidance allows patients to retreat from uncomfortable unimportant relationships in order to prevent discomfort in these relationships from spreading to contaminate and destroy potentially important social and personal contacts. (Healthy avoidance is discussed further in Chapter 6.)

Healthy denial, to cope with criticism and rejection and to overcome anxiety about becoming intimate—short of turning into an extremist frantic gregarious hypomanic who pushes too hard and acts too precipitously because he or she is terrified of acting at all.

Healthy projection, an "It's you, not me" fantasy, particularly useful in an emergency when one's self-esteem falls and badly needs a temporary lift.

Healthy identification, becoming like others who are less fearful and less guilty, more self-tolerant, and more self-assertive. While this is controversial, a therapist can, in selected cases and in a limited way, share his or her personal experiences with his or her patients, encouraging them to identify with the therapist by telling them how the therapist warded off or actually resolved his or her own problems with avoidance.

One therapist contrasted himself as "the back-slapping administrator who succeeded because he complimented his employees for a job well done" with the
"back-stabbing administrator who criticized his employees for their shortcomings." "With him they want to avoid their work out of hate. With me they want
to do their work out of love." "Flattery," he reminded his patients, "will get you
everywhere."

However, sharing experiences, life stories, life problems, and personal
triumphs over being avoidant, while likely to be safe and effective with
dependent avoidants who hang on a therapist's every word, and with *obsessive-compulsive* avoidants who are so paralyzed when it comes to making any interpersonal progress that they beg to be told what to do (even
though, at least in the beginning, when they are most resistant, they plan
to not do it, or to do the opposite) is likely to be a bad idea for *paranoid*
avoidants, who suspect their therapists of wanting to talk about themselves on their time and dime, and for alarmist *histrionic* avoidants who
see signs of avoidance in the supposedly healthy therapist as indicative
of the complete hopelessness of their own situation.

Act Positively

Avoidants should strive to be nice, generous, undemanding, empathic,
act in a healing way toward others, and avoid putting others off.

Being nice is an especially good idea for avoidants because it encourages
others to be nice to them back. Being nice involves becoming less critical
of others, or at the very least criticizing them in a way that leaves open
the possibility of going back, apologizing, and making amends.

Above all, being nice requires managing anger. Avoidants can *feel* less
angry by understanding others' motives so that they can take others' humiliating and rejecting behaviors less personally. Avoidants can *get* less angry by consciously becoming more compliant for the sake of their
relationships (again, short of becoming a pushover). Avoidants might consider taking a lesson from the politicians who backslap and kiss babies, tell
people what they want to hear, and give them what they ask for, this way
winning more elections than they might otherwise win if they were merely
competent and credentialed. In practical terms, instead of complaining that
a lover doesn't fill the ice-cube tray after using the cubes, an avoidant might
consider unselfishly filling the tray him- or herself. Giving a partner this
little gift undercuts and bypasses hostile intramural power-struggles. Next
time a partner fills the cubes on his or her own, out of love.

One avoidant, a vendor out of the morning newspaper, reacted to the question,
"Do you have any more of these newspapers?" with "It's not my fault that I am
out of them—why is every one bugging me?" As his therapist I suggested that he
instead try a shorter, sweeter, less interpersonally divisive, more accommodating,
reply: "Sorry, no."

Shortly after a man's wife died he received a notice from the internist who took care of her, asking her to please come in for her annual physical examination. The man was at first outraged. Then he understood the reasons for the screw-up, saw that it was nothing personal, and realized that the doctor, however misguided, was concerned about his patients' welfare. So instead of getting mad, and even, he called to tell the office that his wife had died, that he wanted to thank them for treating her, and that he wished to commend them for their continuing concern, however misguided, for the state of her health.

Avoidants with passive-aggressive tendencies should be especially careful to avoid expressing their anger indirectly in the form of Freudian slips. Most people can understand what they mean. This was the case when one man revealed his hostility to his wife by referring to himself as impudent when he meant to say impotent. Also to be avoided is brutal honesty for honesty's sake.

Being generous involves giving others something, if only in order to get something back:

An older patient, who needed to be realistic about what could be accomplished at his advanced age, recognized that he had to effectively bribe people to give him something because this was the only way he could get anything at all. Desperate for love, he decided to pay for it in small ways—with gifts. Then, instead of complaining that people only loved him for his money, he complained only if nobody loved him even for that.

Being undemanding involves expecting less to get more. At the very least, one should make one's expectations of others a negotiating point for, rather than a stumbling block to, relationships.

Being empathic involves forgiving others their small transgressions while allowing those who have made them to save face and make repairs. It involves appreciating the good in others by becoming more sensitive to their feelings, needs, and motivations in order to seek out benign explanations for others' presumably malignant behaviors.

A psychiatrist felt passed-over when an internist called not on him but on a psychologist colleague for a consultation with the internist's patient. He remained angry until his own therapist pointed out that he knew (for personal reasons) that the internist was merely living out a positive relationship with his own psychotherapist, also a psychologist.

It involves addressing others' emotional needs, short of being manipulative. For example, *paranoids*, who tend to feel that people who are at all mysterious are therefore involved in a conspiracy, tend to respond well to simple, open, and above-board explanations and reassurances. *Depressives* like being treated in a noncritical fashion by people who take special care to remind them of their good points, not of what they lack. *Narcissists* like being flattered, idolized, and catered to, not slighted and overlooked. Of course, catering to others should stop short of discounting one's own feelings and needs completely, say, by allowing oneself to be a trinket or plaything to be toyed with, and dropped at will.

A depressed hardware store salesman told self-deprecating jokes on his first date. He related how he handed out a flyer for his sale merchandise, and then said, "Read this only if you are having difficulty sleeping at night"—a bad joke and a worse business practice. His date countered, in essence, with, "Stop knocking yourself; when I was in your store I saw your merchandise and it looked pretty good to me. And you don't have anything to be personally ashamed of, either." Alas, this emboldened him to become too narcissistic, to feel too good about himself, to the point that he put her instead of himself down, using the criterion of her availability as a main negative measure of her true worth, criticizing and humiliating her simply for being too easy to get. She then had to counter not with apologies or explanations but with limit setting by aggressive self-promotion.

Perfectionists who destroy viable relationships because of a small flaw that keeps them from seeing the overall good in others tend to react positively to others who are on their very best behavior. *Parsimonious* individuals who only do Dutch treats, inexpensive restaurants, or midnight walks on the beach not because these are romantic, poetic things to do but because as cheap people they like things that are free, often respond well to being reassured that, "I am not a gold-digger" to soften the blow they feel over having to part with money. *Contrary* people favor people who expect or want little or nothing from them. They give the most to those who want or demand the least. Making demands on them triggers their oppositionalism. They respond negatively when pushed for a firm commitment too early in a relationship. They respond positively when handled like a fish being reeled in: given some play so that it may be safely landed.

Passive-aggressives often respond well to others who set limits on their covert hostility, asking them to either stop being hostile in the first place or, if they must be hostile, to at least be hostile out in the open. *Histrionics* with a parent fixation who, unable to get their parents out of their bedroom, drop lovers either because they aren't enough like a parent or because they are too much like a parent, often respond well to being reminded, in word and deed, that "I am your lover, not your mother or father." *Sadists* who make their victims suffer just for the fun of it and *masochists* who get others to make them suffer for the gratification to be obtained from renunciation and loss often respond well to being told that with so much necessary and unavoidable pain and suffering in the world there is no room at all for the kind of pain and suffering that is deliberately induced.

However, sometimes relationships with sadists are actually hopeless:

One patient recognized that her relationship with a sadist was hopeless because when she asked him to spend the night with her for a second time he replied, "I already did that last night." She properly responded not with pleas and tears but with, "Right. Why bother. I already did that, too."

Acting in a healing way towards others fixes relationships instead of abandoning them because they are broken. Avoidants can act in a healing way by becoming peacemakers who soothe ruffled feathers. Keeping the greater good in mind, they can disrupt vicious cycles of strike and counterstrike based on tit-for-tat by ignoring a certain amount of abuse, and instead of getting angry back, responding with a patient, forgiving, "That is just the way he is/she will get over it."

Not putting others off may mean not acting suspicious, worrisome, complaining or hostile on a day-to-day basis, but instead saving these off-putting behaviors up and discharging them only during therapy sessions.

Enter the Best Possible Profession

I sometimes advise avoidants to think twice about entering/pursuing professions that might be avoidance-enhancers, such as: post office mail sorter; writer/indexer; mountain climber; grave digger; philosopher/poet; professional critic (who cannot help but make enemies because inevitably he or she will have something bad to say about someone's work); animal trainer/pet-shop worker; circus performer; and of course, any profession that is illegal. In contrast, professions that might not intensify and even help reduce avoidance include: worker in a charitable organization such as a homeless shelter; greeter in a funeral home; real estate broker; host on a cruise ship; sports instructor in a gym; politician; healer; salesperson; and cab driver.

Turn Over Nonavoidant Resolutions

Here is a list of possible resolutions I ask my patients to consider making:

I will focus on, and single-mindedly make, relationships my ongoing concern. I will not allow myself to be sidetracked in my quest for nonavoidance, making it a one- or a part-time interest. Without being frantic, I will fix on my nonavoidant goals like the concert pianist fixes on his or her career, and head for my nonavoidant objectives in a straight line, with few side trips or vacations, and without letting anyone or anything get in the way. For example, just as a concert pianist should go to bed early and not drink excessive alcohol the night before a performance, I will arrange my life so that I am rested and have enough energy to accomplish tomorrow's nonavoidant tasks. I will then go about achieving my avoidant goals guilt-free, and certainly without first asking for others' approval. I will do something nonavoidant every day even if that only involves picking up the phone instead of letting the answering machine take the call. I will keep one eye open for who might be looking at me so that I can react positively, for not noticing is as bad as not reacting. Each day I will review my progress and ask myself, "What have I done to avoid whom today?" If I don't give myself a satisfactory answer, I will ask the question again, because almost certainly I have done something that I should not repeat. I have looked right by someone good to see. I have antagonized someone who would love me if only I would let them. I have ignored someone who is right for me, using a flimsy excuse—because he is a longtime friend, because she is someone I met on a blind date, or because I have left little room for his or her human frailties. I have not listened hard enough to someone else's positive feelings toward me. Perhaps I have heard their words without listening between their lines, and as a result have taken the negative arm of their ambivalence too seriously, over-emphasizing the base motive of someone with mixed motivation when instead I should have seen the good in the other person and rescued the relationship by being a little more charitable and understanding.

I will think in less avoidant ways. I will distinguish what I *do* fear from what I *should* fear. Each time I detect I am moving away from others I will attempt to determine if the movement is appropriate or unjustified by listing the evidence for and against my dark forebodings and disjunctive temptations. I will think less catastrophically about being criticized, humiliated, and rejected. If I am criticized I will ask myself if the person criticizing me is really important enough for the criticisms to really matter, and if they do really matter, tell myself, "So what." If I am humiliated, I will ask what it is about the other person that makes it so necessary for him or her to do that to me. If I am rejected, I will tell myself, when applicable, "That's their problem, and loss, not mine."

I will be more permissive toward myself. I will allow myself to simply be human. I will relinquish my need to punish myself for imagined, and even for real, miscalculations. If I have failed at a relationship, I will accept my failure as integral to, not an unfortunate complication of, the process of connecting and not use a previous failure as an excuse to create a feared (or desired) permanent setback.

I will enhance my self-esteem by behaving in less avoidant ways. If my behavior does not warrant my being kinder to myself, I will behave better so that I can give myself more of a vote of confidence. I will become prouder of myself by helping others become less avoidant. I will work for a less avoidant society. I will work to overcome bigotry, gay-bashing, and spousal abuse. I will do these things in full awareness that helping others is a royal road to helping oneself.

I will meet a challenging reality head on. Each day I will attempt to bring one difficult person in my life around. Instead of routinely accepting rejection passively, then avoiding everyone who is rejecting me, each day I will attempt to get one previously rejecting person to stop rejecting me and to accept me instead. I will also make what life changes are necessary and indicated. If I feel stuck in a small town I will travel to a large city to try to meet new people, and if I feel isolated in a large city I will try to visit some small-town friends and have them put me up, then take me around.

Bad Advice

Advice Helpful Only for Nonavoidants

Advice good for nonavoidants, such as do your own thing; don't say yes when you mean no; get your anger out; play hard to get; and make complete honesty your best policy, can be routinely bad for avoidants. Generally speaking, avoidants need to become more, not less, connected by saying yes when they mean no; by keeping their anger in, in order to develop and cement relationships; by playing easy, not hard, to get; and by being cooperative, compromising, and even submissive in the hope of getting off the sidelines and into the game.

Advice to Have Sexual Fantasies about Others When Having Sex with Your Steady Partner

As I note throughout, advice-givers often suggest various forms of mental cheating as a way to preserve a marriage. They imply or state that mental infidelity discharges tension or even ultimately increases sexual desire for, and improves performance with, one's regular partner. But mental cheating is not the liberating aphrodisiacal experience many advice-givers suggest that it is. At the very least it involves insensitivity to others' feelings and needs, while at the most it is a form of emotional treachery. Using fantasies about others/pornography as an aphrodisiac is right for an individual only after he or she has carefully considered his or her answers to the following questions: Will you yourself feel flooded and out of control? Do you think your wife/husband cannot tell if you are thinking about another woman/man? Will your spouse know that you are, or actually see you, cruising, undressing others in your mind and in real life with your eyes, and if so, how do you think he or she might feel/react? Will you and/or your partner dislike seeing the other get excited over someone else, only to fall into your arms to consummate an arousal that originated with, and so still belongs to, someone else?

Type III avoidants contemplating cheating in the setting of an ongoing relationship should, as previously noted, disregard the advice from psychotherapists and self-help books to "cheat on your spouse to bring the two of you together," advice that may be right for some people but is almost always wrong for avoidants. Here is an example of such advice, from a television character on the *Brini Maxwell* show named Philomena, advice that is completely wrong for avoidants:

Dear Philomena,

I know that men tend to sleep around and gay men have more opportunity to sleep around than straight men. But my boyfriend and I would like to make our relationship work. Can you give us any idea of what's going on here and suggestions for how we can deal with it? Signed, I can't say no.

Dear ICSN,

I'm glad you asked that. In a recent research project it was found that the gay marriages that seemed to last were the ones where the participants were not so rigid about their sexual fidelity. Gay men who enter a relationship expecting to have a 1950s *Donna Reed* style marriage of complete sexual fidelity were frequently disappointed. You know, of course, anonymous sex is one thing, but actually dating other people, which includes the possibility of an emotional involvement, is much more of a threat. And, as always, honest communication is still the key to relationship longevity.

The following, taken from W. Robert Beavers (1982), is another, related example of advice that is misguided for avoidants: "I believe that affairs can hold stuck marriages together probably as often as they rip them asunder. If reasonably gratifying, the affair may avert emotional illness in the involved spouse" (p. 474).

Advice As to Who Exactly Is Right and Who Exactly Is Wrong for You

Therapists who tell patients who specifically is right or wrong, good or bad for them are often asking these patients to condemn specific relationships prematurely, and on some abstract principle. In my experience, compatibility studies as those to be found in Jon P. Bloch's (2000) *Finding Your Leading Man* do not always take into account a multiplicity of factors, chief of which are individual preference and individual pathology on one or both sides, and how, when one or both people in a relationship are motivated they can make that relationship work. A relationship between almost any two people can be rescued and developed. Instead of telling avoidants who is right and who is wrong for them, mostly therapists should limit their advice to general principles about how to make and implement good decisions when selecting partners. Here are three examples of such generic rules. Avoidants should:

- Take special care to pick people who understand, appreciate, and love, not reject, them. That is a good idea even if rejecting Mr. or Ms. Wrong on the way to Mr. or Ms. Right temporarily requires becoming more, not less, avoidant.

- Not stay overlong in a relationship that isn't working and keeps them from finding another one that might work better.

- Not pick someone wrong for them because they are too guilty to be happy, because they are masochistically fixated not on connecting with the people who love them but on trying to change the minds of those very others who are most set against them, or in order to further specific avoidant goals. As an example of the latter, one avoidant patient almost literally planned to have traumatic relationships so that afterwards he could suffer and make others suffer by having posttraumatic flashbacks about them.

CHAPTER 18

Pharmacotherapy

Clinicians who believe that avoidance originates primarily in biological processes will offer, or even emphasize, treatment with medication. As mentioned in Chapter 2, there are biological theories of the cause of avoidance that point to specific targets vulnerable to medication. Thus the literature suggests correlations such as the ones between externally oriented aggression as manifest in fights and temper tantrums in affective and personality disorders and serotonergic dysfunction; between increased irritability in response to provocation and increased responsiveness of the noradrenergic system; and between disengagement from an environment and a reduction in noradrenergic efficiency. (While the literature emphasizes how serotonergic and noradrenergic dysfunction cause aggression, irritability and disappointment, it is not particularly vocal about the reverse possibility, that the aggression, irritability and disengagement are in fact the cause of the serotonergic and noradrenergic dysfunction.)

I find psychopharmacotherapy to be especially helpful for two groups of avoidants: shy Type I avoidants who cannot initiate relationships and phobic Type I avoidants who suffer from symptoms of a Social Phobia. This will be evident to anyone afraid of attending a party who has effectively self-treated with alcohol before entering the room. I find medication less helpful for Type II and III avoidants, individuals who are undecided and ambivalent, and who give up relationships they have begun, often over a trivial matter, and for Type IV avoidants whose avoidance predominantly consists of being regressed in a codependent relationship with one person for the purpose of not having satisfactory relationships with all others.

Specific medications found to be helpful in AvPD include beta-blockers for stage fright, benzodiazepines, and the antidepressant serotonin reuptake inhibitors and monoamine oxidase inhibitors (MAOIs). Specific schema to help the physician determine which medication is better for which avoidant are beyond the scope of this text.

Several difficulties associated with pharmacotherapy are worth noting. First, anxiety may falsely appear to be biological when it is really psychological, therefore suggesting pharmacotherapy when psychotherapy is really indicated. This sometimes happens because anxiety without words is mistakenly though to be anxiety without content—and contentless anxiety a reliable indicator of chemical imbalance—even though a patient's paucity of associations merely means that the patient isn't reporting his or her associations because he or she doesn't think them worth mentioning, or is suppressing them because he or she feels frightened or guilty about them, or because he or she fears punishment for saying what is really on his or her mind.

Second, many of the medications recommended for avoidance actually have unwelcome protoavoidant psychological side effects. As examples, medications can variously becloud an avoidant who needs to concentrate on nonavoidance, imparting a fuzzy feeling to an avoidant who is better off bright and alert; reduce energy needed for making friends and lovers; and make the avoidant feel too well to need to solve his or her problems, giving him or her a false sense of comfort that decreases his or her need and motivation to go out and meet people.

Third, benzodiazepines, often used for avoidant anxiety, are (though this may be somewhat overdone) both addicting and capable of losing their efficacy over time, so that some patients need to keep increasing the dose. Also, avoidants on benzodiazepines have to stop drinking because of the additive effects of benzodiazepines and alcohol and the increased risk of addiction from the combination of the two. That means: no healthy social drinking and no using alcohol to reduce social anxiety. This is unfortunate for, in my opinion, when used in moderation, alcohol is a safe and effective way to self-medicate to surmount both general relationship anxiety and specific Social Phobia.

CHAPTER 19

Therapeutic Modifications for Treating Avoidants

The suggestions in this chapter are for both psychotherapists who are inexperienced and psychotherapists who are experienced but not yet familiar with the special treatment requirements of patients with AvPD.

BE CAUTIOUS ABOUT SUGGESTING THAT THE PATIENT GET HIS OR HER ANGER OUT

Avoidants distance themselves from people by getting angry with them and then by expressing their anger openly. Expressing anger openly hurts others. Also, expressing anger can intensify, not reduce, anger. As Charles Keating (1984) says, "Recent studies suggest that, contrary to popular opinion, it is not always helpful to express our feelings, to strive for a catharsis or to 'talk them out.' Sometimes such efforts only intensify feelings. It may be best to distract ourselves with other interests. Hostile feelings, at least, seem to dissipate more quickly this way" (p. 150). Therefore, avoidants should take their cue from the magnificently nonavoidant Baltic folktale. They should get others to "take off their heavy coat," and they should do so by being more like the sun that warms than like the harsh wind that blows.

A patient said her sister-in-law made a date to join her for dinner but then didn't show up at the appointed time. When the patient called to ask when and if she was coming, her sister-in-law's daughter answered the phone and told the patient that her mother wasn't home, having gone out to dinner with some friends. The patient's therapist told the patient to tell the sister-in-law in certain terms how much she was hurt and to warn her, "Do this again and we are through." He said, "You must insist on being treated well. You should never allow yourself to be abused this way." Of course, the sister-in-law, instead of apologizing, claimed that she wasn't to blame because she had an ironclad excuse. She said, "I didn't show up because I thought you were to confirm first, and I didn't hear from you." Next the sister-in-law stopped talking to the patient, increasing the patient's isolation and worsening her depression.

Assertiveness training, never a good idea for avoidants, is especially problematical when it is a guise for narcissism training. For example, having a showdown about what *you* want to order for *your* Chinese dinner, a familiar example from Bryna Taubman's (1976) much-followed assertiveness training book of the 1970s, is for avoidants (and for some others as well) less healthfully assertive than it is pathologically divisive.

USE EXPOSURE/TOTAL PUSH WITH CAUTION

Exposure has to go at a rate that the patient finds comfortable. Therapists need to be patient and not push avoidants too hard too fast toward nonavoidance. Patients did not become avoidant overnight and they will not become nonavoidant overnight. Becoming nonavoidant can take months or even years of stop-and-start movement toward the goal. This is for at least five reasons. First, like most everyone else, avoidants both like and need the way they are and fear the alternative too much to yield their problems up easily and immediately and just on the therapist's say-so. Avoidants like their avoidance because, as with any personal philosophy, it is an entrenched much-beloved ego-syntonic personal value system. Avoidants need their avoidance because it is a defense that reduces anxiety. In particular, it reduces anxiety the same way a time-out reduces emotionality: by offering breathing room in interpersonal crises, giving the avoidant an opportunity to regroup forces in preparation for making one's next move. Second, almost all new behaviors require practice before they can become perfect, and second nature. Third, pushing avoidants prematurely into feared encounters can make them anxious, depressed, and negativistic. They then might either leave treatment in order to reestablish comfortable distance or stay in treatment but resist it. This is exemplified by issuing excessively favorable progress reports or by developing sacrificial-lamb, minor nonavoidant successes created and emphasized to hide and keep secret major avoidant failures. Fourth, avoidants who are hypomanic are easily pushed beyond healthy counterphobia/denial into frantic excess that hides but does not overcome inertia. Fifth, avoidants who are at all paranoid (many avoidants) are suspicious of excessive therapeutic zeal. They perceive overeager therapists as motivated by a need to dominate and control them and to use them for their own selfish purposes.

The following is one therapist's comeuppance for pushing a man with AvPD too far too fast to "get out and do things" and "socialize with your family."

A patient, who was actually in satisfactory physical health, was told to "get out more, go to new places, meet new people, and get to know your son once again." Instead of following the suggestions offered he replied with the following letter: "Your prescription . . . I cannot follow. In the first place, you are obviously not aware of my physical disabilities. My energy reservoir is very low, and just a few hours out simply exhausts me. Added to that is the fact that the severe arthritis in my left foot makes it impossible just to walk around the block. Furthermore, my urinary tract problems require frequent emptying of the bladder (anywhere, frequently, from every ten minutes to every half hour). So, besides the fatigue factor, I cannot consider long trips. But possibly the severest problem is my unpredictable physical instability (dizziness, loss of balance, etc.). This is due to a cerebral deterioration, the onset of which I expect will be proved on a CAT scan I am to have shortly.

While it is true, as you suggested, that I would like to live on the Upper West Side of Manhattan, because of the easy access to many cultural events, a goodly number of them free, such as the Juilliard Concerts and the weekly library concerts at Lincoln Center, a hop, skip, and a jump there and back would have no benefit for me, even if it were physically possible.

Furthermore, my contact with my son is, to say the very least, tangential. So even if he were inclined to eke out a couple of hours for a visit, the event would be both superficial and painful.

The following is one therapist's comeuppance for pushing a patient with AvPD too far too fast to get married:

A patient who complained she couldn't meet men said she had begun to meet them, but forgot to say that they were all married. When this avoidant ploy was discovered, instead of meeting married men she met a single man and got married to one—selected for being close to death from terminal cancer.

Generally speaking, total push techniques are most helpful for shy and phobic Type I avoidants, and least useful for ambivalent Type II and Type III avoidants. Type II and Type III avoidants do not need to be pushed. They need to be urged to stay where they are, that is, they need less action and more reflection. To avoid burning bridges, Type III avoidants should stop and think before they act, and perhaps not act at all. Instead of getting an immediate divorce they should postpone their divorce (or other avoidant behavior) and think their plans though so that any action they take is for rational reasons. Before getting that divorce, they should ask themselves questions designed to reveal any role they themselves might be playing in their marital discord, such as, "Do I want to divorce my husband/wife to find a bigger and better man/woman because of blind ambition, to please others instead of myself, to get back at him/her for slights I imagine because I am paranoid, because I think my self-esteem will magically improve if I were married to an artist instead of to a carpenter, or because I have an oedipal fixation and he/she is no real substitute for my actual father or mother?" Even when a clear and present reason for a divorce exists (such as infidelity deemed unacceptable), slow action is always preferable to long repentance. Therefore, some with Type II and III avoidant patients, the advice, "Make a decision and I will help you with it," should be changed to, "Don't make any decisions for a while because you might make the wrong decision now, and if you do, I may not be able to help you with it later."

BE CAUTIOUS ABOUT BECOMING AN ADVOCATE FOR (OR A SPOILER OF) SPECIFIC RELATIONSHIPS

As outlined in Chapter 17, therapists have to be extremely cautious both about recommending specific relationships and about countermanding others. No one, even a therapist, really knows who is right for someone else. The following case illustrates how unwise it can be for a therapist to egg a patient on to give up on a relationship.

A man's lover called and left a message saying her cat had cancer and asked him to call her back. He didn't call her back because he had recently left her the message that his cat had died, and she didn't call him back. He made the point, "I won't give her what she won't give me," and she made the point, "I think he could have been a bigger man about it." The therapist said the relationship was doomed. Disregarding the therapist's gloomy predictions, the patient rescued the relationship simply by forgetting all about who did what to whom, first, and most, putting petty squabbles aside for the well-being of the relationship as a whole.

Many therapists have made the serious mistake of buying into an avoidant's declaration that a relationship is so bad that it should be abandoned. These therapists have often fallen into one or more of three classic traps avoidants set so that they can pursue their avoidance, now with the imprimatur of authority.

The first trap is allowing oneself to become convinced that a relationship should become a casualty of trivial incompatibilities such as, "We differ about what time we like to go to bed." Avoidants set this trap by elaborating trivial negative interactions into hair-raising stories about lovers and spouses ("he abuses me") while simultaneously being especially sweet to their therapist ("and I look to you to rescue me")—being sweet less because they feel positively towards their therapist and more because they know that the therapist uses his or her reaction to the patient to decide whose side to take. Also they want the therapist on their side all the better to mop up the floor with their partner. Such patients sense where the therapist's rational/irrational likes and dislikes lie and speak to them. In some cases, the manipulation of the countertransference begins even before therapy starts. Some patients select a therapist in the first place based on how he or she fits an avoidant agenda, guessing from the therapist's reputation, from things said at the time of the referral, or from the name of the therapeutic group, what therapist will make the best coconspirator for a patient desiring to carry out an avoidant plan already in place.

A woman who sensed her therapist was a highly moral person listed and exaggerated her husband's amoral peccadilloes to get the therapist on her side in her quest for a divorce. Her therapist then said, "You can do better than him," and "there are plenty of fish in the ocean" so "find someone more suitable." His remarks catalyzed her abandoning what was a potentially redeemable relationship with a man who, even though he was a bit imperfect, truly loved her.

Therapists who tell their patients whom to love and when to leave should explore their personal motivation for doing do. Are they overly ambitious for their patients; overly grandiose in their belief that they are able to advise and make choices for others; too perfectionistic for their own and their patients' good; believers in the questionable theory that there is a one and only perfect soul mate for everyone, and at all stages of that person's life; or overeager, overly ambitious advocates for patients, insisting that they do better when they are already doing the best that they can?

I believe that ultimately only the patient can decide who is desirable and who is wrong for him or her. Therefore, many patients should be asked to make that decision for themselves, with the therapist limiting him- or herself to helping the patient implement any decision he or she has made on his or her own. At most some Type II avoidants should be informed of the wisdom of flexibility and compromise, and some Type III avoidants of the wisdom of patience and stick-to-itiveness. When making decisions of this sort all avoidants need to take their personal and interpersonal reality into account, particularly what real opportunities exist in life due to their age, appearance, wealth, family background, professional standing, and availability of support systems such as that provided by a warm, loving family—all factors that influence what gambles, if any, the avoidant can and should reasonably attempt to take to stabilize or improve upon his or her present situation.

The second trap is criticizing a partner and running the risk of severely antagonizing that partner. Avoidants who have a fight with their partners predictably get their therapists to agree with them that their partners are horrors. Then when they have their next fight they throw the negative things the therapist said about their partner up in the partner's face. During a fight some even report a distorted version of, or actually lie about, what was said in order to cow their partner into submission. A favorite avoidant exercise in misquoting is omitting qualifiers, such as "some," "perhaps," and "maybe."

The third trap is criticizing a partner and running the risk of having the criticism backfire should the patient perceive the criticism of the partner as an indirect criticism of the patient—for making such a match—and a threat to a marriage that, in spite of all its problems, offers the patient the possibility of a better life than any available alternative.

USE SEVERAL THERAPEUTIC APPROACHES SIMULTANEOUSLY

When it comes to understanding and treating avoidance, some therapists oversimplify, becoming like a surveyor who reduces a terrain to a series of lines and triangles and then equates the terrain with those lines and triangles. Such therapists miss significant aspects of avoidance by reducing complex human sensibilities, preferences, longings, dreams, fears and sorrows to one or a few factors, such as cognitive errors, negative feedback, or the straight-jacketing influence of the past on the present. Then these therapists only correct cognitive errors, only analyze Oedipus, or only focus on a patient's difficult reality, past or present ("you are the way you are because of early trauma"). They intervene without even consulting the patient's wishes about the kinds of interventions he or she might need, want, think appropriate, or actually require.

One doctor, instead of talking at length with his avoidant patients, gave them an activating medication for their withdrawal and a sedating medication for their anxiety and for the anxiety-based somatic symptoms that often appeared when they tried to socialize. Another got only avoidant therapists to work at his clinic by screening job applicants with the question, "What drug do you give to an elderly lady who wants to leave a retirement community because she doesn't like it there?" and, "What drug do you give to a patient who is grieving for his mother who died suddenly from a heart attack?" (In my opinion in each case psychotherapy should be a main, if not the only, mode of intervention.)

RECOGNIZE THE DOWNSIDE OF REASSURANCE

Ill-advised reassurance can create either too much or too little hope, come across as belittling, or cause an avoidant patient to let down his or her guard and become too accepting of his or her avoidance. Too much hope can lead to disappointment down the line. However good the intention, however positive the immediate emotional impact, soon enough there is a price to pay for the deception. Statements to the effect that "you will find someone right for you if you are just patient" may easily prove to be inaccurate. Predictions that cure can be expected if the patient just takes a few easy steps may not come true. Trivial remedies presented as if they are momentous and guaranteed effective may not work, or may even make things worse. All these things satisfy the therapist's desire to do something for the patient more than they satisfy the patient's need to have something done for him or her. A case in point is excessively simplistic behavioral conditioning that is based on a childlike wish fulfillment that sometimes reminds of the magical ideas of primitive man. For example: make a list of all the things that frighten you about people, then master your fears by tearing up the list (or, for therapists who believe they are being surgically precise and radical—burning up the list).

An avoidant whose therapist promised to cure his avoidant bisexuality by simple behavioral conditioning fought internal, interpersonal and social condemnation as well as his therapist to retain his powerful ego-dystonic sexual attraction. Ultimately he gave up his therapist instead of giving up his bisexuality. That is, he responded with another avoidance—the polite flight out the door. He said, "I'm all better" in order to get away from treatment, overstating the degree of his improvement so that he would not hurt his therapist's feelings. (Behavioral therapists need to remember that flight into health is the real reason for some supposedly positive therapeutic outcomes. Psychoanalytically oriented psychotherapists admit this possibility, though not necessarily for the right reasons. They admit it first, because the presumed cleverness of the formulation is on its own a feather in their cap, and second, because it shifts the entire responsibility for a patient's premature termination of therapy from the therapist onto the patient.)

When trivial remedies go beyond the merely silly to the harmful, they can make things considerably worse.

A sex therapist suggested that a couple cuddle instead of having sex until the desire to have sex returned. But there was as little desire to cuddle as there was to have sex. She also suggested that the worrisome, alarmist, hysterical wife schedule appointments with her husband—times when she could be worrisome and alarmist, so that at other times she could spare her husband from her worries and alarms. The result was unintended: a sense of artificiality was injected into the relationship, and the wife's worrisomeness actually increased as she brooded all day about whether she could control herself until her appointed time to worry.

A therapist asked a patient suffering from symptoms of Posttraumatic Stress Disorder to go to the symbolic equivalent of the original place where the trauma first occurred—to a Vietnam War memorial, in order to relive the trauma to "get it out of your system." This procedure is risky. It can give some patients with PTSD a measure of relief. In this case it intensified the problem because this patient felt re-exposed to an unmanageably noxious stimulus.

Finally, reassurances/sympathy of the more-fish-in-the-sea sort given after a relationship is botched can play into an avoidant's defensive who-cares attitude about screwing up relationships, creating an unhealthy attitude that there are always other fish to fry, when in fact the last fish may have been the biggest and the best catch of a lifetime.

In the realm of too little hope, therapists who say the equivalent of "Being alone, being by yourself, isn't so bad, there are worse things than being alone, I even envy you your going alone to your condominium in the country" can seem to be warning the patient that things will never improve. And finally, in the realm of coming across as belittling, therapists who reassure their patients that "things are not so bad after all" can seem to be saying that "your problems aren't important, you are entitled to little, and you can expect even less."

BE CAREFUL NOT TO CREATE NEW AVOIDANCES

Avoidance creation, sometimes, is an unavoidable complication even of well-done psychotherapy. Psychoanalyses prolonged, or overly prolonged, especially when carried out in a state of abstinence, can cause current relationships to deteriorate and discourage the formation of new ones. Long analyses in a state of abstinence are rarely suitable for avoidants who need to form new relationships starting with nothing. Short-term treatment and cognitive-behavioral therapy (which is often inherently time-limited) solve this problem (while raising some others, as described, in the case of cognitive therapy, throughout). These forms of therapy aren't so involving on their own; they do not act so much the substitute for real living; and the therapist does not ask the patient to waste good years of his or her life in the therapist's office on the couch.

Some therapists unwittingly encourage avoidance by encouraging their avoidant patients to keep busy to deal with their loneliness. For most avoidants, "get a hobby (or a pet) and you won't miss not having friends" should be changed to "get a friend and you won't miss not having hobbies (or a pet)." Like pets, hobbies are suitable for supplementing, but not for replacing, loving relationships with another human being. Although avoidance can be made more tolerable with hobbies, it is usually a better idea to make hobbies more tolerable with nonavoidance, so that the patient doesn't while away lonely hours keeping busy instead of busying himself or herself working toward making the hours less lonely. Solitary activities can also increase the distress of isolation by acting as reminders of how much the patient is missing. The next hobby in such cases can become somatic symptoms/hypochondriasis due to an increasing preoccupation with one's own body. Finally, the therapist who tells the patient to get a hobby is sometimes perceived as a defeatist who says, "Get a hobby if you can't relate," as if he or she had said, "Get a wheelchair if you can't walk."

One psychotherapist suggested, "Get a cat, you will feel less lonely," implying that this was the best his patient could do. This solution created not a less lonely patient but a patient with a cat that was a hated symbol of his loneliness. "I wouldn't need a cat," he told his therapist, "if you had helped me to find a real lover."

Patients who are grieving provide an exception to the rule that hobbies can make avoidance worse. Patients who just lost a significant other are usually not ready to look for, find, and get close to substitutes. For them "keep busy" is a good idea—an even better idea if they can do their busy things with comforting old acquaintances and friends.

Some therapists create avoidance in their patients by treating them as Benjamin's (1996) "interpersonal methadone" (p. 302) for the therapist— as substitutes for a long-term relationship the therapist lacks, or even as an annuity that provides the therapist with a reliable income stream. Such therapists can discourage outside relationships in very creative ways. For example, one therapist, advised by a homosexual patient that he planned to marry a man somewhat his junior, replied, "Men that much younger than you are only interested in your money"—clearly a projection.

BE INVOLVED AND DIRECT

Therapists should avoid being overly intellectual with avoidants. They should avoid getting lost in philosophical ruminations, standing by while their patients eddy their own waters, catch themselves up in the maelstrom, and drown. What some avoidants really need is a directive nuts-and-bolts lecture on what the therapist believes constitutes being avoidant and how and why to stop being that way. That is, the patient needs to be told what to do that he or she isn't already doing, and what not to do that he or she already is doing. Therapists who avoid lecturing their avoidant patients, whether they do so by overanalyzing, overcorrecting thinking, overmodifying behavior, overgiving drugs on the assumption that the problem is biological, not psychological, or doing biofeedback instead of giving positive feedback, should consider the avoidant's cry, "I'm afraid of rejection" as an opportunity to say something trite but true, like, "It's better to have loved and lost than never to have loved at all."

DO FAMILY THERAPY WITH CAUTION

Therapists should be cautious about seeing the avoidant in family therapy. While there are advantages to family therapy, with avoidants these are sometimes outweighed by the disadvantages. For example, seeing two people together can make it difficult for one to express his or her hostility toward the other. With her husband in the room a patient couldn't tell her sex therapist that sometimes she felt that her husband was a creep, and that this was the reason she was frigid. She quite rightly expected that her husband would resent it, be hurt, and take it out on her later.

HANDLE NEGATIVE COUNTERTRANSFERENCE THERAPEUTICALLY

Countertransference, according to Stephen S. Marmer (1988) in his article on the psychoanalyst Karen Horney, is a useful descriptive/diagnostic and hence therapeutic tool because it can reveal the patient's unconscious motives by reflecting them in the therapist's reactions. But counter-transference *problems* create the reverse effect—obscuring diagnosis and interfering with therapy. Here are four categories of harmful countertrans-ference response.

Becoming *impatient* with avoidants. Some therapists find avoidants frustrating. Perhaps therapy is going too slowly and the therapist is tempted to lower expectations in a rush to closure. Perhaps the patient is deliberately being difficult to provoke the therapist to declare, "impasse, let's take a vacation from therapy." The therapist suggests marriage is the goal and the patient counters that he or she prefers a long-term committed relationship because marriage isn't right for everyone, or the therapist suggests a long-term committed relationship before, or instead of, getting married, and the patient counters either that "All I want is a circle of friends and acquaintances, not anything more intimate," or "Marriage is my goal, and that by suggesting otherwise you are trying to humiliate and defeat me." Impatient therapists at best cut corners, cow the patient into saying he or she feels better, dismiss the patient prematurely from therapy, or, at worst, as happened in one case, "throw the patient out of treatment" without notice, and in the middle of a session, because "we aren't getting along very well and it's better if we cut our losses short."

Becoming *critical* of avoidants. Some therapists dislike and become overly critical of avoidants because avoidants are distant and remote; because they are stubborn; because the avoidant's guilt about his or her sexual instincts arouses like feelings in the therapist, enhancing the therapist's sheepishness about having a body and the sexual desires that go with it; or because, as one therapist suggested, the patient is "full of detestable, shameful sloth," a "crock faking somatic symptoms," or a "crybaby unable to tolerate even a little social anxiety."

Critical therapists often use interpretations to hurt. One therapist used the truth that avoidants are partly responsible for their fate not for purposes of imparting insight but to blame the patient for actively causing every rejection he experienced passively. Since all interpretations have a critical aspect, whenever possible with avoidants (as with most patients)—at least in the beginning—therapists should interpret from the side of the fear instead of from the side of the wish. For example, interpretations of avoidant guilt are often more palatable than interpretations of avoidant hostility/misanthropy, especially for patients who tend to be paranoid and depressed.

Becoming too *sympathetic* toward the avoidant. Overly sympathetic therapists view avoidants solely as the innocent victims of less than ideal circumstances. Therapists at particular risk here are therapists disinclined to believe in the existence of unconscious masochistic self-destructiveness; therapists who believe that asking a patient to take responsibility for him- or herself is the same thing as being cruel and heartless to a helpless person; therapists who conceptualize avoidance as a "disease" over which the patient has no control; and therapists who blame early trauma exclusively for a patient's present plight, thereby excusing the patient for actively participating in the avoidant process in the here and now, supporting the patient's desire for the world to change, thereby going along with, and so condoning, his or her reluctance to do anything to change it.

Taking the patient's *negative transference personally*. Patients who complain, "You are criticizing me" make some therapists feel uncomfortably like a critical parent, and patients who disagree with everything the therapist says, responding with faint praise to brilliant, apt, insightful, and decisive formulations by damning them into oblivion, make some therapists feel like a misguided little child.

CHAPTER 20

Treating Depressed Avoidants

This chapter describes methods for treating avoidants who are significantly depressed—in particular, shy, lonely, isolated Type I avoidants whose self-esteem is so low that they do not relate to others because they think that they are not desirable enough to inflict themselves on the world and the people in it. For example, a gay man wrote the following letter actually asking me if I thought he should even consider pursuing what to nonavoidants would at least seem to be a promising relationship opportunity:

The new man in my life is a vice president of a large media company here in Chicago. The person who introduced us said he was just looking for an average guy but I was concerned when he got into his Mercedes and all I have is a 1990 Honda. In other words, he lives a much higher lifestyle than I do and I am worried that I will not be able to keep up with him. My friend says I am worrying about nothing. He is also very good looking and I am just average in looks and make a lot less than he does but we seem to be hitting it off so far, no sex or anything like that, but enjoying each other's company and I actually like him, to date anyway. I just work as a welder in a large construction company but I am not after his money or anything, I would rather live poor and be happy than live with someone I do not like.

Treating depressed avoidants means focusing on resolving the problems they have with low self-esteem; excessive anger; excessive guilt; inertia; panic and agitation; intense feelings of loss; character problems such as paranoia, envy and jealousy, ambivalence, and narcissism; and—a diffi-

culty that looms particularly large with avoidants who are depressed—
hypersensitivity to criticism.

DEALING WITH LOW SELF-ESTEEM

Helping depressed avoidants overcome their low self-esteem starts with
asking them to distinguish low self-esteem that is *rational and appropriate*
from low self-esteem that is *irrational and inappropriate*. Low self-esteem
that is *rational and appropriate* originates in self-criticism and criticism from
others that is well-deserved. To get better, avoidants who criticize themselves and whom others criticize appropriately need to do things differently so that they can feel more positive about themselves. In particular,
they should be less hurtful to people who do, or could, like or love them.
This was the appropriate solution for the following patient:

An overly competitive patient wanted others to fail so that they did not threaten
his number one status. As a result, when he sensed that they were doing better
than he, he set out to defeat them. If a friend asked for a recipe he would alter it
slightly so that the friend's results wouldn't be as good as his own. If a coworker
needed assistance he would delay giving it as long as possible, and then give it
grudgingly, hoping it would come too late to be of any real value. Once he was
in line at the checkout counter in a drug store when the manager told the people
waiting in line to feel free to take any one of a number of plants that were about
to be thrown out because they were not selling. The patient said, "No, thank you,"
only to have the man standing in front of him, trying to be friendly, and funny,
point to a little plant and encourage him to take it, adding, in a humorous way,
"That little plant is *you*." To that friendly overture the patient snidely, and hurt-
fully, replied, "You don't know me well enough to decide what is, and what is
not, me."

It was also the appropriate solution for the acquisitions editor of a music
publishing company who wrote the following letter (here somewhat edited) to a composer complaining that the composer sent some images via
e-mail instead of putting them on a CD and mailing them via snail mail:

When my e-mail downloading was grabbed for over an hour and a half—I suspected that it was your music. If I stop the downloading, to access it again I have
to start from the beginning for another hour and a half. Then it creates duplicates
of everything—another pain in the butt. I told you to MAIL THE MUSIC—I am
not a slave to you and your CONCERTO—but you seem to think so. So much for
NOT following instructions. I simply do not feel like wasting all of this time on
the grunt work you created for me. Like I said I AM NOT YOUR SLAVE and you
load me down with all of this time-wasting baloney. Worse, you are a little teen-
age boy who doesn't even fight me when I am overdoing it, making it even easier
for me to be the mean daddy—which I get guilty about afterwards. I resent work-

ing with composers and you will be the last, because I should be doing my own concerto instead.

Low self-esteem that is *irrational* appears when avoidants dislike themselves, or feel that they are disliked, for little or no reason. Avoidants with irrational low self-esteem do not have to change their behavior. They have to change their minds about themselves. They have to treat themselves better, as more worthy objects of their affections. This was true for the following man:

A patient, neither more nor less human than average, walked around muttering the words "useless dog" over and over again, not only to himself but also loud enough for others to hear. On one level he was speaking affectionately to his recently deceased dog, which, when she was alive, he would often humorously call "useless" out of love. But on another level he was chastising himself—he was the useless dog of which he spoke. He convinced himself of his uselessness by ruminating for days on end about how he had taken the wrong turn in life professionally, hurt his parents by being remote and uncaring, and hurt a former lover by blaming him for mistakes that he himself had made. He would constantly bemoan the fact that he could never undo the damage he had done, and would have to live with its consequences forever. Then after each negative thought about himself he would call out the words "useless dog" both to excoriate himself and to seek the self-absolution which he felt was his just reward for recognizing and confessing his sins.

Here are some things that avoidant patients with irrational low self-esteem can do to make their self-esteem higher:

- Expose the distortive nature of low self-esteem by understanding its past origins. In my experience many avoidants with low self-esteem speak of having had critical humiliating parents who withheld deserved compliments. These avoidants-to-be fought for their parents' love only to have the parents either not respond at all or respond by becoming even more critical and humiliating. Then the avoidants-to-be sulked and, instead of just giving up and accepting that their parents had problems of their own, continued to fight for parental approval. Today they continue this pattern with parental clones. They go through life feeling completely disliked if even one person feels at all negative toward them. Then they seek to be made whole again by finding unconditional love with someone else. They do not even attempt to enter into a relationship unless they feel completely reassured that it will work out. Soon enough they discover that such reassurance is almost never forthcoming. So they give up, withdraw from relationships, and become shy and remote due to their conviction that no one can ever truly love them.
- Interrupt vicious cycles where low self-esteem creates self-esteem that is even lower, ad infinitum. For example, a patient couldn't go to parties because he did not feel worthy enough to attend social events, and he did not feel worthy

enough to attend social events because he was the sort of person who couldn't comfortably socialize. As is often the case in such situations, forced exposure leading to satisfying small successes can break through the impasse.

- Give oneself an evidence-based pep talk. Some patients benefit from making a two-column list in which they identify their positive features in Column A and install these beside the negative features they document in Column B. This way they create a more balanced, and hopefully more positive, overall self-view.
- Talk back to one's critical, punitive conscience. Patients should strive to be less critical of, and more positive toward, themselves. They should become more tolerant of their minor imperfections. They should be more willing to accept their sexuality and sexual deviancies (within reason), without having to repress how they feel (and without becoming a world savior expecting others to repress how *they* feel). They should strive to be the opposite of a patient's lover who insisted that she and the patient cross the street each time they were about to pass a Greenwich Village shop that sold sexual paraphernalia so that neither would see and somehow be contaminated by having seen what was in the window. They should also be more willing to accept their anger. Instead of blaming themselves for being angry, then suppressing their anger and possibly taking it out on themselves, they should accept that from time to time everyone feels hostile and that most hostile feelings are run-of-the-mill, at least when they are occasional, mild, and at a minimum partially valid. (Dealing with anger is my next topic.)

DEALING WITH ANGER

Many depressed avoidants are seriously angry people. Some of their anger is a secondary response to being rejected. However, some of it is primary—that is, it is a temperamental, or inborn diathesis that takes the form of a readiness to disparage, ridicule, criticize, reject, and wreak vengeance on others.

After accepting the invitation, a patient just didn't show up for a dinner party. When the host called an hour into the party to see what had happened, the patient told him, in effect, that an old friend dropped by at the last minute and wanted to spend some time with him. The host got angry, but, feeling that discretion was better than expression, just said, "Okay." The next day the two ran across each other in the street. Now the host was slightly cold, though still cordial—at least as cordial as he could be under the circumstances. Unfortunately, instead of apologizing, the patient attacked the host for being cold and remote, compounding the initial error of not showing up for dinner by blaming his victim for not handling his victimhood better.

As noted throughout, angry avoidants should think twice before getting their anger out, hoping to unburden themselves and clear the air. A better solution is for avoidants, particularly those who are depressed, to avoid getting angry in the first place. Should they get angry anyway, they should try to suppress at least some of their anger. When that is not possible they should at least try to feel angry without actually getting angry. When that is not an option, they should at least express their anger with care, keeping one eye always open to the disjunctive effect that anger has on a relationship. Yes, anger is an acceptable emotion, but expressing anger antagonizes people, and avoidants can use all the friends that they can get.

On one patient's list of people to get angry at was "the kid who stares at me in the halls and will not speak to me but instead looks at me with a sour expression on his face." The patient thought to curl his lip in a gesture of disdain to tell the boy that he isn't as great as he thinks he is. He also thought that instead of holding doors open for the boy he would let them slam in his face. I suggested that that curative would simply get him a reputation around the building for being nasty, and that would lead to his being even more isolated, lonely, and angry than before.

Here are some ways avoidants can keep from getting angry in the first place or, when that is not possible, better manage the anger they cannot help but feel. The exact method selected will depend on individual preference, personality, and in the case of therapists, training and orientation.

Keep from Getting Angry in the First Place

Avoidants can keep from getting angry in the first place by picking others who do not make them angry. They can expect less from the others they do pick so that they won't be so disappointed with what they actually get. They can treat others more carefully to avoid riling them. For example, they can avoid crossing them so as to not provoke them to anger. They can say "yes" when they mean "no," without being a pushover or a sucker. To avoid disappointing others and making them resentful, they can tell others in advance what to, and what not to, expect from them. For example, they might state in advance that "if I seem shy and detached it is because I suffer from social anxiety." Finally, avoidants can apologize for their shyness after the fact so that others will forgive instead of resenting them for being isolated and remote, and will not take their isolation and remoteness so personally.

Better Manage the Anger You Cannot Help but Feel

Avoidants should attempt to suppress the anger they cannot help feeling. Though it is considerably shy of a curative, they might try making a list of ten people they would like to get angry with, write down what they would like to say to them, then tear up that list as a symbolic gesture that affirms their desire to not say or do anything negative to anyone on it. They can cover up their anger by going to the opposite extreme and instead of flaring being as nice as they possibly can be. Or they can learn to express their anger in new, less off-putting, less avoidant ways—sublimating their anger by punching a punching bag, or, if that is the best they can do, expressing their anger not directly but indirectly, by being passive-aggressive.

DEALING WITH EXCESSIVE GUILT

Depressed avoidants are guilty people who dislike themselves, expect that others will share their self-dislike, and then avoid others to spare them unpleasantness. Instead of disliking themselves they can see themselves, when applicable, not as "bad" but as "different." They can learn to make creative excuses for themselves, for example, telling themselves not "You shouldn't have done that," but "I did that because it was what I wanted to do," "I was being true to myself," or "I couldn't help myself." They can envision the bright side of what they perceive to be their flaws. For example, many people like depressive clinginess, schizoid remoteness, or hypomanic overactivity. They should certainly resolve to rid themselves of a rigid morality that dictates that enjoying themselves is a sin. This way they can then give themselves permission to do healthy but enjoyable things formerly forbidden. They should attempt to reduce *survivor guilt*. Instead of experiencing guilt over doing well when others are doing poorly by comparison, they should view themselves as separate entities entitled to fulfill their destiny regardless of whether or not others fulfill theirs. They should reduce *guilt over success* by rethinking their belief that the world is a zero-sum place where because there is a finite quantity of x, anything they get by definition they got by taking it away from y. In general they should lighten up, and two good ways to do that are to stay away from people who make them feel guilty, such as people who have their own problems with guilt and are looking for company in their misery, and to always remember the two magic words of guilt reduction: "so what."

DEALING WITH INERTIA

Avoidants who sulk and retreat can benefit from taking themselves in hand and self-starting. Mood improving and activating medications, the exact indications for which are beyond the scope of this text, can help move avoidants from here to there—to a new, more strategic, position from which they are likely to find it easier to take the next step.

DEALING WITH PANIC AND AGITATION

Depressed avoidants often panic and become agitated when, thinking catastrophically, they come to believe that because all is not entirely well, that means that all is lost. For example, one avoidant kept thinking, "I ruined myself" over the slightest, and often entirely imagined, interpersonal misbehavior on his part, such as asking a waiter to take back a cold cup of coffee and bring him a hot one. Panic and agitation tend to respond positively to cognitive therapy, to calming behavioral techniques such as deep breathing and saying reassuring mantras to oneself, and to psychotropic medications as prescribed by a physician.

DEALING WITH LOSS

Depressed avoidants who do not seek interpersonal gains for fear of experiencing interpersonal losses should recognize that their defensive disengagement predictably creates the very losses that they are attempting to avert. Avoidants who are grieving over actual losses should try keeping busy, structuring and organizing their day to avoid getting even more depressed and retreating from life completely.

DEALING WITH SPECIFIC CHARACTEROLOGICAL PROBLEMS

Depression in avoidants is often the product of covalent difficulties with paranoia, envy and jealousy, ambivalence, narcissism, and hypersensitivity to criticism. *Paranoid* depressed avoidants feel depressed because they abandon ships they only imagine to be sinking. They do so because they suspect that others who are in fact trying to get close to them have a hidden disjunctive agenda. Their suspicions originate in at least three ways. First, they originate in a lack of basic trust. Second, avoidants arrive at their negative assumptions after scanning for negativism in others, proving their own point by blowing transient, critical notions they are bound to discover way up out of proportion, or by uncovering, and taking to heart, meaningful critical thoughts that are there but were meant to be kept hidden. Third, there is a proneness to projective assumptions such as the belief that others are as down on them as they are down on themselves. For example, someone cruising a patient in a singles bar merely asked him, "What do you do?" meaning, "What do you do professionally?" (that is, not sexually). Already concerned that he was a failure sexually he took what was probably just an attempt to make conversation as a criticism for being a homosexual, and walked away. Sometimes extreme delusional thinking prevails. When that is the case, professional assistance may be required. For example, a child believed that all the animals in the world hated her to punish her for her hatred of one of her cats. A patient asked a book vendor the price of a book. Told it was $80, he loudly uttered a series of disapproving curse words, then said he would have to pay up because he needed it to "find out what the people on the bus were saying about me." Next, dramatically giving himself the finger, he said, "On second thought, I won't need the book; I already know what the people on the bus have in mind." Treatment of this level of paranoia is beyond the scope of this text.

Envious and jealous depressed avoidants feel depressed because they feel helpless and despairing due to the belief that everyone is better, and better off, than they are. As a remedy, instead of comparing themselves to others unfavorably they should start viewing themselves as individuals whose value is unique though their status in life may need some improving.

Ambivalent depressed avoidants feel depressed as a result of the unstable relationships they have because they fear commitment or because they alternately overvalue and devalue others. A remedy consists of 1) deciding to be in or out of a relationship, then, if in, staying the course, and 2) trying hard to work things out.

Narcissistic depressed avoidants feel depressed because they need everyone to admire them—in the real world, an absolute impossibility. They can benefit from becoming less preoccupied with the possibility of feeling unloved. A good place to start is by carefully defining what not being loved actually does, and does not, consist of, so that they can be more realistic about their expectations of others and thus avoid being constantly disappointed about not getting the lofty things they think the world owes them.

DEALING WITH CRITICISM

While no one likes to be criticized, avoidants have a special problem with others' negativity to them. All avoidants, as the *DSM-IV* suggests, hesitate to look for interpersonal intimacy because they fear being "exposed, ridiculed, or shamed" (p. 662), and subject to "mockery or derision" (p. 662). Depressed avoidants are particular alert and hypersensitive to criticism and hesitate to look for interpersonal intimacy for this reason. Here is a step-by-step guide on how avoidants can deal correctively with their extreme hypersensitivity to criticism.

Step 1: Recognize Criticism Wherever It Exists

So that they can deal with criticism effectively, avoidants need to be realistic about being criticized. While on the one hand, they need to be reassured that people are not being as critical of them as they think they are, on the other hand, they need to be honest with themselves and identify those situations where they are actually being criticized. Even though they might prefer to go into denial, they need to fully recognize both the critical assaults directed toward them and also the harmful personal effects those assaults can have on their emotional state.

In the realm of recognizing the critical assaults directed toward them, avoidants can benefit from understanding that some behaviors of others that look superficially benign can in fact be deeply hostile. That means: mind-reading the negative as well as the positive motives of others; blaming loved ones they would prefer to spare even though that requires temporarily becoming more, not less, avoidant; and not thinking of themselves as paranoid for seeing criticism where there is none—not giving people who do not deserve it the benefit of the doubt, and not making excuses for others whose behavior is inexcusable. In other words, avoidants owe it to themselves to see not only the best in others but also the darker side of human nature that an overappreciation of the brighter side of human nature may have blinded them to so far. Avoidants need to recognize *covert* criticism hidden in the form of such nonverbals as: raised eyebrows, eye rolls and shoulder shrugs; socially acceptable rationalizations such as, "I am merely asking a question," or "just playing the devil's advocate"; hedge words such as "but," as in "My complaint is not significant, but"; disqualifying words like "simply," as in "I was simply asking you when you were finally going to get around to cleaning up your room"; vehicles for constructive correction such as, "I wouldn't criticize you if I didn't want you to be the best you can be;" and so-called vehicles for love, such as, "I am leaving you only because I love you too much to ruin your life."

In the realm of recognizing the harmful effects of criticism on their well-being, it helps to spot the following alerting responses to having been criticized: a physical response, such as insomnia with nightmares of being tortured, impotence, headaches, and stomach pains and an emotional response, particularly anxiety and depression accompanied by such thoughts as, "What did I do to deserve being picked on?"; "How will I ever be able to defend myself?"; and "Will my persecution ever stop?"

Step 2: Understand Where Your Critics Are Coming From

Avoidants can use an understanding of how their critics operate to help cope with and master their painful response to criticism. They can ask themselves not only, "What is going on with me" but also "What is going on with my critics?" Understanding critical presumption, prejudice, cognitive error, and outright gaffes can help the avoidant recognize that it is "them, not me, with the problem." That makes criticism seem less overwhelming, less personal, and so less meaningful. For one thing, criticism is often as much about the critic as it is about the individual being criticized. Many critics are just living out a personal, egoistic agenda, demeaning others as a way to brag about their own taste, knowledge, intelligence, and refinement, sending the message to their victims that "*I* have the good taste to spot a bad apple" or "*I* have the ability to understand this complicated work, and *you* don't" or, as actually suggested by one critic, "I have the big fly-swatter, and you are just a fly." Sometimes criticism is a transference response by a critic who mistakes his or her target for a prying mother, controlling father, or competitive sibling. Shrill critics in particular have often identified with a harsh hurtful parent and are now abusing others the same way their mothers or fathers abused them. Sometimes a self-criticism lurks behind the criticism of others. Here the critic projects onto and humiliates and demeans others for traits he or she dislikes in him- or herself. Therefore, avoidants can often profitably reframe the negative things critics say about them as negative self-statements on the part of the critic, displaced outwardly, with criticizing others just the critic's way to criticize themselves, with the "you" being an example.

A homophobe's criticisms of gays and lesbians was externalized self-criticism of the critic's own forbidden homosexual wishes—a way for him to appease his own conscience along the lines of "I may be that way too but I want to be clear, to myself and the world that it's not something I approve of in, or like about, myself." This critic's goal was to reduce his own guilt and shame by a self-congratulatory disapproving of others for being and doing what the critic felt guilty about, and so hated in, himself. Not surprisingly, this critic regularly found others most unappealing when he saw what he liked about himself in them. With him, as with all such critics, the formulation, "It takes one to know (and criticize) one" held a special truth.

As previously mentioned, sometimes the criticism of others is self-justification by a critic who is defending him- or herself against a perceived attack. For example, once a gay patient, having perceived my not-so-gentle suggestion that he get his act together, simmer down, institute some self-control, and stop acting out promiscuously and having unsafe sex, struck out at me critically for being controlling, demeaning, and devaluing his gay identity—his way to defend his own rebellious, disinhibited, behavior that he either had no intention of stopping, or would have liked to have stopped but could not get under control.

Step 2 often involves recognizing specific pathology in one's actual or potential critics. Avoidants can simultaneously affirm themselves, develop a semi-scientific method of self-defense, and, if they like, improve their relationships with their critics by recognizing specific emotional disorder in their critics and speaking to that. In the realm of self-affirmation, as Keating (1984) suggests, avoidants can lessen their "difficult feelings by understanding some of the syndromes of difficult people [who] may be feeling depressed, guilty, fearful, etc., and refus[ing] to admit such feelings even to themselves" (p. 150). In the realm of self-defense, avoidant victims of criticism can take protective measures based on an awareness of the specific pathological nature of the potential or actual danger they are in.

For example, to be safe, gay men have to be extremely careful not to cruise a latent homosexual, thereby catalyzing serious conflicts about to erupt about homosexuality. In the realm of devastating their critics brilliantly, the fly who was the victim of the critic with the big fly-swatter pointed out what Freud might have noted about this critic's self-image—that the critic was attempting to overcompensate in fantasy for a specific physical lack he had in reality. Finally, in the realm of improving relationships with one's critics, patients, if they choose, can act in a constructive way with their critics using time-tested therapeutic methods gleaned from the world of known interpersonal curatives. For example, predictably, *paranoid* critics tend to respond positively to reassurance that they are not in danger ("I would never cheat on you because I love you too much to do that"), to a positive spin put on their paranoia ("I know you only keep me on a short leash because you love me," or, "suspicious people like you make good detectives"), or to the victim's taking some or all of the blame on him- or herself (not, "You didn't hear me," but "Perhaps I didn't make myself clear."); *depressed* and *narcissistic* critics tend to respond positively to compliments for their perceptivity; *competitive histrionic* critics tend to respond positively to a compliance on the part of their victims that suggests an at least partial if only transient willingness to be dominated and subjugated; and *sadistic* critics tend to respond positively to having limits set on the amount of hostility they will be permitted to express and act upon. Of course, a caveat is that there is a trade-off involved in coddling critics: compromising one's own identity for purposes of maintaining a relationship, or one's professional status.

Step 3: Understand Where You Are Coming From

Avoidants can maintain a more positive self-image by understanding why they respond so negatively to criticism. Is it their submissiveness and self-punitive attitude that leads them to overvalue others' negative opinions about them as compared to their own more positive opinions about themselves? Are they parentalizing critics as omniscient and omnipotent mother or father clones to the point that they feel as if they are undeserving, bad little children too small and weak to even consider challenging others' negativity to them? Are they compliment junkies who, having been as children either criticized too much or loved too well, as adults need to sustain a completely unflawed self-image based 100%, at all times, and no matter what, on positive feedback?

Step 4: Learn to Respond in a Healthier Way to Actual Criticism

Avoidants can harden themselves to criticism. They can ignore negative people who reject them. They can remind themselves that no matter who they are, not everyone is going to like them or approve of what they do. They can tell themselves that if they do get rejected it is not the end of the world but a part of, that is, an unfortunate complication of, having active relationships. They can put unjustified criticism into perspective by developing a sense of humor about it, seeing the amusing and unimportant side of what looks at first glance to be an interaction of tragic proportions. I sometimes ask my patients to think of every episode of being criticized in terms of its significance in the infinite scheme of things. I tell them, "When you are criticized, it sometimes helps to think universal thoughts. Every once in a while look up at the stars and realize what a small thing you are compared to it all. I don't advocate your doing that to see yourself as a meaningless speck, or to diminish your significance in your own eyes. I just want you to be less upset about things that don't really matter, which is most things, and criticism certainly. Turn off that alarm bell in your head. Not everything is a catastrophe. Don't panic. Recognize that what seems so important today often turns out to be unimportant tomorrow. Make everything a matter of life, not a matter of life and death."

Of course, avoidants should not harden themselves to, ignore, or belittle *constructive* criticism. Instead of becoming automatically and reflexively defensive in the face of any and all criticism, they should distinguish constructive from negative criticism. They should reexamine themselves to see if the constructive criticism is warranted, accept it if it is, and change accordingly. That doesn't mean seeing oneself as a bad person. It just means trying to be a better person the next time. Blaming others less and themselves more can seem like a bad idea for avoidants with low self-esteem. However, while their self-esteem might temporarily fall as a result of the increased self-blame, it will predictably soon rise again as new, satisfactory, rewarding relationships develop with people who now find the avoidant more likeable simply because he or she is acting more likeably.

Avoidants, if they choose, can also try to turn criticism into a positive, creative, growth-enhancing experience. Avoidants can make criticism work for them by taking it to heart and doing better the next time, then making certain their critics hear about their positive accomplishments.

Step 5: Meet Criticism Head On

I sometimes recommend that avoidants respond to criticism not like a turtle pulling back into its shell (flight) but like a lion turning on those who trouble it (fight). Here are some of the things avoidants can do to act more like that lion.

Discount your critics. Avoidants can blank their critics out *indirectly* by focusing away from them and onto their supporters. Alternatively they can blank their critics out *directly* by being assertive instead of passive. I might advise my avoidant patients to plan their repartee in advance of an anticipated attack. I might suggest that they make a list of their positive points and reel them off to themselves or to the critic when the critic is being negative to them. I might suggest that they remind their critics that it is not only "who will accept me," it is also "whom I will accept." I might suggest that they set limits on what they will permit their critics to say and do by identifying with the aggressor and becoming as aggressive to the critic as the critic is being aggressive to them. There are three ways to identify with the aggressor. The first is by having demeaning fantasies towards one's critics but keeping them to oneself. For example, one way to overcome a fear of public speaking is by thinking of the audience as fools, perhaps in the nude, thus demeaning the audience so that it makes little difference if they demean you. The second way involves living well as the best revenge—having an extremely pleasurable life to spite all those who want you to be miserable. The third way is turning tables, fighting fire with fire, and giving the critic a taste of his or her own medicine by squelching the critic in kind, and in turn. They can simply tell their critics that, in effect, they do not know what they are talking about. Particularly helpful here are tu quoque mechanisms where the victim tells his or her critics, "You are one, too," or "you did it first," even if, or especially when, the logic is unsound. For example, an individual responded to criticism for pirating software by pointing out that a software company's monopolistic practices were just as bad, or worse, than what she did.

I reassure avoidants who fear that being assertive with their critics ensures further criticism and rejection that they will likely discover that the opposite is true. As suggested above, they will likely discover that sadistic critics perceive their victim's submissiveness as weakness, and that inspires them to further attack. Therefore, giving sadists carte blanche—then a second and third chance—condones their sadism complicitly, and that encourages it indirectly.

I help avoidants who have difficulty being assertive even with those who are in a position to do them serious harm discover why that should be so. Possible causes (with remedies implied) are low self-esteem and such of its accoutrements as a fear of success; some equals all thinking, characterized by the inability to distinguish setting limits from getting annoyed, getting annoyed from getting angry, and getting angry from committing murder; an excessive need for a positive self-image with that positive self-image too easily shattered by even the slightest hint of negativity in the form of inner anger, no matter how mild or justified; and an excess of empathy and altruism where saying "no" is believed to be hurtful to others in situations where a "yes" is even remotely possible.

On the downside, however favorable the risk-reward ratio may be, being assertive, or counterassertive, works imperfectly with the many critics who know how to foil attempts at self-defense. In particular it can backfire

when the critic responds by becoming even more humiliating and rejecting, making the avoidant's worst fears come true. It also works imperfectly with critics like literary critics who have made themselves
revenge-proof, who, like homophobic teenagers driving by and yelling
antigay epithets at gays on foot from the safety of a moving car, hide
behind one or another impenetrable fortress, throwing darts at their hapless victims from a high perch, comfortable in the knowledge that all the
victim can do is write letters of protest to the editor, letters that the editor
will never publish.

Step 6: Manipulate Your Critics

Avoidants can manipulate their critics in one of several ways. They can
make them feel guilty by loving them more the more critical they are
("that's okay; the negative things you say about me don't change how I
feel about you"), or by beating them over their heads with their bloody
bodies ("look what you have done to me"). Or they can disarm their critics
by saying a "mea culpa," getting their first with a self-criticism, as in "You
are right, I know that that's the way I am, but what can I do about it, I
don't seem to be able to change." They can humor, coddle, or cater to their
critics to bring them over to their side, a method that few people are even
willing to try even though it works especially well with those critics (most
critics) who like to be loved, however roundabout the way they have of
expressing that.

A patient told a music critic that he liked the opera *Martha*. He didn't know that
the critic disliked the opera and had just said so in print. Thinking that everyone
read his words, the critic became offended that the patient, a big nobody, was
disagreeing with him, a well-regarded professional. Feeling disrespected and unloved, the critic got back at the patient by diminishing him, doing so by calling
him "very opinionated." The patient, feeling that the relationship with this critic
was important to his career, and more important than winning this particular, not
very important, battle, swallowed his pride and agreed with the critic that he
should have never given him an argument in the first place.

Step 7: Have a Rational Discussion with Your Critics

When being criticized, refuse to accept global criticism—the equivalent
of name-calling. Instead ask for the details. Demand specifics so that you
can know exactly what you are being criticized for. Now you can create
the best possible point-by-point defense.

Step 8: Put Third Parties between You and Your Critics

Third parties can advise avoidants what to do to stave off criticism and
suggest ways to recover from criticism that the avoidant was unable to

escape. They can be supportive confidants who take the avoidant's side and provide him or her with a comfortable, safe haven at times of stress, a retreat where the avoidant can go to be reassured that he or she is not as bad as the critics say and, when applicable, to hear that it is the critic, not the avoidant, with the problem.

Step 9: Just Walk Away from Your Critics

Avoidance can be a healthy, self-protective mechanism for dealing with situations that cannot be prevented or turned around. Avoidants should lose interest in meeting only the difficult challenges of life, in only winning the hard games, and in only making the hard conquests. They should focus away from changing the minds that are most set against them, and from making the difficult people in their lives the ones who count the most. They should instead focus on their most fervent admirers, and their truest and most loving friends.

When walking away physically is not possible, it might be possible to walk away emotionally. One can shun a troublesome person on site by saying the following magical mantra to oneself, one that is in fact applicable to, and useful in a general way for, almost all avoidants in almost any avoidant crisis:

"That is just the way some people are.

It's their problem.

And I will simply refuse to let it bother me."

References

American Psychiatric Association. (1987). *Diagnostic and statistical manual of mental disorders* (3rd ed.). Washington, DC: American Psychiatric Association.

American Psychiatric Association. (1994). *Diagnostic and statistical manual of mental disorders* (4th ed.). Washington, DC: American Psychiatric Association.

Anthony, M. M., & Swinson, R. P. (2000). *Shyness & social anxiety workbook: Proven techniques for overcoming your fears*. Oakland, CA: New Harbinger.

Auden, W. H. (1960). The more loving one. *Homage to Clio*. New York: Random House. Available at: http://www.poets.org/poems/poemprnt.cfm?45442B7 C000C07060075.

Ballenger, J. (1991). *Masters in psychiatry*. Kalamazoo, MI: Upjohn.

Barlow, D. H. (1992, Spring). Cognitive-behavioral approaches to panic disorder and social phobia. *Bulletin of the Menninger Clinic, 56* (Suppl. A), A14–A28.

Beattie, M. (1987). *Codependent no more*. San Francisco: Harper/Hazelden.

Beavers, W. R. (1982, December). Indications and contraindications for couples therapy. *The Psychiatric Clinics of North America: Marital Therapy, 5* (3), 469–478.

Beck, A. T. (1990a). *Cognitive therapy of the personality disorders*. New York: Guilford Press.

Beck, A. T. (1990b). *Psychotherapy of an avoidant personality* [tape]. New York: Guilford Press.

Beck, A. T. (1999). *Prisoners of hate: The cognitive basis of anger, hostility, and violence*. New York: HarperCollins.

Bellafante, G. (2002, March 10). Some who needed holding after 9/11 are now holding off. *New York Times*, sec. 9, pp. 1, 2.

Benjamin, L. S. (1996). *Interpersonal diagnosis and treatment of personality disorders*. New York: Guilford Press.

Berne, E. (1964). *Games people play*. New York: Grove Press.

Bloch, J. P. (2000). *Finding your leading man*. New York: St. Martin's Griffin.

Burns, D. D., & Epstein, N. (1983). Passive-aggressiveness: A cognitive-behavioral approach. In R. D. Parsons & R. J. Wicks (Eds.), *Passive-aggressiveness: Theory and practice* (pp. 72–97). New York: Brunner/Mazel.

Capote, T. (1993). *Breakfast at Tiffany's: A novel & three stories* (1st Vintage International ed.). New York: Knopf.

Coleman, E. (1992). Is your patient suffering from compulsive sexual behavior? *Psychiatric Annals, 22*, 320–325.

Dostoyevski, F. (1969). *The idiot*. New York: New American Library.

Fenichel, O. (1945). *The psychoanalytic theory of neurosis*. New York: Norton.

Flaubert, G. (1964). *Madame Bovary*. New York: New American Library.

Frances, A. & Widiger, T. A. (1987). A critical review of four DSM-III personality disorders. In G. L. Tischler (Ed.), *Diagnosis and classification in psychiatry*. New York: Cambridge University Press.

Freud, A. (1946). *The ego and the mechanisms of defense*. New York: International Universities Press.

Freud, S. (1936). *The problem of anxiety*. New York: Psychoanalytic Quarterly Press and Norton.

Freud, S. (1950). *Totem and taboo*. New York: Norton.

Freud, S. (1957a). Certain neurotic mechanisms in jealousy, paranoia and homosexuality. In J. D. Sutherland (Ed.) and J. Riviere (Trans.), *Collected papers* (Vol. 2, pp. 232–243). London: Hogarth Press.

Freud, S. (1957b). "Civilized" sexual morality and modern nervousness. In J. D. Sutherland (Ed.) and J. Riviere (Trans.), *Collected papers* (Vol. 2, pp. 76–99). London: Hogarth Press.

Freud, S. (1957c). The economic problem in masochism. In J. D. Sutherland (Ed.) and J. Riviere (Trans.), *Collected papers* (Vol. 2, pp. 255–268). London: Hogarth Press.

Freud, S. (1957d). Libidinal types. In J. Strachey (Ed.), *Collected papers* (Vol. 5, pp. 247–251). London: Hogarth Press.

Freud, S. (1957e). The most prevalent form of degradation in erotic life (from Contributions to the psychology of love). In J. D. Sutherland (Ed.) and J. Riviere (Trans.), *Collected papers* (Vol. 4, pp. 207–216). London: Hogarth Press.

Freud, S. (1957f). On narcissism: An introduction. In J. D. Sutherland (Ed.) and J. Riviere (Trans.), *Collected papers* (Vol. 4, pp. 30–59). London: Hogarth Press. (Original work published 1914.)

Freud, S. (1957g). On the sexual theories of children. In J. D. Sutherland (Ed.) and J. Riviere (Trans.), *Collected papers* (Vol. 2, pp. 59–75). London: Hogarth Press.

Freud, S. (1957h). Some character-types met with in psycho-analytic work. In J. D. Sutherland (Ed.) and J. Riviere (Trans.), *Collected papers* (Vol. 4, pp. 318–344). London: Hogarth Press.

Freud, S. (1957i). A special type of choice of object made by men (from Contributions to the psychology of love). In J. D. Sutherland (Ed.) and J. Riviere (Trans.), *Collected papers* (Vol. 4, pp. 192–202). London: Hogarth Press.

Freud, S. (1957j). The taboo of virginity (from Contributions to the psychology of love). In J. D. Sutherland (Ed.) and J. Riviere (Trans.), *Collected papers* (Vol. 4, pp. 217–235). London: Hogarth Press.

Freud, S. (1957k) The theme of the three caskets. In J. D. Sutherland (Ed.) and J.

Riviere (Trans.), *Collected papers* (Vol. 4, pp. 244–256). London: Hogarth Press.

Freud, S. (1957l). Thoughts for the times on war and death. In J. D. Sutherland (Ed.) and J. Riviere (Trans.), *Collected papers* (Vol. 4, pp. 288–317). London: Hogarth Press.

Fromm-Reichmann, F. (1960). *Principles of intensive psychotherapy.* Chicago: University of Chicago Press.

Gabbard, G. O. (1992, Spring). Psychodynamics of panic disorder and social phobia. *Bulletin of the Menninger Clinic, 56* (Suppl. A), A3–A13.

Galvin, R. (1992, March–April). The nature of shyness. *Harvard Magazine, 94,* 40–45.

Haley, J. (1976). *Problem-solving therapy.* San Francisco: Jossey-Bass.

Hardy, T. (1981). *The mayor of Casterbridge.* New York: Bantam.

Hass, N. (2002, January). A haven for women is no longer quite home. *New York Times,* sec. 9, pp. 1, 6.

Hendrick, I. (1958). *Facts and theories of psychoanalysis.* New York: Knopf.

Jones, E. (1953–57). *The life and works of Sigmund Freud* (Vols. 1–3). New York: Basic Books.

Kantor, M. J. (1998). *Homophobia: Description, development, and dynamics of gay bashing.* Westport, CT: Praeger.

Keating, C. J. (1984). *Dealing with difficult people.* Ramsey, NJ: Paulist Press.

Landro, L. (2002, April 25). If doctors prescribe information, will patients pay or surf the web? *Wall Street Journal,* p. D4.

Laughlin, H. P. (1956). *The neuroses in clinical practice.* Philadelphia: Saunders.

MacKinnon, R. A., & Michels, R. (1971). *The psychiatric interview in clinical practice.* Philadelphia: Saunders.

Marmer, S. S. (1988). Theories of the mind and psychopathology. In J. A. Talbott, R. E. Hales, & S. C. Yudofsky (Eds.), *The American psychiatric press textbook of psychiatry* (pp. 123–162). Washington, DC: American Psychiatric Association.

Marshall, J. R. (1992, Spring). The psychopharmacology of social phobia. *Bulletin of the Menninger Clinic, 56* (Suppl. A), 42–49.

Millon, T. (1981). *Disorders of personality: DSM-III: Axis II.* New York: Wiley.

Millon, T. (1999). *Personality-guided therapy.* New York: Wiley.

Millon, T. & Davis, R. D. (1996). *Disorders of personality. DSM-IV and beyond.* New York: Wiley.

Norman, E. C. (1990, September). Letter to the Editor. *American Journal of Psychiatry, 147,* 1253.

Nunberg, H. & Federn, E. (Eds.). (1962). *Minutes of the Vienna Psychoanalytic Society.* Vol. I: 1906–1908. New York: International Universities Press.

Oldham, J. M., & Morris, L. B. (1995). *New personality self-portrait: Why you think, work, love, and act the way you do.* New York: Bantam Books.

Pinsker, H. (1997). *A primer of supportive therapy.* Hillsdale, NJ: Analytic Press.

Portnoy, I. (1959). The anxiety states. In S. Arieti (Ed.), *American handbook of psychiatry* (pp. 307–323). New York: Basic Books.

Quality Assurance Project, The. (1991). Treatment outlines for avoidant, dependent and passive-aggressive personality disorders. *Australian and New Zealand Journal of Psychiatry,* 404–411.

Rapee, R. M. (1998). *Overcoming shyness and social phobia: A step-by-step guide.* Northvale, NJ: Jason Aronson.

Rosenthal, E. (1992, August 18). Troubled marriage? Sibling relations may be at fault. *New York Times,* pp. C1, C9.

Siever, L. J. *Serotonin and psychiatric disorders: New vistas.* Unpublished manuscript.

Sullivan, H. S. (1953). *The interpersonal theory of psychiatry.* New York: Norton.

Sullivan, H. (1954). *The psychiatric interview.* New York: Norton.

Taubman, B. (1976). *How to become an assertive woman.* New York: Pocket Books.

Thompson, C. (1959). An introduction to minor maladjustments. In S. Arieti (Ed.), *American handbook of psychiatry* (pp. 237–244). New York: Basic Books.

Wharton, E. (1987). *The age of innocence.* New York: Collier.

Widiger, T. A. (1988). The DSM-III-R personality disorders: An overview. *American Journal of Psychiatry, 145,* 786–795.

Index

About the Author

MARTIN KANTOR is a psychiatrist in private practice in Boston and New York City. Dr. Kantor has served as Assistant Clinical Professor of Psychiatry at Mount Sinai Medical School and at the University of Medicine and Dentistry of New Jersey, New Jersey Medical School. Dr. Kantor has been active with residency training programs at hospitals including Massachusetts General and Beth Israel in New York. He is the author of 11 other books, including *Passive Aggression* (Praeger, 2002) and *Homophobia* (Praeger, 1998).